THE LIFE
OF
OTHER DAYS

Tim Cramer

I

Published by The Collins Press, Carey's Lane, Cork.

Printed in Ireland by Colour Books Ltd., Dublin.

Typesetting & cover design
by Upper Case Ltd., Cork.

ISBN - 0-9516036 -6 - 3

British Library Cataloguing-in-Publication Data.
A catalogue record for this book is available from the British
Library.

Author's Note

All of those mentioned in this book are or were warm, real, living people. In one instance only have I used a pseudonym, to prevent any possible embarrassment to a very fine young lady whose unfailing good humour enlivened all our days in Inchigeela long ago. 'Kate' is not the real name of the lady concerned in the narrative, nor was there anybody of that name employed in Creedon's Hotel in the time of which I write.

Contents

Dedicated to my dear wife and my family who like to laugh with me at the 'good old days of the shiny penny in the Christmas stocking'.

Is ní raibh rud ar bith sa domhan
Nach ndearnas (dá mba mhaith liom é);
Do léim mo bhád ar bharr na habhann
Sa ghleann inar tógadh me...
(Dúbhghlas de hÍde)

And there was nothing in the world
I would not do if I so cared.
My boat upon the river surged
Down in the glen where I was reared.
(Trans. - author)

THE LIFE OF OTHER DAYS

In the golden age of Irish history, in that great period of the 'Island of saints and scholars', in a remote settlement some forty miles from the sea, a cool mountainy breeze ruffled the ice-blue waters of the little lake at Gougane, sending tiny ripples darting towards the small oratory, like minnows rushing for shelter. The first rays of the limpid sun caressed the high peak behind narrow stone cells as the monks rose to the sound of the bell for Lauds.

One by one, they emerged from the hard beds built into the thick walls, wincing momentarily as bare feet landed tentatively on cold stone, shaken into wakefulness more by this than by the insistent clangor of the bell, the keeper of the Rule. 'Laudamus Dominum' they whispered individually as, shivering and stretching, they prepared for yet another day of work and prayer. Then, cowled, with hands hidden in the folds of hair-shirt sleeves against the morning chill, they walked in slow, deliberate procession towards the chapel.

To the west stood the looming majesty of Cam Rua, the Red Peak, glowering mightily over the forest and the valley below. North and south were other mountains, leaving the only gap to the east, for the rising sun to penetrate as it would, in its own time. Downhill behind the oratory rushed a number of small, white waterfalls, tumbling headlong into the lake like liquid lemmings bent on their own sublimation. In the intense silence could suddenly be heard the first piping notes of the blackbird, in a soprano counterpoint to the tenor and baritone cadences of the monks as they chanted the beautiful Latin psalms in praise of the Creator. It seemed no different from any other morning. Yet it was different. This morning, Brother Finbar, setting sight on the rising sun for the hundredth time in recent months, had come to a decision. It was time to leave.

And so it came to pass. In due time he and a few others left Gougane Barra, the place of prayer and sacrifice named after him, and followed the path of the rising sin and the River Lee, from its fountainhead under the Cam Rua and along the fertile valley where contented cows grazed and corn grew in abundance, where fine grazing sprang perennially from the good earth and the crops bore easy and heavy fruit. For several days they journeyed in Biblical fashion, taking night shelter where it was offered, eating where they were fed and then but little, according to their regime, until finally they arrived at a large marsh where the river widened and spread itself, creating in the process a number of islands on the low, soggy ground. On the south side of the this marsh, they found a slight eminence and there decided to settle, building in time a small church and yet another monastery. In due course, people and houses gathered round the settlement and, because of the nature of the

1

place, they called it 'Corcach', the marsh, which over the passage of time became translated and abbreviated into 'Cork', the city built on the marsh.

At first it was small, consisting of but one central street running north and south and from which sprang a number of tiny, unwholesome alleyways, noisesome with the odour of human detritus and teeming with activity. The whole was surrounded by the twin encircling arms of the Lee and had its main street guarded at each end by fortified bridges. In time, as more and more people crammed in, and as the port city began to develop and purvey the produce of the surrounding hinterland to the world at large, more bridges were flung across the Lee, bigger ships began to arrive, bearing fine wines and spices and taking away the rich, creamy butter for which the city was famed. Further, beyond the northern hills, grew an area which became known as Blackpool, with the stress on the second syllable, as is common in Cork. The name derived from the Irish 'linn dubh', literally the 'black pool', after the many tanneries and dyehouses that existed there, the effluent from which gave life to the myriad small industries of the region.

This place is germane to my tale only insofar as in its picturesque surroundings lies one of the entrances to the Glen, the once-wild valley carved out of the hills when the glaciers swept down long before the time of Finbar, leaving in their wake little but a deep rift in the landscape and the little Glen stream, meandering along narrowly to burst out of the valley at Blackpool itself, finally to join the mighty Lee at a place with the improbable local name of Pouraddy Harbour. Needless to mention, there is no harbour there, just the confluence of a tiny stream and a large river. Neither, of course, is there any truth in the rumour that the same non-existent harbour housed non-existent Irish submarines during World War Two.

The other, and more easily accessible, entrance to the Glen is by way of a little lane which is an offshoot of the Ballyvolane Road, one of the exits from the city in the north-eastern suburbs. This lane is officially known as Sun View East, but in the time of which I write, it was unofficially known as the Glen lane, or simply the 'Fac', since it led to the big Goulding fertiliser factory at the Blackpool end of the Glen valley.

It is on this lane, on the Glen itself and on the surrounding hinterland, both urban and rural, that most of these reminiscences are based. This beautiful wild place of stream, lake, quarry and hill, of fascinating indigenous and migratory wildlife, was the place of our youth, our Tír na nÓg or Valhalla. Here were our pirate coves, our Indian plains, our rough playing pitches. Here we learned to swing a camán and to kick a ball, to hurl ourselves across the wildest parts of the stream in a daring and often very wet game of 'chicken' and even to swim, in a pool formed by a home-made dam.

It is all changed now. Nemesis in the form of progress has taken its toll and the once wild Glen of our youth is today a city park, tasteful and still pleasant, but no longer wild, tamed into submission and conformity, and in part desecrated by the gaping maw of the excavator tearing sand from its northern hillside. The Doctor's fields behind our old houses now bear crops of new dwellings and a school, a through-road and a Corporation depot. The Glen Lane itself has long since been levelled and concreted; Paddy Buckley's stable under the old elm has been swept away along with the tree itself, and John Murphy's huge garden houses two bungalow's, one occupied by his youngest daughter and her family. Dan Murphy's farm has vanished with many others under the sprawling sweep of urbanisation as the growing city has spread its concrete tentacles into what was once rich agricultural land.

The sunlight still sparkles on the little Glen stream of my youth, but that too is changed, having been developed into a series of man-made lakes, lovely, swan-bearing and environmentally perfect... a little too perfect, perhaps?

Sic transit gloria.

ACKNOWLEDGEMENTS

Like every author, I owe a debt of gratitude to those who have helped in the preparation of this book, either materially or by way of encouragement, My sincere thanks go to:

The Collins Press, my publishers, whose enthusiasm from the outset made it all possible;

My friends Father Liam O'Driscoll, Walter McGrath and Seán Dunne, who read the first draft and encouraged me to continue, and to Walter also for his typical generosity in allowing me the use of the fruits of some of his own research, especially in relation to the history of the Glen;

My editor, Phil Murphy, whose expertise was invaluable and who saved me from the horrors of tautology and other dreadful literary excesses;

My colleague and friend Ted Crosbie, Chief Executive of Cork Examiner Publications Ltd., and my fellow Directors for generous permission to select from *The Cork Examiner* archival photographs, and to Stephen Coughlan and Lillian Caverley for their assistance.

The majority of the photographic illustrations reproduced here are by kind courtesy of Cork Examiner Publications Ltd. However, there are a number of places and objects long since gone of which I could find no photographic record.

In spite of all this assistance, memory can be a fickle jade, and I alone must assume responsibility for any inaccuracies of time or incident which may have slipped in.

In the words of P.G. Wodehouse, 'OK Con, you can let 'em in now!'

INTRODUCTION

This is not an autobiography, nor is it intended to be, Neither, despite nearly forty years in journalism, is it a chronicle of great events or major personalities. Readers seeking those things will have to look elsewhere, where they have already been well chronicled. True, little pieces of history do intrude where they seem appropriate and the account is personalised, but only insofar as I am the loom on which the tale of people and places of an age now gone by is woven. From this it will be gathered that it is a journey back in time to a particular place which is characteristic of many places, both urban and rural, in an Ireland and indeed a world now gone forever.

There is little extraordinary in this journal, except insofar as the ordinary of yesteryear has become the extraordinary of today, and will become the social history of tomorrow. So why bother to put it all on paper? First, because it is gone and should not, I believe, be forgotten - all this apparent inconsequence, all this minutiae of daily living. In attempting this chronicle, I have been very fortunate in a number of respects. First, I was born and reared with one foot in the country and the other in the town, so to speak, in a proud place in a fiercely independent city, old, beautiful, battered by the ravages of a turbulent history as well as by fire and flood. Secondly, I grew up at a time of enormous change, when the old industrial order had to give way to new, and in the event, humanly devastating technology, when the last of the old sailing ships left the quays, when the last steam locomotive chugged away into history, and when the lovely Clydesdale pulled the last dray back to the stable.

Thirdly, because of my various occupations before becoming a journalist, I was in something of a privileged position to be involved in a number of the old ways of life and to notice their disappearance. Inevitably, this involvement has left its indelible mark, a deep concern and sadness at the destruction of both town and country, before the preservation counsels now prevailing emerged from the follies of yesterday. Finally, I was simultaneously both honoured and traumatised at presiding editorially over the changeover of our own regional newspapers from the old 'hot metal' printing system to the bright new offset technology of today, a process which is continuing to develop even as I write these words.

Though I have lived through this period of enormous change, I am not naive enough to deny that much of it was for the better; that in many ways, conditions have greatly improved for the ordinary people who form the bulk of this account. There is nothing worthy or glamorous about dire poverty, bad housing, endemic disease and all the other social ills of the time under consideration.

And if the past was not all black, the future is not all bleak, Medical advances alone, for instance, have made a staggering difference to the quality of life. So too have better education, a greater awareness of physical fitness and, of course, far easier availability of travel facilities which have made this old world a much smaller place. The old, twin curses of unemployment and emigration remain with us, however, as if to remind us that not everything changes....

In spite of all this, I am convinced that we have lost an old and easy contentment and a more gentle, leisurely way of life that is now very difficult to re-create. In an age of instant entertainment and information, we have lost some of the ability to wonder, some of the time to stop and talk to each other and, perhaps most of all, some of an old morality that respected person, property and creed. There are times when I feel we would do well to heed the little gem of advice given in Eric Cross' book *The Tailor and Ansty*: 'Take the world fine and aisy and the world will take you fine and aisy'. This, in our time, we did, and this is how we did it.

THE LIFE OF OTHER DAYS

It was the sort of place where time stood still, a little hamlet on the edge of a village connected in turn to the city proper by long, winding, hilly roads, along which grew still other villages that, in the century before, had been taken over and absorbed by the inevitable growth of the years and the expanding conurbation. But our hamlet, on the border of the city, had resisted all the blandishments of the developer and stood small but proud, a little collection of houses strung out along a lane that was curiously split down the middle by a low stone wall for half its length, one half giving access to the houses, the other leading to the place known simply as 'the Glen'.

It was as if the planners of another time had blundered, so that we had two lanes instead of one, neither of them clothed in anything but the stone and soil with which nature had provided them. If you ignored the detached home of Mr. Bowen, the insurance agent, which stood in its splendid isolation at the very entrance to the Glen, there were only six houses, one of them a part-time shop, another reputedly a one-time monastery, three-storied, high-gabled, its various rooms and stairs rambling all over the place like something from a mad architect's dream, a strange house to find in a place like this.

Our house, Number Five, was a moderately-sized, two-storey home, what would probably now be called lower middle-class, though doubtless in our time it would have been called simply working-class. Even then, it must have been very old, though nobody could tell just how many winter gales had lifted a few slates from its tired roof, how many torrents had battered wetly and noisily against its tall windows. Solid slabs of stone for window sills suggested its age, but did not date it; neither did the three-foot thick walls, one of which, an internal dividing wall, had sunk a little with the years, so that the upstairs rooms in particular had sloping floors. Mother had to put blocks of wood under one end of her bed to keep it reasonably level, and somebody had once shaved pieces off the end of the bedroom doors so that they could be opened inwards fully against the slant of the floors. This meant that when they were closed, there was a large gap at the bottom that admitted draughts.

There were three bedrooms, two with fireplaces, the smallest room without. Downstairs, the accommodation consisted of a fairly large room with an ancient Black Prince cooker, connected to the city gas system, an aged sink in another corner with a single, cold-water tap and a black range, on which simmered for a few hours every night in winter, a large pot of porridge that was re-heated for the following morning's breakfast. Both before and after the cooking of the porridge, the pot was replaced with a huge black iron kettle,

7

so that hot water was available on an almost constant basis.

Several times a week the iron range was coated with black lead and brush-polished, as one would polish boots, its few steel parts being buffed with emery paper until they shone brightly, producing a silver contrast with the glossy black. When the fire in the range was lit and the big kettle steaming busily, this was a cosy little room, especially on dark winter's evenings, and I had my own little stool by the fire, tucked away in a corner where I read without interruption, while our black cat dozed contentedly on a ledge in front of the oven door, relishing the heat as only cats do.

The front room was rarely used when we were young, largely, I think, because we all preferred the kitchen, where everything was to hand and where the washing – of both clothes and people – was done in a big steel bath, which I once succeeded in toppling over on myself from its rather precarious perch on a chair, this being just the right height for scrubbing clothes. Fortunately, the water in it was only lukewarm and I escaped with no more than a thorough soaking. The parlour, or as we called it, simply 'the room', was used for highdays, holidays and visitors and its furnishings included a huge mirrored sideboard, a three-piece suite of unknown vintage and little comfort, a large dining table and its attendant chairs, ornate and very heavy, an old photograph of my maternal grandparents and a print of Richard Jack's famous painting, *The Toast*. I did not particularly care for this print – it seemed to me to have very little to do with our style of living – and much preferred two other prints in the high hallway, depicting colourful Arabs in Middle-Eastern bazaars, with towers and minarets in the background!

In the tiny front garden, my father, before his death, had cultivated a few climbing roses, a hydrangea which later threatened to take over the whole patch and some 'London Pride', delicate and beautiful, together with a Canadian currant bush which occupied its own corner for many years, bringing a splash of vivid pink to the area every spring. Apart from the fact that it contained the outside – and only – toilet and a small shed, the back garden was unremarkable except for the fact that its southern wall was high, an old chimney breast showing clearly that it was part of a long-demolished cottage or house. It also helped to establish in my mind the fact that the whole place was built when homes were constructed higgledy-piggledy, huddled on top of each other, with little consideration for space.

Sometimes, when we were attempting to cultivate this part of the garden, remnants of the life of the former occupants would surface in the shape of old implements and kitchen artefacts and once I found a very old penny, which set me digging industriously for days in the vain hope of discovering a hoard. This then was our home, semi-detached, well worn, but snug, cool in summer because of those thick walls and not too difficult to heat in winter, even when the bitter northerlies blew up the lane from the Glen, unhindered in their frozen progress by many miles of relatively flat land.

So, in Number Five, on a morning in August 1935, my long-suffering mother brought me and my twin brother bawling into a world even then trembling on the brink of a terrible holocaust. There too, just a month before, my father, a fireman on the Great Southern Railway, had been taken ill with appendicitis, and rushed to hospital, where he died, suddenly, of peritonitis. So our arrival cannot have been an occasion of any great joy, the more so since a few days later my twin brother, having viewed the world with a jaundiced eye, decided that this place was not for him and returned to his Maker, leaving only Mother, the pink squalling bundle that was myself and my sister, five years older. It was hardly the most auspicious start in life, but like it or not, we had to make the best of it. If there were any compensations, they were hard to find, except perhaps for the fact that Mother, then aged thirty-four, was a gentle, easy-going person who worked hard, worried a lot and cared for us as best she knew, indeed as only a mother could, at a time when nothing came easy.

Of course, I remember none of this early trauma, my first conscious memory being, extremely vaguely, of a trip to Bridlington in Yorkshire in the summer of 1939, where I had two aunts. I seem to recall coming home on a tossing ship with everybody around being very sick, and I later gathered that we just got out of Britain in time, only weeks before the declaration of war. But these few scattered memories are hazy, like those of somebody waking from anaesthetic and repeatedly dropping back into slumber, seeing only passing images and fleeting glimpses.

But I do recall quite vividly my fourth birthday, sitting on the front step on a sunny morning, no doubt placed there to await the arrival of Mr. Rooney, the postman, tall, ever cheerful and, on this particular morning, simply bursting with goodwill as he handed me several of my own special envelopes with my own special birthday cards, and telling me what a big boy I was now. It was, I suppose, the first watershed, the first time when I really began to sit up and take notice, as I supposed big boys must. It was also the first of many glorious mornings spent at the front of the house, from where I had hitherto been banned, on the grounds that I might wander off while Mother attended to the household chores. The responsibility of staying within certain strict limits – 'You are not to go out into the Big Lane' – had its corresponding compensations, because from the limited confines of the Small Lane and the front garden, I could watch the daily kaleidoscope of everyday living in our neighbourhood.

Small as it was, it would be wrong to suppose that nothing ever happened here. Indeed, it was simply packed with minor incident from early morning until nightfall, with arrivals and departures, with people and animals, with deliveries being made and goods and services being offered, with the vagrant poor who were soliciting from those almost as impoverished, with strolling musicians from afar, with the unemployed yodelling and paper-and-comb amateur minstrels from the village of Dillon's Cross, just a few hundred yards away.

For a four-year-old, morning came gently to this place, after a night cocooned in the swaddling clothing of a benevolent Nature; sometimes awakening for a while to the sighing of the big old elm across the lane, the distant braying of a donkey, the raucous 'craak-craak' of the landrail or corncrake from the reeds in the Glen or the surrounding meadows, and the strangely comforting sound of a heavy goods train chug-chugging its way, gasping and wheezing, up the long gradient from the tunnel outside Glanmire station, en route to Thurles or Dublin. This sound indeed, was to be the start of a lifelong fascination with railways. On some nights, much earlier, before I settled down for the night, Mother would bring me to the upstairs back window of the house to show me the huge orange glow in the sky over the distant tunnel and to hear the furious pounding of the Night Mail as, double-headed, it tackled the fearsome bank in a cacophony of sound and billowing smoke and steam, and I was much too small then to realise why there was a tear on her cheek as she tucked me in and kissed me goodnight.

But morning brought nothing of the drama of the night before. It began with the soft clop of Michael Daly's horse on the unmetalled lane as he began his milk round, having left his home in Rathcooney, high in the heart of the hinterland, at dawn. With the first rays of the sun he arrived from the east, like a Magi, bearing not gold, nor frankincense, nor myrrh, but the very essence of our staple diet, and certainly of mine. The soft snort and stomp of his horse mingled with the clatter of pewter as he drew the precious liquid from the tap in the churn at the back of his high-wheeled cart, marked 'Bainne ar díol', into his gallon, then to be re-distributed into the quart or pint as the occasion and the customer required. There were, of course, no customers to greet him at that early hour; he simply took the key from above the door and entered, pouring the milk into the large jug in the hall, closing the door and replacing the key as he went. And since those pre-pasteurisation days, no milk has ever tasted so good, cool, rich, creamy and full of the intimate smell of calm, contented cows and herbaceous country grassland.

Scarcely had Michael gone on his way, his horse wandering the familiar route untended, when Paddy Buckley arrived, rotund, gaitered, clad in waistcoat and old battered soft hat, to lead his own steed from the little stable under the elm. Dragging out the large-wheeled but this time low-slung cart which he used for his daily haulage, Paddy set about the business of tackling up, slowly and carefully, working at the particular pace of a man who has done this same task thousands of times and who will not be hurried – the same deceptive pace that I was later to notice many times in people who worked the land and the animals, and in skilled craftsmen with respect for their trade and their materials. Soon, bridle, heavy collar, hames and reins all ready, off they would go on their leather-creaking way, to another day's labour.

I was never quiet sure what exactly Paddy and his cart carried, or to where, because he always left empty and arrived home in the evening equally devoid of goods, but I understand he was a small-time, private haulier, contributing as much to the economy of our own locality as to the great commercial ventures of the city – a suite of old furniture to an auction, a bit of low-priced house moving, a load of hay for a local farmer, or the collection of a tierce or two of stout which one of the local publicans needed in a hurry.

These were the things of little drama but sound economy that filled his life and ours. As he went, he would lift his hat and shout a greeting to the Sunbeam girls, chattering like bright sparrows as they wended their way down the lane to the Glen, through Goulding's fertiliser plant and on to Blackpool, to Willie Dwyer's brand new hosiery factory which was to become one of the corner-stones of the industrial scene in the city for many years. Sunbeams indeed, always bubbling over with high good humour and arm-linked bonhomie, they bounced along, in cheerful contrast to the Goulding workers who would quietly follow them; Mick Nagle and his cohorts, bent from carrying heavy loads and the burdens of the day, their overalls snow-scattered with the white dust of their employment, sure that their steady steps would bring them to the factory gate before the five-to-eight siren sounded.

With their departure, the place settled into its morning routine, like an old man putting on a comfortable pair of slippers, or a well-worn cap. With breakfast came my boiled egg, eaten with its little 'soldiers' of bread and butter, dipped in and stickily extracted, to accompanying exhortations to 'eat it all up now so that you'll be a big, strong boy to look after Mammy'. Fortunately, I loved boiled eggs anyway! When the postman had come and gone, I pottered around, holding my precious birthday cards and wandering over to Nana Mac's little shop window next door, to see what goodies I might expect on this, my special day, because certainly there would

11

be something, in spite of the frugality of the times.

Nana Mac was elderly, grey and gentle, her tiny shop consisting of part of her living room curtained off for some privacy, and its outer portion stuffed with sweets, chocolate, cigarettes, lemonade and, frequently, little home-made cakes with which she supplemented her meagre income. Mostly they were scones, with jam in the middle and a little coloured icing on top, and she sold them for a penny. Now and again, when business was slack and when she was unflustered, she would take me by the hand and bring me into the inner sanctum to see her treasure, the biggest egg in the world. It was, in fact, an ostrich egg, coming from heaven knows where, but resting in a large jar on the mantlepiece, to be taken down to four-year-old level so that my wondering eyes could get a proper view of this marvellous object from some far corner of the globe. In her little garden outside grew flowers and shrubs, the latter almost hiding a large enamel sign that proclaimed *Lyons Tea – A Packet For Every Pocket,* and others extolling the virtues of Players Weights, Woodbines and Kerry Blue cigarettes.

Nana Mac and her sister Nurse Eaton occupied the ground floor of the house. Upstairs lived her son, Phil McCarthy, a large, portly railway driver, quiet almost to the point of shyness, his Kerry-born wife Nora, dark-haired and beautiful, and their family, who were my playmates for many years. There must have been some sort of tenancy conspiracy among the railway fraternity because, across the way in the large old house that was Number Three, and reputed to have been the monastery, lived yet another railway fireman, John Murphy, brother of Séamus, the famous Cork sculptor, his wife Sarah and a large family of, at that time, five girls and one boy, yet another girl being born later.

Between us and them, in a house strangely more set back from the lane than the others, and thus having a longer front garden, lived the Linehan family. The parents were both tall and angular, but the children, all of them strong personalities, were robust in both activity and nature. One of the girls subsequently became a nun. The first two houses were occupied by the families of Quinlan and McLoughlin, with whom we had little dealings, first because they were 'grown-ups' and secondly, because of the peculiar way in which our little hamlet was structured, their front entrances were not in the lane, but on the main road.

As the morning wore on, there were other commercial arrivals, always by horse cart, the most visually spectacular being the bread men, of whom several came to different customers in the lane. Their carts were things of beauty with large, delicately-spoked wheels on light springs, bearing the square boxes that held the bread and on top of which sat the driver, majestic in his aerial grandeur. But his must have been the very devil of a job in bad weather when he still had to sit there, unsheltered and open to the worst the elements could fling at him.

These carts were always almost luminous in their gorgeous liveries, green and yellow for Thompson's, dark blue and gold for Simcox and so on, mobile advertisements as well as mere conveyances. Inside, when the driver-salesman opened the rear door and poked them out with a long stick with a nail on the end, were the most mouth-watering artefacts of the bakers' endeavours: pans, skulls, baskets, ducks, and plain or 'batch' bread, which came not in loaves, but rather in semi-separated rows from which chunks were broken off according to customer requirements. There were small cakes too, in big trays, but they were hardly ever for us; fresh, crusty bread kept the hunger away and economy dictated that volume rather than delicacy was better value.

Scarcely had they gone when, on certain mornings, would come the laundry wagon, similar in style but more sober in livery, and driven by one of the best-loved characters in the area, little Frankie, whose tiny frame in no way reflected his stature in the community or, indeed, his outlook on life. Frankie was unfailingly cheerful, full of banter and jokes, which were always against himself. He would draw himself up to his full five-foot-nothing and solemnly pronounce; 'Now, I remember when I was in the Shanghai Police...' or 'My family must be the only one where the son's clothes are cut down for the father'. Much later, the powers that be replaced Frankie's cart with a motor van and strong rumour had it that a policeman on traffic duty on St. Patrick's Bridge almost ran for his life when he saw what he imagined was a driverless van approaching him. Frankie's excuse was typical; 'If I sit on the seat without a cushion, I can't see through the windscreen. If I use the cushion, my feet can't reach the pedals'. The response from the policeman, who was known as Fingers because of the manner in which he summarily flicked the traffic on its way, is not recorded!

It was usually afternoon or evening, depending on the time of year, before the more eccentric arrivals drifted into the lane, the human flotsam of a not too affluent society, seeking no more than a bite to eat or perhaps the small price of a roof over their heads for the night. We never got to know them in the way that we got to know the strolling musicians, and any feeble attempts at friendship were usually rebuffed. Our elders may have known something, perhaps a tale of exceptional hardship or ill-luck, but if they did, they never confided in us, and it was at our absolute peril that we attempted to play any pranks on these walking ragbags of humanity, because the parental consequences would be dire indeed. Browbeaten and battered by the storms of life, they came shuffling into our lives, mainly male and elderly and always ill-clad and pinched, and we watched them in fascination, not so much for what they were, but for what they did.

Having received some little solace, be it food or money or perhaps even an old coat, they would pause at the outer wall of the house, take a nail from inside a tattered pocket and scratch a mark on the wall. Then, without a further word, they would shuffle off from whence they came, ghostly figures disappearing into the evening mist. Try as we might, we could never decipher the strange symbols scratched on the wall. Almost certainly they were some sort of written code left for those who might follow, or perhaps even to serve as a reminder to themselves on future visits that here might be obtained assistance, there a dog to be watched, or there again a house not worth bothering with since the inmates were almost as poor as themselves. Either way, we never did learn the key to the code, just as we never learned who these desperate people were, and I still wonder if the expression of awe and wonder common around the neighbourhood, 'put a mark on the wall', stemmed initially from the scratches of these unfortunates.

Much more happily, we would greet the arrival of the various musicians, many of whom came time and again to entertain us, often with considerable talent, for the few scarce pennies that would come their way. A husband and wife team of violinist and harpist would set up stage in the middle of the lane and proceed to go through their repertoire, to the great enjoyment of a small audience. At the end of every tune, we would applaud enthusiastically, whether we knew the air or not and, of course, there were special nursery rhymes for us smaller ones, who would bellow them out in time to the music.

There was more than a touch of old gentility about this accomplished duo, the graciousness of another age, as they bowed and plucked busily to enrich our lives; he magnificent in a flowing beard and she slim and elegant on her little stool. And when the performance had finished, before the cardboard box was passed around, they would smile and bow, as though to a packed concert hall, and condescend to give a few encores with all the aplomb of accomplished performers, which indeed they were. This caused many of our elders to remark, after they had gone, what a pity it was that such a lovely old couple were reduced to this, 'ag seinm cheoil do phócaí folamh', playing music to empty pockets, like the blind poet Raftery.

Now and again an accordionist would appear, another elderly man who had special love for us children, and who took great pleasure in playing for us. 'Now I'll play "The Blackbird",' he would tell us. 'It's an old Irish dance tune, and one of these days, when I get the time, I'll teach it to you.' And his dancing fingers would caress the keys of the ancient instrument and the music would come, tripping and skipping into our ears, to stay forever in the cadences of the mind. But he never did get around to teaching us the dance, and for a long time he did not appear at all.

Then late one evening, he appeared again in the lane, much older now, bent and white-haired, and without the accordeon. Instead, he had an old tin biscuit box on which his rheumatic fingers tried to diddle out the half-remembered notes and rhythms. His old accordeon, he told us, had become broken beyond repair and he could not afford another one, so he was reduced to lilting and drumming on the old tin box, and 'tisn't the same thing at all, but 'tis the best I can do for ye, God help us'. God help him indeed, for after that last sad evening of mouth music and the heartrending performance on the old biscuit box, we never saw him again. Only his farewell wave as he turned the corner remains in the mind, and the memory of 'The Blackbird'.

Much more raucous and unmusical were the Friday night fish women who came peddling the very last of their wares, choosing this neck of the woods to try to get rid of what was left before going home, usually without doing too much in the way of business. On their backs they carried large baskets, strapped on in the way hikers now carry knapsacks, holding with both hands the front straps as they bellowed what sounded to us like 'Awk, Awk, Maak-er-el', when in fact they were probably extolling the virtues of hake and mackerel. Their stentorian tones filled the evening air, causing one local to remark; 'Well, the fish mightn't be great, but she has a fine pair of lungs, God bless her'.

Why they came here at all heaven knows, because it was a long way from the city centre and it was all uphill. But come they did, and off they went, usually profitless, leaving the now quiet evening to us and to the bats that swooped and dipped over Murphy's high gables and drove the girls indoors lest they became entangled in their hair, according to local legend. But we boys knew better and would throw stones at the little creatures to test their in-built radar and watch them adroitly dodge even the most accurate of our missiles at the very last moment.

*   *   *

By the time I was almost, but not quite, old enough to go to

junior school, things had changed a little in our small household. Mother had obtained some employment several mornings
a week and, as a result, I was often 'farmed out' to a great aunt,
Charlotte, who was more popularly known in the family circle
as 'Shaddy', and who managed a large boarding house on
Summerhill, on the way into the city. She was one of those
small, apparently frail, but quite indomitable little women who
tend to have an influence on things out of all proportion to their
size. The old house was a high, four-storied affair, the bulk of
which was taken up by bedrooms where her guests lived, all of
whom were from banking or insurance circles. 'My gentlemen'
she called them, and treated them accordingly. They were as
much her family as her patrons – and indeed her living, because
without them she could never have maintained the huge house,
which she rented on a weekly basis.

It was moderately, rather then luxuriously, furnished, with
the usual large lounge and dining room and what was even then
a huge kitchen. It backed on to Wellington Road, where there
were many similar houses, but had a very long garden in front,
running down to a flight of steps and an old wrought iron gate
leading to Summerhill. In the garden grew some fine roses, since
one of her guests was a rose fancier. I was in dire trouble with
Shaddy one day when, playing with my sister, I slipped and fell
into the rose bed, ruining one of his special favourites, but the
good man himself never said a word about the matter.

Another one of her guests was a noted local rugby player
who was later to die tragically when somebody stamped on his
stomach in a maul. His name was Charlie and he was a particular friend and adviser to Shaddy, keeping in touch with her even
after he had been transferred to Limerick, and on his death she
missed him as a mother would miss a son. A third was an amateur carpenter, and my sister and I used to look in wonder at the
fine furniture he created in his spare time. Yet another was a
watercolour artist of some talent, and I used to marvel at the
lovely landscapes he produced, apparently without effort,
thought I know better now. Without exception, they were cheerful, nice people and of course, they would have been in the
upper echelons of Cork society in those days, when bank clerks
and insurance men had far more status than they have today.

But for me the great attraction of the big house was the fact
that on fine mornings I was allowed to sit on the steps at the gate
on Summerhill and view the morning parade; busy housewives
making their way towards the city with shopping bags or baskets, postmen on their rounds, errand boys from the city stores
wearily pushing their huge basket-laden bicycles up the hill to

the big houses in St. Luke's and Montenotte, and whistling as later they freewheeled wildly downhill to begin yet another trudge to Blackrock or Douglas, Sunday's Well or some of the better-class suburbs. Horse carts came and went too, wheezing up the hill to St. Luke's where there was a water trough from which the animals could drink, guzzling noisily while they rested. Those coming downhill had special steel 'slippers' that could be put under one wheel to keep them from running away on the steep slope, and it was one of these unfortunate horses which first brought me into close contact with the reality of death.

I was sitting on the step as usual, when about a hundred yards away, down the hill, a poor horse was quite unable to make the grade with its big cart and went down under the heavy load. A group of men came and tried to get the animal up, releasing the shafts and dragging the cart clear, but it was no good. The horse lay there, unable to rise, despite a few pathetic efforts. After some time, another man appeared with what I thought looked like a gun. There was a loud bang, the horse's head jerked upwards and crashed down again and, in the sulphurous silence that followed, Shaddy came rushing down to drag me away.

The doorstep adventures did not stop there. Some days later I was back at my old station, drinking in the morning scene, when a van came downhill from St. Luke's, travelling fairly fast for those days. As it came nearer, I thought one of the front wheels was wobbling and with all the confidence and concern of a five-year-old, stood up and waved to the driver, pointing frantically to the erratic wheel. He, doubtless thinking I was a friendly little lad, waved back and cheerily shouted something, until suddenly the wheel came off and went bouncing down the road, while the van careered across the street and crashed into the kerb with a resounding bang. Once again Shaddy came running, terrified no doubt that her small charge had been maimed, or worse. And again I was dragged away from the fascination of the ensuing scene and sternly confined to the upper garden 'where I can see you, you little rip'.

But essentially Shaddy was a kindly little person, who would take me on the greatest adventures of all, her shopping trips to the city – though I must, on reflection, have been a confounded nuisance to her. So off we would go, hand in hand, first to the Post Office at St. Luke's Cross, one of the lovely little villages that had become subsumed into the city, with its old toll house, its horse trough, its magnificent and much under-rated Church of Ireland edifice – the rector of which is also, incidentally, the rector of the famed Shandon – and its plethora of fine houses and shops, prominent being the elegant grocery store-cum-pub of the Henchy family, ornate in its Victorian finery.

There was wealth here at one time, when the old city was expanding from its marshy roots and when the prosperous merchants and upper-middle class could afford to build tall and strong, as in the high, above-the-road houses of Árd Áluinn and Árd na Gréine, protected across the way by an old police barracks, then inhabited by a sergeant and one garda. One of its four exits led to the other village of Mayfield, by way of prosperous Montenotte, home to the truly wealthy, who built fine, almost great, houses on mini-estates overlooking the benign Lee, its twin arteries rejoined and flowing along the busy quays of the upper harbour.

Our business with the kindly, bespectacled postmistress over, it was off again, down Wellington Road, one of the many streets in this area commemorating the grandeur of the old Empire, and destined to retain its name in spite of changes elsewhere, as in MacCurtain Street below, which used to be King Street. Off Wellington Road were other large houses and avenues proclaiming that this whole area was once a bastion of colonialism, at least in the minds of those who built it; terraces like Belgrave Place and others still singing of battles long ago. Such thoughts, of course, never crossed my juvenile mind as we made our way down Wellington Road, but I did notice the sheer size of the houses, their blind, high north-facing windows on the left hand side – one of which was Shaddy's – contrasting with the sparkling glasses of those on the other, where the morning sun shimmered off the glass as it would off the calm waters of a distant lake.

Indeed, this place reflected the curious anomaly that was then Cork; on one hand the fierce, independent republicanism of a city and a people who had been to the forefront in the struggle for freedom from a 700-year yoke and, on the other, a continuing presence, in the form of architecture, of Imperial glory and a hankering, among some, after the old days. In those days there were still many elderly men who had served with distinction in the First World War, and even perhaps in the Boer War, wilting figures who had once been ramrod-straight, and who still tended to maintain that 'a man is never broke when he has the King's shilling in his pocket'.

Living now on small army pensions, they epitomised, more than anything else, more even than the surrounding colonial buildings, the Irish contribution to British ambition. Against the tide of nationalism, they stood four-square, a pathetically small group of people who had made their own choice in life and above all, a living reminder of their dead comrades on the bloody fields of the Somme and Passchendale, slaughtered in furtherance of the spurious promise of 'freedom for small nations' – and all of this at a time when the stormclouds were again gathering over Europe and a world trembling on the brink of another catastrophe.

But as we strode this fine, broad street on a bright sunny morning, taking in the housewives and the few dwindling maid-servants polishing their brasses and pram-walking the children, any such sombre reflections were far from the mind of a small boy. I was far more interested in the delicious, tummy-aching smell wafting from Thompson's bakery in York Street, where the day's batches of fancy cakes and other goodies were being completed. I was then unaware that across the road at the top of York Street hill, Mary and Annie MacSwiney, sisters of the hunger-strike patriot Terence, were conducting their classes in Irish in their private girls' school known as Scoil Íte, an educational establishment that was to become something of an institution in the city. A little further on I knew was the school of the Christian Brothers, tall and red-bricked and catering for those who could afford to go there; for those who couldn't, it was the North Monastery or Sullivan's Quay. The Brothers, it seemed, felt they had to cater for all classes, but there was always a certain distinction about 'Christians' and it was related purely to ability to pay, plus, of course, the fact that here they played rugby and cricket, while other Brothers' schools concentrated on Gaelic games.

At the end of Wellington Road we came to the junction with steep St. Patrick's Hill, then haunt of the medical profession, almost every door of the four and five-storied houses bearing a brass plate polished almost to extinction, at least of the name and qualifications of the occupant. A few steps brought us to the Baltimore Stores for fish, and then it was over the wide arches of St. Patrick's Bridge – the second on the site, the first having been swept away by floods even before it was finished – and into the city proper, where the big double-decker, red and white buses ran, and the drivers of the few cars of the time parked wherever they pleased. There too the driver of the horse-drawn 'sidecars' dozed in the morning sun, waiting for business at the Statue (to Father Mathew, the Apostle of Temperance), one of the landmarks of the city. The same sidecars have long since gone from all but the tourist resort of Killarney, where they are known as 'jaunting cars', but in the Cork of 1939 they were an integral part of the city transport system.

As when I was with Mother, shopping soon became a bore, except for the fascination of visiting the different shops and watching with some juvenile awe the everyday commerce of the city at work. The grocers' were the best, and while Patrick Street may have been the main street, Princes Street, just off it, was the most entertaining. There, while Shaddy bought her bacon and cheese, butter and eggs in O'Donovan's, I would watch enthralled as the man in the white coat spun the huge hand-wheel to cut the rashers on to a gleaming, reciprocating steel tray, in slivers of red and white, streaky or loin, thick or thin, according to customer requirements.

Further up, Barry's famed tea and coffee emporium was a nose-twitching Aladdin's cave of aromatic wonders from the furthest corners of the world, the smell of roasting coffee blending with that of the various teas and spices. The teas were kept in huge bins and scooped out, when requiring to be weighed, into paper bags with an illustration running across the front of a little Indian boy in pantaloons bearing a tea tray. I became very fond of that little boy; he looked so happy at his work, with a big beaming smile, and I used to imagine that I would like to have him for a friend. Then, as a special treat if I was very good, Shaddy would take me into Thompson's restaurant for tea and a sticky bun, where for a little while we would sit among 'the best people', before going on to Lipton's to complete the morning's purchases.

Lipton's I think I loved best of all, even better than Thompson's, because it had a high wire system running across the ceiling of the entire shop, from the various counters to the cashier's office. The sales assistant would take the money, write a docket and put both into a capsule which she screwed into a container. Then she jerked a handle and off it whizzed, with a high-pitched scream of metal on wire, to the cash box, where the money and docket were removed, change placed in the capsule and with another scream, back it came again, to stop with a clang at the counter.

On those occasions when I was with Mother, rather than Shaddy, there would always be the chance of one final treat, a trip to the toy counter at Woolworth's, where stood leaden toy soldiers and farm animals from the firm of Britain's. There, eyes out on stalks, was the delicious indecision of what to choose, bearing in mind the financial constraints of the day. Eventually, after a great deal of dithering and changing of mind, I would come away clutching another little lead cow, or soldier, to add to my small collection, Mother having handed over 'a big white money' (sixpence). Finally, the shopping done, the inner man satisfied, for the time being at least, and the toy in the pocket, it was time to head for the Statue, and the bus home.

Unlike the modern, one-man, auto-change vehicles of today, the buses of my youth were usually double-deckers, with Leyland 'Lion' or 'Tiger' petrol engines, crash gearboxes and huge steering wheels, because they had no power steering. On the upper deck, the front jutted out over the driver's cab, so that next to his little home, which of course was on the right-hand side, there was a sort of an alcove which contained the engine and the left-hand wheel, before the lower deck of the bus proper began. No streamlining here, just a blunt, solid front end, seemingly full of power and the might of the huge engine. The entrance was at the rear, with curved steps to the upper deck, where the seats were built to hold five or six people, depending on size, with a side corridor. This, of course, made things very difficult for the conductor, who had to develop very long arms in order to reach the innermost passengers for their fares, to the accompaniment of much banter and arguing among the women about who was going to pay for whom. 'Let me get this... No, no, let me...' so that eventually the poor harassed man would roar 'For God's sake will ye make up ye'er minds and don't have me standing here all day'.

The driver sat in splendid isolation in his cab, in a little world of his own, connected to the rest of the machine only by a bell code; two for go, one for stop, and a little sliding hatch that nobody dared open except for the conductor. Occasionally the conductor would open the hatch and poke his head in while the bus was in motion, and I used to wonder what could be so important that he and the driver had to talk about it while on the move. Then one day we made an unscheduled stop outside the tobacconist's and the conductor, complete with ticket machine and money bag, dashed away for a minute...

Mighty these buses may have been, with a fine healthy roar from the engine, but it was all uphill on the way home and with a full load, including a number of standing passengers, progress tended to be slow. Mostly we ground along in low gear, only now and then getting into second with a thump and a lurch, so that those standing swayed forwards and then backwards like a chorus line as the bus snatched and jerked, like a horse taking the strain of being asked for even more effort. The regular conductor, of course, knew everybody. Those who travelled on our local bus were not customers but friends, and Jimmy would pause for a word with all his clients as he dispensed the tickets from his magic machine. Sometimes when we were leaving, he would give me the end of a ticket roll, which could be used as a streamer – that it had a red line down the centre served merely to indicate that the roll was about to become exhausted, but it made it appear quite exotic when blowing in the wind.

We got off at Dillons Cross, named after the Fenian patriot Brian Dillon, and there the bus would turn, the driver grunting as he swung the huge wheel to full lock so that the vehicle could negotiate the half-circle in one attempt, without having to reverse. Another bus went even further uphill, to the outlying village of Mayfield, up the very steep incline to the Three Horseshoes pub and the chapel. Late at night, I would lie tucked up, listening to the last bus groaning its weary way up this hill, with an increasing roar from the engine and the loud whine of the bottom gear, until finally, almost with an audible sigh, it came to rest at the pub. From there on it was all level ground to Mayfield – and it was time for me to go to sleep, lulled into slumber by the song of the newly-arrived house martins in the eaves above my window. It was a gentle sound that was to stay in the mind forever, later reinforced by enacting in school Padraig Pearse's poignant little story 'Eoghainín na n-Éan' (Little Eoin of the Birds).

THE LIFE OF OTHER DAYS

At the very bottom of John Murphy's garden, just before the hedge separated the sloping, brown earth from the small but smelly open sewer that ran behind the houses along the boundary of Jim Bowen's patch, stood a young and very virile chestnut tree, rearing its ever-rustling foliage upwards, as if reaching for sustenance to the omnipotent sky. Serenely confident of its own stature, it stood firm against the wildest of weather, its roots holding it steadfast in the teeth of the most vicious southwesterlies, its young, flexible branches bending easily before the gale, offering ready if see-saw perches to blackbird and thrush, to sparrow and linnet.

It seemed to grow at an extraordinary rate, shooting skywards year after year, reflecting our own growth, our own progress towards strength and a sort of maturity. Like us, it was in the green years, with us for as long as any of us could remember. When we were too small to do anything but rest beneath its benevolent shade in summer, we longed for the day when we would be able to climb into its uppermost branches, to become part of the tree that was already a part of us, as indeed was the whole of John's garden, that veritable cornucopia of all living things that never ceased to delight our young eyes and senses.

Fortunate indeed were we to have such a place to go and even more fortunate to have a man who tolerated our almost daily intrusions into his life and his valuable spare time. It may very well be true that one is nearer to God in a garden than anywhere else on earth, and certainly to us, John's half-acre was a truly magical place, divorced from his house and hidden behind a high corrugated iron fence on top of a four-foot stone wall. While Mother and my sister, and I, in my tiny, tin-pot-way, struggled to produce a few drills of potatoes, some cabbage and a little lettuce from our own back garden, respectably sized but back-breakingly untended, John's patch was full of horticultural delights, both vegetable and floral, not to mention the fruit which he grew in great abundance. How he managed all this industry in addition to his physically demanding full-time job as fireman on the railway is one of those mysteries to which none of us had any solution, though it did puzzle us from time to time, the more so since it was entirely a one-man operation.

At the bottom of the garden was a hen-run where he kept a variety of fowl, through which we were first introduced not only to hens, but to geese, ducks and the few turkeys which were kept specially for Christmas. But the hen-run was largely the domain of his wife, Sarah. The garden was John's and his alone. There we first learned the mysteries of a bountiful nature, in our tinier years, from the body of an old, heavy wooden wheelbarrow, in which this busy man somehow found time to cart us about, to squeals of pleasure. I suspect that he built the barrow himself, as he built almost everything else in sight, including the large greenhouse in which, among other things, he grew a vine, which at times we helped him feed with copious quantities of manure-water from a big wooden butt, together with ox blood, which he swore was essential to the well-being of the black grapes.

John was one of those people with an instinctive feel for the land and its needs, the archetypal Mr. Greenfingers for whom just about everything seemed to shoot from the earth. His vast knowledge of growing was natural rather than scientific and he treated his garden accordingly. He was what would nowadays be called an organic grower, annually forking tons of manure into the ground, to put back what the growing plants had extracted, and it was simply by watching him that we learned much of what we applied to our own little plots. A large-framed, very strong man, he patiently and unceasingly tilled the earth, producing every conceivable type of vegetable, together with fruits such as apples, gooseberries, raspberries, loganberries, blackcurrants – but not strawberries, which he said occupied too much room for the return they gave.

In addition, we learned the names of the flowers: the lupins, the red hot pokers, the asters, sweet-scented stock, roses, and the beautiful 'Love Lies Bleeding', a name that intrigued us all. Whose love? And why was it bleeding? To say that John was generous with his produce is an understatement. Often in winter he would sell some of it off to us neighbours at bargain prices, and it was not unusual to get the ingredients of a good, rich soup or stew for a few pence. For the rest, we ate heartily of his fruits and if we ate too much, he rarely complained, except when we took apples or tomatoes that were not quite ripe. 'For heaven's sake, will ye give them a chance to grow!' he would say in exasperation.

Almost every hour that God sent he would be found there, digging and cultivating, resting from his labours only to take the odd pint, often with his brother Séamus the sculptor, or to listen to operatic records, of which he had a fine collection. There we watched and there we were unwittingly educated, even in such gruesome matters as how to wring the neck of a hen properly, or more cheerfully, how to find the nest of a bird that was 'laying out'. There too was the hilarious day when his daughter Veronica and I were sent to select a turkey for the Christmas dinner and, having opened the gate of the pen, ended up by being chased about the garden by a particularly vicious bird, squawking and spitting.

The garden was at once our playground and our schoolyard, for we learned as much there as we did in the classroom, following the constant, slow rhythm of the changing seasons and taking entirely for granted the fact that the various crops and fruits would blossom in due time. It never occurred to our unconscious minds that they only did so because of the labour lavished on them by the gardener. Once John took up fishing, taking a bunch of us down to the little Glen stream where, armed with a trout rod, he flaked the water unsuccessfully for the better part of an evening while we watched fascinated as he tried fly after fly, bait after bait. Then, with uncommon impatience, he declared that this business was a total waste of time and he promptly returned to his garden, where the fruits of his labour were far more certain.

Inevitably, all the hard work eventually took its toll. In the early sixties, John died suddenly at home, of a massive heart attack. By then, half of the garden had become the site for a new bungalow. The remainder was industriously tilled by his family for a number of years until finally, it too disappeared under the foundations of another bungalow for his youngest daughter and her husband. Only two small portions of our Garden of Eden now remain. Gone forever are the hen-run, the greenhouse of the grapes, and the concrete slab where we played shop. With their going we lost part of ourselves, though I still cannot bite into a Cox's Orange Pippin without conjuring up a flood of memories, while night-scented stock comes wafting on a wave of nostalgia.

*   *   *

They could not last, of course, these idyllic days in and around the lane and in John's garden. Life is real and life is earnest and, apart from the conflict that had erupted in Europe, my own little Sword of Damocles had been hanging over me for some time. On a bright sunny morning in June it finally fell, though not without some warning. I had noticed little things, like a new pair of shoes being bought even though we were in high summer and I often went barefoot. And there was the matter of the satchel, or backsack, as we called them. That had appeared, together with a small pencil case which, while its contents intrigued me, also contained a certain menace. Anyway, after breakfast one particular morning, I was scrubbed and clothed, shod and sacked and taken off by Mother to the infants' school which I had so often passed on happier trips to town.

Situated behind a very high stone wall at St. Luke's cross, it was an old red-bricked building which even from outside smelled of an odd mixture of smoke, chalk and stale urine. I disliked the place on sight, but there was nothing for it but to allow myself to be led in. There I was put in the charge of a bright young lady named Miss Tubberty – although I am quite sure now that her proper name was Tubridy – and together with a dozen others, some of whom were bawling, we were seated at old wooden desks and given

'márla', or plasticene, to play with. This would later be exchanged
for dried peas, or 'púiríní', with which we were expected to count
up to five.

It was, on reflection, not a bad way to start the business of
education for life, the more so since Miss Tubberty was a kindly
young lady and the surrounding walls were full of interesting
things, like pictures of strange places and glass cases of small toys
which, however, we were not allowed to touch. Our room held only
the junior infant class, but behind that was a larger room which had
two classes, that on the ground floor being run by Miss Barrett, the
Headmistress, while elderly, gentle Mrs. O'Connell was in charge of
a group which was tiered upwards in a wooden gallery. In yet
another room, Mrs. Nolan had the senior class. That same gallery
was a strange place, because underneath was the turf store, to
which, when our time came to occupy the wooden tiers, we were
sent to bring back a few sods for a gloomy fire that always seemed
to give off more smoke than flame and certainly gave out little in
the way of heat. But the real dread of going for the turf was the fact
that an occasional rat would scuttle away into the darkest recesses
of the undergallery; we, of course, would scuttle off fearfully in the
opposite direction.

Discipline was simple and, to be fair, not at all harsh. The system was basic, and if we were meant to be quiet while the teacher
was doing something else, we simply put our heads in our hands
and pretended to go to sleep. Otherwise, there was marching and
counter-marching around the classroom to the accompaniment of
much off-tune singing, which all seemed to me to be a waste of time
and effort, and there was much chanting of simple lessons in uni-
son. Once, when in the senior class of Mrs. Nolan, I won a sixpence
when the Religious Inspector called and chalked the word 'chesty'
up on the blackboard. I was the only one able to decipher the ana-
gram and tell him that a scythe was a tool used for cutting corn.
Otherwise, despite my early fears, junior school seemed to slip
away without much incident, apart from the fact that the ever-kind-
ly conductor Jimmy would often give me a lift home on the bus in
the afternoon. But even to my juvenile mind, the place was anti-
quated and unwholesome and it was a considerable relief when, on
another June morning a couple of years later Mrs. Nolan lined us up
and marched us up the hill to the 'big boys' – St. Patrick's National
School, commonly called, with much affection, simply 'St. Pah's'.

It was, in every sense of the word, an eyopener. Even as we
approached, the bright morning sunlight seemed to bounce cheerily
off the white walls. There was a huge playing area, some of it concreted, the rest gravel-covered and bounded by a low hedge against
which we would sit during break, sunning ourselves. On the out-

side wall of the separate and very clean toilet block there was the
most marvellous tap that sent drinking water up in an arc when you
pushed the button. Inside was a bright, airy assembly hall where we
would gather for prayers every morning and one of the teachers
would lead us in the hymns, including one which I have never
heard since and which began with the words: 'Full in the panting
heart of Rome, the great Apostle's crowning dome...'. The rest
escapes me, which is probably just as well, because it did not then
and does not now sound like one of the great pieces of sacred music
of our time. In fact, I used to wonder if it was really a military
march!

In St. Pah's the system was that one teacher would take a
given class and continue with it right through the years, from second class to seventh, thus gaining a knowledge of his pupils second
to none, while we in turn came to know his moods and to 'trace the
day's disasters in his morning face' – or at least we thought we
could. With our man, we were often wrong, first because he was
very even-tempered, and secondly because if he was feeling at all
unwell, he never let us see it. Low-sized and to us, middle-aged, in
the common use of that very relative term, his name was Jack
Murphy and we soon learned that he was nicknamed 'Small Jack'.
Looking back, I consider myself most fortunate to have had such a
teacher in what were my formative years, but then, exceptional cali-
bre was one of the hallmarks of that school, where the famed Cork
short-story writer Daniel Corkery had also taught, before my time.

There also was tall Charlie Keane, who surely knew every boy
who had ever passed through the school and who in later years
would stop me in the street for a chat and to know how my mother
was getting along. Paudie O'Driscoll, into whose class we would be
sent on the rare occasions when Small Jack was ill, was something
of a character and would exasperatedly hurl pennies at anyone who
was disruptive – we were not allowed to keep the pennies! Jim
Fennessy, then the youngest of the staff, we all loved. He had a
great rapport with us and was much involved in trying to organise
us into a bunch of sportsmen, with great effort and some limited
success. Finally, there was the headmaster, Danny O'Callaghan, a
tall gangling man of uncertain temper who would ring the bell at
the end of break, long arms and legs flailing all over the place. He
tended to use any piece of wood that came to hand as a cane, and
was treated with more than ordinary respect.

The very basis of our schooling was, of course, the Three Rs,
reading , writing and arithmetic, added to which was a certain
emphasis on the Irish language and whatever other of bits of knowledge a busy teacher could squeeze into a rather full curriculum. The
writing in particular was interesting. We used headline copybooks,

with specimen sentences on the top line of each page, which we had to copy, getting as near to the script as possible, so that ultimately, after a great deal of practice, the majority of us had developed a flowing, almost copperplate line. Small Jack was very insistent on good writing, which he declared was one of the hallmarks of intelligence and anyway, he would constantly tell us, it was both important and only good manners to be able to communicate properly with somebody. 'If you eventually become doctors, you can scribble the same rubbish as all the rest of them', he would say, 'but as long as you are with me you will learn to write so that people can understand what you are trying to say.'

In those pre-ballpoint days, we used old wooden-handled, steel-nibbled pens which must have been a direct derivative of the quill, dipping the nib into inkwells in the front of the desks. These inkwells, of course, were also used for other, more surreptitious purposes when Small Jack wasn't looking, as for instance soaking little balls of blotting paper in ink and then twanging them at a neighbour, using a ruler as a springboard. Woe betide those found indulging in this practice. The nibs themselves varied greatly, ranging from the common, narrow, spiky-writing 'N' to the much broader 'M' which gave a fine, broad, strong line and which our grubby , ink-stained hands found much easier to control. Used nibs, especially the narrow 'Ns', were pulled off the handle, dressed up with paper flights and used as darts.

There were two routes to school from our little hamlet. Each involved going first to Dillon's Cross, where a choice could be made. The 'proper' way lay up Streamhill, along a bit of Gardiner's Hill and into school by way of the back entrance there. More likely, and especially if time was pressing, which it usually was, there was a short-cut by way of an old track opposite Brian Dillon's house, up past an area known as 'the Bandza', or old bandhouse, long since gone. The name reflects the popular Cork practice of abbreviating almost everything and then adding a final 'a', as in 'Pana' for Patrick Street or 'Barracka' for Barrack Street, so adding an element of linguistic mystery to the colloquial English spoken in the city that has baffled many an outsider. A visitor to one of our Gaelic games was once utterly bewildered when, asking his local friend which was the Cork team, was told: 'Dere dere dere!' (Translation: 'There they are, there!'). At all events, having passed the Bandza, the way then lay through Kiely's Field, a large expanse of empty land bordering the school, which was later to become the venue for an annual visiting 'amusements', or fairground.

Across the road from the Bandza, around the hairpin corner that leads to Collins' Barracks, is a row of little cottages. Just beyond them was once a low wall, from behind which, on an evening in 1920 a grenade or bomb was hurled at a truck load of British Army troops on their way from the barracks to the city. The carnage was considerable, with at least one killed and many wounded. The bomb-thrower escaped through the Glen just behind him, but the reprisals began almost at once. Roads were cordoned off, innocent people were taken from their homes and threatened with death. Some of the cottages were summarily burned.

Worse was to come, much worse. The hated Black and Tans, reputed at the time to be the scum of British prisons, went on a midnight rampage through the centre of the city, setting one side of Patrick Street alight and going on to burn the City Hall. In spite of the heroic efforts of the fire brigade, who were seriously hindered in their work by the Tans, the fires continued to rage, until one side of Patrick Street was engulfed. People were murdered in their beds and, in one instance, a man was dragged from a tram and shot.

Subsequently, the most inane efforts were made in the house of Commons to pin the blame for the atrocities on 'the Sinn Féiners'. One MP went so far as to suggest that the burning of the City Hall was due to sparks from the other fires – unaware, no doubt, that City Hall was a quarter of a mile away, separated from the main blaze by the wide south channel of the River Lee. Nobody admitted that the Crown forces were responsible, but the facts were known to hundreds of eye-witnesses. Yet there was some tacit acknowledgement of culpability. In the wake of a public outcry, the hated Tans were ordered out of the city and removed to West Cork.

One morning, as I was making my reluctant way through Kiely's Field, I stumbled on something and, pausing to investigate, found an old revolver, rusty, mud-covered and plainly inoperative, since the trigger was missing. That, of course, was of no consequence whatever. Trigger or not, it would be absolutely marvellous for playing cowboys and indians, the more so since it was the genuine article, making me the envy of all my pals, who had to make do with badly-carved wooden guns. We had at times heard rumours that Kiely's Field, had been used as a drilling ground by 'the boys' during the 'Troubles' (The War of Independence), but bearing in mind its relative proximity to Victoria (later Collins') Barracks, we had always doubted this. The revolver find, however, seemed to put a different aspect on the rumours.

The gun stayed hidden in my schoolbag for the greater part of the day, until, unable to contain myself any longer, I took it out to show it to my school neighbour. Of course, it immediately caught the eagle eye of Small Jack, who took it from me and questioned me closely as to where I had got it. Then he said quietly: 'I think it might be wiser if you left that with me', and I never saw it again, much to my chagrin at the time, though in retrospect he was undoubtedly right. While, on the surface the Ireland of 1943 was going through its peaceful 'Emergency' – by which quaint euphemism we referred to the Second World War – certain elements of society had been interned in the Curragh. To be found in possession of an illegal firearm would certainly have led to trouble with the authorities, and Small Jack was well aware of this, even if I, in my innocence, was not. The gun vanished and was never mentioned again.

I did not then, and I do not now, subscribe to the oft-quoted saying that schooldays are the happiest days of one's life. Schoolchildren, like adults, have problems of their own, and to them they are just as major as their problems are to adults. The mind does not discriminate at any age; difficulties are difficulties, whether one is young or old, and while they may vary in intensity, they do not vary in being there and in being very real at the time. Nor is it a matter of proportion: the want of sixpence to visit the cinema with the pals can be as mortifying to a small boy as the want of a pound for a harassed housewife trying to put a good dinner on the table.

Nevertheless, I was very happy at St. Pah's. It was a good place to be. I was on top of my schoolwork and I liked Small Jack, not least for his unfailing good temper and his dedication to us. It is largely due to him that I became fluent in the Irish language in the first instance, and that I never had any bother with it afterwards. He broadened our horizons too in many ways that had nothing to do with the curriculum, taking us on visits to places like the Municipal Museum, trying to interest us in local history and geography which, in the days when they were not on the syllabus, were almost unheard of at first level. He also tried to teach us the elements of tonic sol-fa singing, and here I was a dismal failure, since Jack very quickly rooted me out as being totally tuneless, one of the biggest 'crows' in the class. Still, I loved to watch him at work with the tuning fork and the scales, and his patience in getting some semblance of harmony into the lovely 'Lark In The Clear Air' was almost saintly. We were often more occupied, I'm afraid, with thinking about the real larks that sang in the high meadows of Rathcooney and, if school was all right, escape from it was even better.

After all, we had the Glen and the fields far beyond and when the summer holidays blessedly arrived, Philip, son of Phil the railway driver next door, and I would hardly be seen at home from after breakfast until dusk. Self-taught in the subject he may have been, but Philip's knowledge of nature was staggering. He it was who, during our ramblings in the Glen, introduced me to the wildlife of the area and imbued me with a love of nature that has never diminished. Philip knew where to find a wren's nest, that small round ball hidden away in a bush and lovingly lined with the most delicate wool and feathers. He could easily distinguish between the song of the blackbird and the thrush, and indeed almost any other species.

He would guide me on expeditions to locate the bullfinch, the willow-warbler, the linnet, the blackcap and a host of others, and it was he who first showed me where the sand martins nested high in Ellis' quarry while the Ruston Bucyrus digger ate into its very entrails. He could even find the elusive nest of the skylark: 'Never look where she lands, because she will not come to earth near the nest, but several yards away' – and so indeed it was. In a few moments, he would locate the little nest in the long grass, but even in our egg-collecting days, he would never allow more than one egg to be removed from any nest , and none at all if there were only one or two present. 'If we take too many, the mother will forsake the nest and the mice will get the rest of them.' I do not know if this logic was sound. Perhaps even one egg was too many to take, but it was typical of the care Philip had for all living things that he would activate this self-imposed restriction.

He had a special affinity with animals too, especially with dogs, and often when going for a walk he would collect not only my terrier, but a whole clan of animals from the locality, all of which would happily follow on his heels as he set off, like some sort of canine Pied Piper, adding to his coterie as he went. When we fished for thorneens (minnows) in the Glen stream, Philip would ignore the more usual method of trawling the river bank with a scoop made from a handkerchief or rags, declaring it to be no sport at all, and instead he would use either a worm on a bent pin – the minnow swallowed the worm and was hauled out before it could disgorge it again. Or he would wade into the water and use his cupped hands to chase the fish, especially the 'redbreasts', into a corner and scoop them out. So in our meanderings through the countryside we became almost inseparable, to the extent that I once got mumps from him when, against maternal orders, I accepted from him the loan of a nature book when he himself was stricken, loudly protesting that I could not refuse it without insulting him. Shortly afterwards I began to feel the beginnings of a huge lump in my own throat!

Even that had its compensations, however, because it was springtime, the Doctor's man was ploughing the fields behind the house and I was away from school and able to observe all the activity. I was well on the road to recovery when the roar of a tractor – the doctor was a very progressive farmer – came from the Top Field, heralding the start of a few days of activity which kept me entertained on my window-sill perch. I should, of course, have been in bed, but Mother was working and I was alone at home. Both the Top Field and the Middle Field were a little too far away to get more than an impression of green sod turning to brown earth, but when at last the tractor entered the Back Field, directly behind our garden, my interest level shot up. Now it was possible to see the carefully adjusted plough biting into the sward and swathing its way along, leaving a bow-wave of turf as it cut its furrow.

Gradually the green field turned to brown, but I noticed that at the southern end of the field, the tractor stopped well short of the headland, where a group of locals whose back yards backed on the field had 'annexed' a few square yards of the Doctor's territory for use as little gardens, fencing off these plots with bits of old iron bedstead and anything else they could lay hands on. Over the grim years of the war, when food was in short supply, the Doctor never once interfered with these little plots. Indeed, since he kept a fine herd of milking cows, he would probably never have ploughed the fields in the first instance except that he was compelled to do so by law, the government requiring that every landowner commit a certain amount to tillage.

*   *   *

We did not have a war in Ireland; being neutral, we had instead the 'Emergency'. Mr. de Valera, to the expressed anger of the British government, had insisted that Ireland would not become involved in another conflict. The nation was still a very young state, with many economic problems and still some remaining bitter memories of British occupation. It was, in any event, not at all equipped for war, and de Valera gauged public opinion perfectly with his declaration of neutrality. The result was the 'Emergency', that strange time when Ireland feared invasion by either Germany or Britain, each of which was presumed to be anxious to establish a secure base on the Western Approaches, and each of which was seen as a potential enemy. This state of national anxiety led to the settings up of the LDF, or Local Defence Force, a sort of 'Dad's Army' home guard, as well as the call-up of all army reservists.

At the time, it was deadly serious for those directly involved, and indeed the men took on the task with great dedication in the face of considerable difficulty, not least in terms of armaments, transport and supplies. But of course it all provided amusement fodder for us youngsters, who would watch them drilling in the Glen, being kept well back from the troops indulging in target practice with old Lee Enfield .303s, collecting what we could find of the spent brass bullet cases afterwards and erupting in hilarity when the ancient Bren-carriers broke down with monotonous regularity.

The more serious side escaped us entirely. Apart from the

occasional bulletin on the wireless, or a picture of a stick of bombs on the front page of the single-sheet *Echo*, we were insulated from it all. We had to submit to food rationing, especially of tea, sugar and butter, but somehow we managed on minuscule amounts of these commodities per week, re-cycling tea leaves, using boiled sweets (when we could get them) as sugar, and getting salted country butter from friendly farmers' wives who were good with the churn.

What we did not then realise was that our own tiny fleet of merchant ships, which were desperately trying to keep the nation supplied with essentials, were being blown out of the water by German submarines, despite having huge Tricolours painted on their hulls, these being floodlit at night. And as the war wore on, it became apparent that, while we may have been neutral officially , it was very much a question of whose side we were neutral on! Stray German airmen who landed here were interned in the Curragh for the duration; RAF pilots were usually smuggled quietly back over the border with Northern Ireland, to fight again.

There were other, better concealed, examples of this strange, one-sided neutrality, and I have since been told tales of meetings which took place in a certain house in Cobh when top British naval experts were present, and where certain strategies were discussed. These I would not expect officialdom to confirm, but they were related to me by a friend who, as a schoolboy, lived in that house and who was summarily dispatched upstairs to his own room when certain people arrived. Be that as it may, Ireland's role in the war was certainly not passive, even if it may have been officially neutral.

We have only to consider the huge numbers of Irish who fought on the Allied side in that conflict and those who manned essential services in Britain during the period, including work in ammunition factories, to realise that our contribution to the war effort was considerable. Certainly it did not merit the venomous outburst of Winston Churchill at the end of the war when he bitterly castigated this country for its neutrality, and was in turn taken to task with great dignity and statesmanship by Mr. de Valera in a radio broadcast that has found its own place in history.

But by and large, the war passed us by, even if the 'Emergency' did not. For instance, we were all issued with gas masks in cardboard boxes, and shown how to wear them. I hated the things, because it was almost impossible to breathe properly in them, and the eyepieces fogged up so that you could not see where you were going. As far as I can recall, the only use to which we ever put them was for playing cops and robbers.

As the war wore on and coal became almost impossible to obtain, gas was rationed, the meagre supply being limited to a few hours a day at mealtimes. Many a harassed housewife broke the rules and lit the gas outside of these hours, in spite of the 'glimmer man', whose arrival in the area would be spread from house to house as the local bush telegraph began to send out a message of warning.

The ill-famed brown bread too, which was baked with flour from which most of the goodness had been extracted, played havoc with our tummies until we became accustomed to it. The few cars in the city belonged to people in essential services like doctors, priests and so on, and many commercial vehicles carried huge gas balloons on their roofs, long before the LPG of today became commonplace. Other silvery balloons, retained by long steel cables, floated high over the few merchant ships in the harbour, the belief being that the cables would act as a deterrent to any marauding aircraft.

But these were all things with which we learned to live. Shortages of drink and cigarettes did not affect us at all. We were far more concerned about the lack of sweets and fruit – some children born early in the war years did not see a banana or an orange until the conflict was over, and indeed had to be persuaded to eat these strange objects when the first of the 'liberty ships' arrived. Meanwhile, we were happy in our youthful pursuits, the materials for which were always ready to hand or could be found by a complicated process of bartering.

* * *

There were seasons for everything, which had absolutely nothing to do with the old Biblical seasons, but which rather depended on our whims and fancies. There was a season for spinning tops, for instance, when the old, much-used 'racers' and 'fat Maggies' were taken out of dark recesses and whipped along the road with vigour until we tired of them and turned to something else. 'Corkers', or chestnuts, of course, had to have their own season, governed by a greater Mind than our own, but otherwise things like marbles, hoops, and street games flourished and vanished as quickly as the flowers of spring as we moved restlessly from one to another.

Most of us youngsters kept dogs, usually terriers or mongrels, since we could not afford the more exotic breeds, but they were as much loved as any of the pampered species that yapped from gateways as we passed the homes of the upper-classes. I am a firm supporter of the belief that every youngster should have a dog, because nothing else will more quickly teach the lessons of responsibility, caring, and consideration, and nothing else will be more quickly rewarded with that peculiar loyalty and affection that only a dog can offer, when properly looked after.

When Rex arrived in our house I was eight and he was a tiny bundle of fluff, whimpering at being separated from his fox terrier mother and a litter of five, from which I had the pick, at the home of a friend of my mother in the famed village of Blarney. I chose him not out of any great knowledge of dogs, but he had a black shamrock on his white back and sides, and he crawled all over me as I fondled the litter in their basket. It was a case of instant mutual rapport and it was to last for fourteen years After a few days the whining stopped and Rex became an integral and much loved member of our small household, in spite of his puppyish depredations, like tearing strips out of everything in sight, not least out of some of my sister's schoolbooks which she had left lying around within his reach.

Very quickly, boy and dog became inseparable companions. When I came home from St. Pah's at lunch-time – I was first in and had the job of putting on the kettle – Rex would come bounding from his bed, yelping and jumping up and down with pleasure at my arrival. Later in the afternoon, when school was over, we would go galloping off to the Glen, like two young things let loose. Mischief was his middle name and he was never out of it. Once he spotted a distant hare and in his mad rush to the chase, he ran into a roll of barbed wire, from which I had to extricate him, bloody but still game for the hunt. Another time, while sniffing out rabbit warrens on Shepherd's Hill, he overreached himself in his exuberance and went tumbling down thirty feet of quarry face, from which fall he emerged unscathed, as I stood trembling on the brink, sure that my beloved dog was dead.

He got both himself and his master in quite another kind of trouble when he once consorted for a brief while with a pedigree cocker spaniel named Rhona, belonging to a young Protestant lass who lived in one of the bigger houses on the Ballyvolane road. Normally we were on the best of terms with our 'separated' neighbours, and indeed we were all very good friends, without any hint of religious or other division. On this occasion however, all hell broke loose. Pauline came ranting down into the lane, loudly declaring that Rhona was pregnant and it was all Rex's fault. When I mildly protested that if her bitch had been in that condition she should not have been left at large anyway, and that it was, 'the quare dog that won't bite a bone', she became even more incensed. Eyes flared and feet stamped and away she went in a blazing temper while we, of course, went into hysterics. In fairness, I must record that Pauline's bout of bad temper ebbed as quickly as it had arisen, nature took its course and, afterwards, Rhona was kept on a very tight rein indeed!

As the years passed, Rex shared every moment with me, his stumpy little tail wagging with pleasure in my hours of outdoor pursuits. When the whole family took off to England for a three-month spell, Rex had to be farmed out, so back to Blarney he went. My sister had to cycle with him in the front basket of her bike, to leave him, yelping and straining at the leash, as she rode tearfully home. We had been away only a week when a letter arrived from Nora McCarhty next door to say that an exhausted Rex had been found on the doorstep, having chewed through his leash and made the long journey home. She fed and cared for him until the people from Blarney came to retrieve him.

When Mother and I finally came home, my first task was to take a bus to Blarney to bring my beloved Rex back. On a rainy, cold September night I found him, standing at the door of the house, staring down the road to Cork, waiting. When he saw me approaching, he gave a bark of sheer pleasure and literally jumped into my arms. When we got home, he rushed around the house like a mad thing, running from room to room as if to reassure himself that everything was still there, that he was home again. We were never separated again, except in death.

It was on a Sunday morning, fourteen years later, when he was quite elderly and probably a little deaf, that he rambled away from his usual seat outside the front door and, busy with breakfast, nobody missed him until a young lad knocked. When I answered, I found him holding Rex in his arms, quiet and shivering. 'He was knocked down by a car on the road and he couldn't get up', said the little fellow, 'so I picked him up and brought him home to you. He seems to be badly hurt, but he didn't bite me.' He was indeed badly hurt, even to my untrained eye. He could not stand on his hind legs and while he drank a little milk, he quickly sank down into a lying position again.

I went to see Tony, a friend who was very knowledgeable about dogs, since he bred Alsatians. He came immediately to examine Rex and then turned to me and said, very quietly: 'Go for a walk in the Glen and come back in a quarter of an hour'. So I went, alone for the first time in many years. When I returned, Tony was holding a .22 rifle in his hands and Rex was lying quite still on the ground. 'I'm very sorry', said my friend, 'and I know how you feel, but you'll see now why I had to do what I did.' He picked Rex up by the front and rear legs, and the little body collapsed in the centre, its back broken. Tony patted me on the shoulder and went away, leaving me to my grief. In the garden where he had grown from puppyhood, I buried Rex on that black afternoon, and with him, a huge part of myself and my boyhood.

The weeks passed and the house seemed empty. Mother, in

particular, missed him when I was working; I missed him all the time and I do not believe I walked in the Glen at all during that period. One day, Tony arrived again, carrying in his arms a busy bundle of fluff that turned out to be a little Cairn terrier. 'Look,' he said, 'this little thing is being murdered by the Alsatians, who are using her as a sort of football in my place. She's a very affectionate little creature and I thought you might like to have her.' 'But,' I protested, 'she's a pedigree dog, I couldn't possibly afford her.' 'Never mind that,' came the reply, 'I want her to have a good home and if you want her, she's yours.'

So it was settled and Vicky became part of us, soothing the hurt and enchanting us with her affection and knowing ways. She came to know the sound of my motorbike and later my car, when I arrived home early in the morning from my night's work, and would jump out of her bed when I was still out of human earshot. One morning, when I was having a cup of tea and reading, about 4 am, just before going to bed, I imagined I heard footsteps on the little pathway into our two adjoined houses. It was, I thought, just Phil McCarthy coming home from a late turn on the railway, and took no notice. But there was no further sound of a door opening or closing, and then I looked at Vicky.

She was standing near the door of the room, quite rigid, and with her hair literally standing up on her back, the only time I have ever witnessed this oft-quoted phenomenon. When I opened the door, she ran into the hall and stood there, quite silent but obviously agitated. In spite of the trepidation that was now creeping over me, I decided I had better investigate. I opened the front door; nobody there, or on the pathway outside. I ventured further out, to where I could see the whole lane in the light of the recently installed electricity standard; nothing there. To this day I have never solved the mystery, the more mysterious since Phil told me on the following day that he had been asleep in bed at the time.

In time, Vicky, given with a generous heart by a good friend, became an integral part of our lives, much loved and loving, but she never quite replaced Rex. The moral, of course, as every dog owner knows, is that these most loyal of friends have a limited life. They age and pass on while we are still merely growing, and they leave us only the memories.

On a blazing bright summer Saturday under a cobalt sky still vaguely tinged with the crimson alizarin of early morning, we crossed the little wooden footbridge with its slender iron railings that led from the Glen to Dan Murphy's farm. We trudged up the hill between the furze bushes and, finding a pleasant grassy area, lay down amid the surrounding foliage on Shepherd's Hill to laze away an hour listening to the songs of linnet and whitethroat, chaffinch and blackcap. Far overhead the skylarks soared from spiralling level to level into the morning light, filling the whole Glen with their chirpings and making us wonder how so much sound could emanate from such tiny bodies. Below, the little Glen stream made its unhurried, winding way between banks of reeds, a silver thread that sparkled in the morning sunlight, seeming almost to send diamonds of pure ice bouncing upwards from its surface.

On the distant lake formed by the retaining wall in front of the Engineer's house, waterhens would be scuttling haphazardly about their aquatic business and in the long rushes which abounded there, little sedge warblers would be clinging to the reeds. We could see the sand martins, which annually nested high in Ellis' quarry only a hundred yards away. Now they swooped and dipped over our heads, flying high - traditionally a sign of good weather - as they sought the flies with which to feed the last of their broods in the deep-holed nests they had burrowed into the sand. Closer to hand, the linnets, which favoured this part of the Glen because of its abundance of ground cover, diverted us with their looping flight, almost as if they were stringing invisible telegraph wires between the bushes.

It was peaceful there. We luxuriated in the warm sun on our bodies, already beginning to tan after several weeks of this glorious summer, soaking up its rays as if we could never get enough heat, as if we were storing the warmth like insulators against the possibility of a cold winter to follow. These were the precious hours, the time when our Glen was all but empty, when we could lie and laze and relax, untroubled by noise, other than the occasional lowing of the cattle from Dan Murphy's or the few belonging to Jim Rice that grazed across the way. It would not last. We knew it and made the most of it while it did. Tomorrow, the Glen would be packed, as it had been every Sunday since summer began and, while we did not begrudge sharing our treasured place with the multitudes, we simply wished that Sunday would come and go quickly, taking with it the milling throng.

For to this place, during these wartime years when there was no possibility of transport to anywhere else, when families could not afford the trains to Youghal or the buses to Crosshaven, they converged from all over the city. The influx began about midday, when the first of the families came chattering noisily down the lane, parents pushing babies in ancient prams that clattered and bumped on the stony path; older children holding young toddlers with one hand, some clutching little fishing nets with the other. We could have told them that these were all but useless; that they would be far better off with a large cloth which could be scooped under the reeds and weeds, trapping the 'thorneens' before they had a chance to swoop away to freedom, but who were we to spoil their anticipation?

Squealing with delight, they set eyes on Nana Mac's shop and began a pell-mell race towards this tiny emporium as parents vainly shouted to them to wait. The lure of sweets and lollipops, lemonade and cakes was too much to resist, and into the small enclosure about her house and ours they would crowd, clinging to the railings of her window and gaping at the goodies inside. It was the beginning of a very busy day for Nana Mac, who would somehow manage to keep her patience as she dealt with a throng intent on spending all their pennies as if there was no tomorrow...

So they went, into the heart of the Glen, to find some little space near the water, where the parents could keep an eye on the youngsters as they paddled and fished. They never came to any harm, because the stream was only about a foot deep, except in the more remote parts, which toddlers could not reach anyway, so that the worst that could befall them was a cut foot from an unseen underwater obstacle, a piece of broken glass or an old bit of iron thrown there by the careless. The strange thing was that no matter how many came, the Glen seemed to be able to accommodate them all easily, swallowing them up and and then distributing them according to their needs: parents with families, young lovers seeking a bit of seclusion, old folk looking for a little shade from the glaring sun, weary workers needing only to lie and rest amid the bedlam of shouts and shrieks before tackling the toil of another long week.

All afternoon they chatted and played, dressed in their light summer finery, so that the whole place became a veritable palette of primary colours. They usually stayed until tea time, soaking up the sun and gossiping, mothering howling children who had fallen into the stream and soothing those with cuts and bruises, until it was time for the long trudge home. Now the children were tired and fractious and if there were a few pennies still left, they would be spent in Nana Mac's, to soothe the youngsters and ease the journey home, for many had come from the far side of the city and not all would be able to afford the bus fares.

Slowly, as the Glen shook off its human adherents, like a dog shaking the water off its back, solitude returned. Only a few remaining lovers now strolled home, arm in arm, as the evening sunlight cast a dying ray on Shepherd's Hill and silence returned to the wild acres.

It was not a big place, this Glen, being about half a mile long from the eastern end near the entrance to musical Dr. Aloys Fleischmann's house, past the old bridge leading to the hill and on beyond the Engineer's house and the old millrace, to the Goulding factory and the railway tunnel at the western end. Before Goulding's came, it was known as Dodge's Glen, after the old corn mill owned by the Dodge family, the ruined remains of which still stood starkly between the high hills that all but blotted out the sunlight at that particular spot. The rushing waters of the millrace were now controlled by Goulding's, who had installed a new pair of sluice gates, behind which was a pool we used for our early attempts at swimming, diving in from the high rocks overhead and spluttering the few yards to the concrete-lined shore.

It was a good place too for sailing model boats, on the very rare occasions such as birthdays when we managed to acquire them, because they could easily be retrieved if the rudder was wrongly set or the sails were caught by a sudden gust of wind. I recall spending a whole evening in August, when I was nine, and had just been presented with a small Triang tinplate model yacht - bright green with a single sail and costing one shilling and sixpence - watching it curve and cant before the wind, while I was skipper of a great windjammer on the long grain haul from Australia. Darkness was falling when we finally reached port and I tucked my latest treasure under my arm and headed home.

The Glen was a favourite walking place of the patriot Brian Dillon, who lived at nearby Dillon's Cross. Of somewhat weak physique and short of stature, he was nevertheless a great walker and, while he usually chose the Glen for his perambulations, he would sometimes undertake the much more arduous hike to Rathcooney, where his remains now lie, past the boreen of Arderrow, home of his favourite uncle, Daniel Dill. His love of the Glen is reflected in a poem he wrote while in Woking Prison in 1870. Entitled 'On Hearing a Robin Sing' it contains the stanza:

> Ah me, this many a year ago -
> How quickly happy time will fly -
> Since songs burst forth of liberty,
> And tender love that ne'er should die.
> 'Twas in the shade of the hanging wood,
> Where murmuring rivulets eddy and flow,
> While the click-click of the old mill wheel
> Made chorus in the Glen below.

The great natural beauty of the Glen gave rise to several plans to convert it into a pleasure park, but they came to nothing until 1985 when Cork Corporation took it over and developed it. In the 1930s, for instance, one Michael Prendergast from St. Luke's, who knew every inch of the Glen from boyhood, planned boating and amusement facilities there, but the scheme never materialised. In Glen House, the home later occupied by Dr. Fleischmann, Professor of Music at University College, Cork, and one of the city's most eminent men, the Hosford family had once built and maintained a small and very private boating pond and island, re-stocking the pond and that part of the Glen stream with trout every year. It was a place we visited rarely and then surreptitiously, by way of the stream itself; going under an old stone bridge across the entrance path and then entering a kind of enchanted wood, to pause in wonder at the half-concealed beauty of the pond and island, before scampering away again from the barking of a very large dog.

It was, of course, a place of natural fascination for youngsters. In addition to the stream that provided swimming, paddling and fishing, the Glen was a natural habitat for wild things, not least colonies of bees, which every summer sent out first their emissaries to scout the land, and then the workers to garner the rich harvest of pollen from the myriad wild flowers. As children, before we got more sense, we would catch them in jam jars filled with flowers, somehow believing that by having these tiny creatures within our grasp, we would hold on to summer forever. There was nothing evil in our thoughts, just that acquisitiveness which is natural to children, though in this instance certainly detrimental to our little charges, the majority of which expired before we were finally persuaded to set them free.

They came in large numbers and in great variety and while we did not know the entomological names for any of them, we could easily distinguish between the tiny honey bees, forever working at a frantic pace, the huge bumbles, the orange variety that stung viciously, and the little black bees with red rearquarters which we commonly called 'red-arsed bees'. Curiously, we discovered, by trial and error, that certain of these did not sting and could be held in the hand. These harmless ones were present in almost every species and they were characterised by one instantly recognisable factor: they all had bright yellow noses, even the little black bees. I have never discovered whether this is a distinguishing mark of the drone, but certainly those of us who caught these yellow-nosed creatures were never stung. I have had considerable difficulty convincing people of this; even in later years my own children were extremely sceptical, until one day during a country walk I gave them a concrete demonstration and they watched wide-eyed as

Daddy actually caught bees in his hand and was not stung.

The whole Glen was crissed-crossed with tracks and paths created by human passage over the generations, and we knew every one of them as well as we knew the stairs at home. We knew too how to watch for and avoid the many old slit trenches that had been cut into the grass, presumably during the Great War, when troops from Victoria Barracks must have been given some brief - all too brief - training before being sent off to the mass slaughter of the mud and blood-soaked trenches; sent off to die under an alien sky far from the singing skylarks or the cry of the bittern, so beautifully evoked in the poignant lament of Francis Ledwidge for Thomas McDonagh.

All around too were the decayed signs of old industries, though in those days our enquiring minds failed to elicit much information about these beyond the response that 'that was some old factory'. Two huge limestone pillars reminiscent of an entrance to a jail guarded the entrance proper to the Glen; further on was a pair of old iron gates, so we reckoned that there must have been something to guard, something from which people should be kept out. Certainly there were at one time at least three mills in the area, and the remnants of these we could find by examining the waterside. But inland, high above the water and next to the two tiny cottages occupied by Goulding workers, were other aged concrete blocks jutting grotesquely out of the undergrowth, so that there must have been some sort of enterprise conducted here which did not need water power. Perhaps it was just an old stone-house, but it left us intrigued.

Near to that place too was the 'black ash', a plateau of red-brick furnace dust long since pounded into a solid mass on which no grass or weed would grow. We used it for playing hurling and for bonfires on appropriate occasions, and during the Emergency, the army found it ideal as a shooting range because behind it reared a high hill to catch the stray bullets of the marksmen - and they were many - whose eye was not 'in'.

It was here too that we learned to play, to the utter astonishment of the unemployed 'corner boys' from Dillon's Cross, that most English of games, cricket. It happened because I had by then become very friendly with three lads who lived on the Ballyvolane Road, Humphrey, Patrick and John, whose father, Pat Twomey, was a master plumber with a business in Paul Street, in the centre of the old city. In the hallway of their house was a large and beautiful, highly ornamented scroll from his plumbers' guild bearing, amid much ornate decoration, the legend *Defence, not defiance*. I had always considered it a thing of some value for future generations, and I am delighted that it has now found a permanent home in the

Cork Municipal Museum, having been presented some years ago by Humphrey to my curator friend, now retired, Aodh Ó Tuama.

In that hallway also were some fine silk screen prints of moustachiod he-men on penny-farthing bicycles and of early railway trains, but they have been lost over the years and none of the Twomey lads now know where they are. They would certainly be quite valuable today. There also, hanging at the very back of the hall, was a fine pencil sketch of one of the Lakes of Killarney, at which I would stare for a long time, because it was the first time I realised that a pencil could be used to achieve such beautiful and subtle effects of light and shade. I determined then that one day I would try it for myself, but it was to be very many years before I actually did begin to sketch.

The Twomey boys went to school to the Christian Brothers establishment at Wellington Road, the 'posh' school, where both rugby and cricket were played, and in due course they acquired a full set of cricket gear; bat, balls, stumps and bails, and we would mark out a pitch on the grassy edge of the 'black ash' and under the tutelage of the lovable but fiery Grandpa Twomey, get a game going. Gramps was often the umpire and when one of the lads disputed a decision, which was frequent, he would fly into a rage and, pulling up a stump, chase the offender, threatening dire consequences and shouting; 'Come back here, sir!' to the great hilarity of the assembled audience. He was a retired master tailor and a gentleman of the old school, carrying his moustached dignity under a straw boater in summer and a Homburg in winner.

So we learned the finer points of the game and would listen for hours to the cricket matches on the BBC, until figures like Denis Compton and Norman Yardley became as much household heroes as Christy Ring or Joe Kelly in the sphere of hurling, while John Arlott's gravel-voiced, slow delivery was as familiar to us as the fever-pitch staccato of the emergent, brilliant Mícheál Ó hÉithir. Joe Kelly, incidentally, was the son of a retired RIC policeman who was locally known as 'Pop', and whose daughters ran one of the most successful and popular grocery shops in Dillon's Cross. One of the team of famed Cork hurlers of the day, he was subsequently ordained to the priesthood and is now ministering in New Zealand.

Pop was a great pitch and putt enthusiast and on a very makeshift course in the same area of the Glen, he would gather round him a group of the unemployed young men from the Cross and sparks would fly as their game progressed. Like Gramps, Pop had a fiery temper and sometimes the lads would wind him up by indulging in a little deliberate cheating. Then the shouts could be heard all over the Glen, but it was all in good fun and I suspect that Pop enjoyed it as much as anybody, even though his face was thunderous as he roared 'blackguard!' at the offender.

In retrospect, it is extraordinary how catholic our sporting tastes were. Cricket, for instance, was the most 'foreign' of games; yet we not only played it but came to love it for its intricacies, and indeed our corner boy audience would sit and watch us for hours. While they did not, perhaps, fully understand the rules, they would encourage us to greater effort as we tore up and down the bumpy crease, or occasionally slammed a 'six' into the far bushes that marked the invisible boundary.

In passing it is necessary to add that these same corner boys tended to be much maligned by those who mistakenly thought that they were shiftless and bone-idle. The truth is that they simply could not get employment in those hard years, and had to while away their time as best they could. So they sat and smoked and watched us play, or played cards, or went for a long hikes into the surrounding countryside, sometimes bringing back a rabbit or two to add to their meagre diet. Some, I suspect, were physically unwell, but even they would undertake odd jobs when they could get them, to augment their miserable dole money. Often they would go harvesting for the local farmers and threshing time was a veritable bonanza for them, with the certainty of free porter thrown in for good measure.

Their language was, to say the least, colourful, and for that reason we were discouraged from associating with them, especially when they were playing pitch and toss, or 'feck' as it was known locally. We, of course, ignored these strictures and we knew them all intimately, though they did not encourage us to join them in pitch and toss, because we were considered too young. There was an elemental decency about them, these half-illicit companions of our youth, Bawnie, Ham, brothers Philip and Ollie, Peter and Toes, and what they lacked in the niceties of social behaviour they more than compensated for in warm humanity. Several of them died relatively young, I suspect because of a combination of illness and malnutrition, because both hunger and disease were never far away, and with their passing, the place lost a lot of its colour.

In addition to the usual games such as marbles, conkers and so on, there were a number of pastimes which, while they were not exactly peculiar to our area, were nevertheless fascinating and probably reflective, in one form or another, of city life everywhere in these islands. Certainly in recent years they have become the subject of exhaustive and detailed study by social historians and others, but to us they were just a traditional and pleasant means of passing the time when no other entertainments were available.

We played shop, for instance, usually on the concrete slab in John Murphy's garden, setting out our wares in the form of

'chaynies' (derived from the word China, as in tableware, and leading to the derogatory expression; 'Go and play chaynies with your
grandmother's false teeth'). All sorts of broken pieces of pottery
were used with great imagination to represent various grocery commodities: broken mixing bowls, because of their colour, would
become pieces of butter; little bits of red glass were much prized as
sweets and so on. There were no limits to the imagination and even
the most unlikely objects would be pressed into service in order to
stock our shops.

From that we would progress to a game called 'gobs', in which
five pebbles, usually smooth and white, were tossed upwards from
the hand and an attempt was made to catch them in their down-
ward flight on the back of the outstretched fingers. There were
many convolutions of this game which involved considerable dex-
terity and at which the girls in particular excelled, as for instance
leaving one pebble on the ground and snatching it while the others
were still in the air, in the manner of a juggler. Then of course there
was 'pickie', better known overseas as 'hopscotch', with the playing
area chalked on the ground and much shoe leather worn out trying
to nudge an old shoe polish tin into the various squares with one
foot while hopping on the other.

Action songs we had in plenty, from the very childish 'Ring-
O-Roses' (though we did not then know it was a commemoration of
the Black Death), to the popular 'London Bridge is falling down'
and 'The farmer takes a wife', while yet another was sung as a ball
was thrown against a wall, and rejoiced in the weird name of 'Plain-
ee, clap-ee, rol-ee, pol-ee'. Again it demanded considerable skill
because it was accompanied by all sorts of gyrations while the ball
was in the air. Doubtless the historians of the years to come will
have as much fun trying to sort out these enigmas as we had when
we were simply playing the games!

There were other, less legal pursuits. We had our own version
of 'runaway knock' which not only reduced the risk of apprehen-
sion and the dire consequences, but introduced an element of mystery as well as fury in its unfortunate victims, and added hilarity for
us. Across the main road from McLoughlin's large garden was a terrace of small houses with sloping gardens in front. Using a reel of
black thread, purloined from a sewing box, we would attach one
end to the door knocker of one of these houses, reel it out carefully
and then clamber into a gap in McLoughlin's hedge, from where we
would gently tug the thread so that it did not break, while simultaneously activating the knocker. The puzzled victim would, of
course, answer the knock, realise that he or she had been tricked,
and dash down the steps into the road to apprehend the culprits,
only to be confronted by an empty, ill-lit street. The real anger and

frustration would build up when the victim, having barely closed the door, would hear the knocker banging merrily again...

An interesting variation was to tie the thread to the railings of one of these houses, at about hat height, and sit and wait until a suitable victim came along, usually a man walking his dog before retiring for the night. At his approach, we would lift the thread, and, on a perfectly windless night, off would fly the hat. His amazement would be expressed volubly and in the most picturesque terms. At times like this, as walking stick beat vainly at surrounding air - because we had of course lowered the offending thread again - only iron will and the knowledge of the certain retribution to follow kept our hilarity in check until the walker, who knew he had been duped but did not know how, had disappeared into the safe, dark distance.

We were, of course, selective in our victims, just as we were secure in our avenue of retreat through McLoughlin's garden in case somebody should just happen to find the thread and trace it to its origin. Usually we chose some of the less likeable neighbours who tended to treat us with disdain, and if the behatted one happened to be just out of one of the nearby hostelries, then the fun was all the greater. In spite of our antics, the elderly were always left untouched, as we felt it would have been unfair to bother them, and anyway, there were plenty able-bodied victims to be had who added an element of extra challenge and danger to the whole enterprise.

*   *   *

But if the Glen was our Valhalla, it was in reality only the jumping off point for further adventure, because immediately beyond it was the country proper, the rural hinterland of the city. On the Ballyvolane road, the city stopped abruptly at Rice's house, a rather stately building with a large, high-walled garden in front and to the side, and a small farm behind, to which was attached a little dairy where the lush milk from the few cows was daily processed and distributed. There the urban housing ended, but the city boundary itself was several hundred yards further out, near the Fox and Hounds pub, a little inscribed tablet set into a low wall on which old men would sit smoking their pipes and chatting, with one foot literally in the city and the other in the country. When the time came to go, they would rise and jokingly say: 'Well, I suppose we'd better go to Cork'.

If you climbed the steep Rice's Lane, past the old barn and up through the fields on either side which constituted the main part of the farm, you arrived at the high Mayfield Road and St. Joseph's church, beyond which the fields were laid out in war-time plots, cultivated by the people from the locality. Mayfield was a totally separate village, about a mile further out, but from the top of the hill, on a clear day, you could see the hazy blue mountains near Macroom to the far west, and nearer, the Ballyhoura hills of north Cork. In between lay the verdant countryside of rolling hills and small farms, laid out like an aerial photograph. It was the sort of view that made you want to get up and go, to travel into these far-off landscapes.

Meanwhile, bereft of anything in the way of transport but shank's mare, it was necessary to confine ramblings to nearer home, to the black hills of Banduff, where the gorse blazed its deep yellow flames across the hillside, and where the blackberries offered an abundance of rich eating on the hedgerows along the way. Or to high Rathcooney, up the steep hill where the lads played the game of road bowling - almost unique to Cork, being practised elsewhere only in County Armagh - with 28-ounce iron bowls which they drove with great skill along the rough surface, the aim being to complete the course in the least amount of throws. The sport had - and has - a vocabulary of its own, with phrases like 'lofting the bend' (hurling the bowl across the projecting arm of a corner so that it landed in mid-road on the other side), or gaining 'a bowl of odds' (going further in one throw than the opponent in two), or 'aiming for the sod' (a wisp of grass placed on the roadway as a marker for the player).

It was all very hectic stuff, and physically demanding, as the heavy bowl was thrown with an under-arm swing that threatened to tear the arm from its socket by sheer force of velocity. Heavy gambling was part and parcel of the whole affair, so that a considerable amount of money might hang on the strong arms and shoulders of the players, each of whom had their own following, vociferous and extremely critical. It also demanded considerable vigilance on the part of the spectators: to be struck by a veritable cannonball in which mass and velocity combined to prove the theory of irresistible force was anything but amusing and could, indeed sometimes did, result in severe maiming.

While it was always diverting to watch the bowl players, our more usual trek was though the fields with our dogs, sniffing and diving into hedges after elusive rabbits, barking excitedly at each scent, and rarely disturbing any living creature besides a few birds. Provided we behaved ourselves and did not plough across fields of standing crops, the freedom of the wide acres was ours. The local farmers, most of whom we knew anyway, were tolerant of our comings and goings, and I can never remember an occasion when we were summarily ordered off the land. Instead, if they happened to be about, we would stop for a chat, or to have a drink of water, while we admired their workhorses and they in turn would have a kind word about our dogs.

Often they would direct us to distant hedgerows where they knew the rabbits were plentiful, their only restriction being that we let the dogs get on with it and did not attempt to tear down the earthen banks with iron bars 'like that crowd that came last week'. But it was obvious that we did not have any crowbars, and we were always careful about closing gates and generally respecting the farmers' hospitality and the land itself. This had been drummed into us in school and it paid rich dividends. Our farmer friends knew we could be trusted not to do anything careless and in turn, we had unrestricted access to their fields, so that they became almost our own, to wander where we would in God's clean air. Little wonder that we came to love the countryside in all its variegated grandeur and to recognise the slow turning of the seasons.

Undoubtedly the most exciting time to be in the country was at harvest, when the ripening corn waved and danced in the breeze so that the fields looked like golden ponds across which raced sunlight and shadow, bringing ever-changing hues to the rippling mass of stalks. We would keep a close eye on the fields behind our own house, waiting for the morning when the Doctor and his man would come to inspect the crop, taking a few ears of corn and rubbing them in their experienced hands, blowing away the chaff and perhaps chewing a few grains, as indeed we ourselves had already done, tasting the soft inner ear as well as the hard outer husk, and knowing that the harvest was really nigh. We were by no means experts, yet the appearance of the Doctor merely confirmed our own opinions.

Next morning, the peace would be shattered by the roar of the tractor-drawn reaper and binder, tackling the Top Field as a few men cleared the headlands with scythes in the two lower fields. Almost before we knew it, they would be upon us, the tractor chugging slowly around the edges of the Back Field, the binder flailing along behind, spitting out stooks of golden richness as the whole place droned with the sound of rhythmic activity. Gradually the circle of standing corn would grow smaller as little birds flew terrified away, mice scuttled out of reach of the machines, dogs barked as they chased the little creatures, and all the while the relentless machine disgorged itself of its bundles.

These we were allowed to arrange in stacks of three or four, ears uppermost, because the Doctor was above all a practical man and if there were youngsters willing to help, he was not going to object. The work was hard on young hands unaccustomed to such labour, but we carried on, happy in the knowledge that we were

helping and that we were, for a little while at least, being taken seriously in a world of men. Only when it was all over, when the last
few sheaves had come tumbling out of the maw of the binder, when
the equipage had gone trundling away and the Doctor to his tea, did
we really begin to enjoy ourselves. Then, in a world of stubble, we
raced among the stooks, chasing the few remaining field mice with
the dogs and catching some, dropping them down the frocks of the
girls, whose screams of terror drowned our raucous laughter.

Soon, a strange quietness would descend on the shorn land
and, as the evening sun shimmered on the heads of the standing
sheaves, we would lie in the stubble, watching intently as the elder
lads from the Cross patiently showed us how to make Harvest Knots
from corn stems, twisting and looping them into heart shapes in a
ritual that must have been as old as time itself. Next day we would
wear our own badges in our shirt buttonholes with a certain pride.
We had been to the harvest. We had worked the land. We had par-
taken of the richness of the good earth.

Early September brought those mornings when it was good to
be alive, when the overpowering heat had gone from the sun, when
the cooling breezes of autumn sent the first russet leaves fluttering
and the first grey-tinted clouds scudding lightly across the azure
heavens. It also brought the threshing machine to the nearby farms,
where, nature having done its part, the ricks of corn now awaited
the mechanical, man-made process of separation of the ear from the
husk and stem.

The other signs of autumn were all around: the fields of stubble, as yet not burned off or ploughed in: the orange glory of
Shepherd's Hill, where the bracken was giving a final, brazen display before retiring for winter; the luscious blackberries festooning
all the hedgerows, before the October 'fairies came on them' and left
them cocooned in cuckoo-spit and, according to old tradition, no
longer fit to eat. But it was the arrival of the threshing gear that
evoked the real excitement. The good Doctor, having harvested his
crop, had it transported to we knew not where for further process-
ing, so we had to look east towards Rathcooney, to the O'Connell's
or Dill's, for a great day out, even though we were judged too young
to be allowed become actively involved.

By the time we arrived, which was usually in mid-morning,
the place would be in a flurry of activity. In the haggard near the
rick was the wooden threshing mill, built by the famed Ransomes
company of East Anglia, Britain's granary. It had been in use many
years now but was still good for many more, its bright red standing
out against the more sombre shades of ochre all around it. It was
driven by a Fordson tractor of uncertain vintage by way of a long,
looping belt, but some of the old men present could remember the

day when the prime motive power took the form of a steam engine, either stationary and trailed around from farm to farm, or else one of the magnificent self-propelled Fowler machines, resplendent in its green and bright brass, with a tall chimney, a great flywheel and a symbolic leaping horse on the smokebox door.

If there was apparent chaos, it quickly became clear to us that it was very organised chaos indeed. Every man had his task and stayed with it through the long day. The pitchers on the rick deftly tossed the sheaves to the men on the threshing mill, one of whom quickly sliced the binding with a sharp knife and passed them to his companion, who fed them into the maw of the mill, where the mysterious process of mechanical winnowing took place. At the rear, another man cleared away the straw to still more workers so that it could be built into a new rick, and yet another looked after the big sacks which hung from the rear of the engine and into which splashed the grain like a river of pure gold. When these were full they were tied and carted away by yet another burly worker.

All of this frenetic activity was accompanied by the steady drone of the tractor and the rumble and boom of the threshing mill itself, by the shouts of men talking above the din and the constant clatter of pitchforks flashing bright steel tines in the morning sun. It was thirsty work, of course, so there was a tierce or two of porter at the ready, which would be tapped at intervals and glasses or mugs handed to the perspiring workers, and we would marvel at how quickly a pint could vanish down a dry throat. Some of the workers were very skilled, moving from farm to farm with the contractor; others were the local unemployed, hired for the day and glad of the work. Theirs was the relatively unskilled part of the job, the carting away of the loose straw or assistance with the building of the rick, which was an art in itself.

A hearty lunch would be taken in the farmhouse, or in the outbuildings, or perhaps even in the open haggard, because some of the men were too shy to go inside and would prefer to eat in the shade of an overhanging elm or chestnut, resting until the restarting of the tractor called them back to their labours. There was no question of stopping until the work was finished; the good Lord might not send another such day and it was well to get the work done while the weather remained fair and dry. In any event, the contractor was promised on another nearby farm tomorrow and he was anxious to keep to his schedule while the weather held. By evening, one rick was gone and another built in its place. The season's crop had passed through the mill and the farmer and contractor had consulted on the yield and quality of the grain. The yard had been tidied up and the last of the workers paid off.

Now they stood around in little groups chatting and joking

and finishing off the last of the porter. The few neighbours who had come to help, in the old tradition of the 'meitheal', would be thanked and assured of support when their turn came, and then the tractor would be hitched to the threshing mill and the outfit would be drawn slowly out of the gate, on to the main road, and its next job. We, who had watched with awe, would stand until it had creaked and shaken its way up the hill, over the top of which a pale harvest moon was just beginning its soaring arc into the evening sky. Somehow, as we made our way home, we too felt a certain sense of completion. The annual ritual of sowing, growing, maturing, harvesting and threshing had ended and we had been part of it, even though on the fringes. Its fruits would soon end up on our table and, like the crop, we too had matured a little.

We did not understand, ourselves, at the time, how deep were our rural roots, and how full we were of superstition and 'piseógs', though if anybody had suggested that we came from 'the sticks' or were mere 'country boys' - usually with some ungenerous connotations - we would probably have assaulted them. The truth is that though we considered ourselves urban, perhaps even a little sophisticated when in fact we were anything but, the countryside was on our very doorstep and we loved it deeply. Just beyond the Glen, at the top of Shepherd's Hill, was Dan Murphy's farm and behind that again was the tiny cottage of elderly Maurice Hayes and his wife Mary, growing out of the side of a narrow road that is now a motorway, and bounded at the back by the Glen stream, by the side of which Maurice tended a tiny, triangular garden. A more rustic place it would be difficult to imagine, the more so since the side gate of the cottage led into what we called 'McAuley's wood', which in truth was merely a double line of tall elms and sycamores, though it did also have a little well of very cold, clear water.

On summer days, as a treat, Mother would make the special effort of getting ready a small picnic and taking us there, beyond the realms of the crowded Glen, into the balming shade of the tall trees, to sit on a grassy bank and fill our cups with nectar from the well or to explore the wonders of hedgerow and stream, until it was time to make our way homeward. But no such outing would be allowed to end without a visit to the Hayes' cottage, where Mary, stout and beak-nosed, would gossip amiably to mother, while my sister and I gazed, tip-toed, into the high left-hand window of her little cottage, where she kept a few boxes of sweets for sale to a very uncertain passing trade. Maurice, now bearing the burden of his years, was a gentle fellow who worked as a sort of odd job man for our landlord, old Mr. Rice, calling every now and then to put a new slate on the roof, patch up a broken door or put in a new pane of glass. Nothing seemed beyond his talents and for a man of his advancing years, he would erect a ladder and shin up it with surprising agility.

Our usual way home was by way of the little roadway that led from the Hayes' cottage, past Daunt's farm with its red farmhouse, well hidden behind a high outer wall and known locally as 'the red house', to the Fox and Hounds crossroads, named after the long, low pub of the O'Connell family. This was a favourite stopping place for funeral-goers on the way to and from Rathcooney cemetery, burial place of the patriot Brian Dillon, high up in the hills where in summer the skylarks filled the air with a song, and where stood the ruins of an old St. Leger pile in a place called the 'castle field'. Funerals, of course, were horse-drawn and it was a very long and thirsty walk from St. Joseph's church to Rathcooney, so that 'the Fox' would be guaranteed a large clientele, at least on the way home - though some of the hardier spirits would also slip in for a pint on the outward journey. Nor was it unknown for the deceased to have stipulated that such a stop should be made, 'to give the lads a rest and a drink before tackling the hill'.

Bereavement was very much a communal affair. Once news of a death in the locality became known, an invisible, unwritten, but very definite formula was followed. The priest was called to administer the Last Rites, a local lady noted for her expertise in this direction was summoned to lay out the corpse, and usually only then was the undertaker called in to make the final arrangements. Meanwhile, from the houses all round, kind neighbours could be seen scurrying back and forth, with extra chairs, candlesticks, crucifixes, bottles of holy water and, hidden away under cloths, items of food such as fruit cakes which they had baked specially. If the deceased had little or no means and had not provided for the funeral by way of the 'penny death', collected weekly by the insurance man, a collection was taken up. Death had its dignity and nobody was allowed to go to the grave unhonoured and unsung, although some care was always taken to protect the reputation and the circumstances of the family concerned.

In the house of the deceased, which was always marked by a black crepe on the door knocker, to show that death had gained admittance, the body lay in state. Neighbours filtered in and out, saying a few prayers and muttering their muted condolences to the bereaved. Some close friends stayed to offer continuing consolation, and to sit up with the relatives through the long night before the removal to the church and the eventual funeral. Food and drink would, of course, be provided, together with snuff, and there would be a great deal of reminiscing, mainly about the deceased, all of which very real support helped to dull the pain of separation.

In spite of the inevitable gloom, it was impossible not to be impressed by the elegance of the funeral procession, with its finely-crafted hearse drawn by two jet black, plumed horses, the driver also clad in black, but wearing a white sash from shoulder to waist and a tall hat, polished and buffed until it shone. The lightly-sprung mourners' carriages too, likewise horse-drawn, were master-pieces of the coachbuilders' art, the thin spokes radiating outwards from the hub, and angled so that the wheel rim was several inches further out than the hub. So fine were these spokes that they seemed almost incapable of supporting the weight of the coach, let alone its occupants. But this, of course, was the real test of crafts-manship, strength wedded to beauty, delicacy to functionalism, and it was impossible not to marvel at the sheer skill of the hands that had taken the bare wood and transformed it, with saw, plane, chis-el, mallet and spokeshave, into such intricately and accurately jointed and mortised artefacts.

With such vehicles, we felt, it would be impossible for any-body not to have a good funeral and, there being an element of humour in everything, I once heard one old fellow say to another, as the pair sweated along uphill behind the hearse on a summer's day: 'He's a damn sight more comfortable in there than he ever was - and he's certainly more comfortable than us!' To which, in due time, were added such comments as 'Ah, if he could only have been here to see the turn out' or 'He would have loved to be here with all his pals'. Unconscious humour perhaps, but it did reflect the fact that people had a deep respect for the dead and not least, that they should be sent into the after-life with some decency.

For many people, especially our country neighbours, funerals were a great social occasion, an outing, an excuse to get away legiti-mately from the daily grind for a brief period, to meet friends they had not seen for some time and to engage in long conversations which were utterly inexplicable to us youngsters. How could peo-ple talk for so long about so little when there were far more interest-ing things to do, like playing surreptitious hide-and-seek among the gravestones or looking for birds' nests in the old walls and grasses of the cemetery? Death has little relevance to the young and, while we may have offered due reverence to the deceased, the ceremonies and the final burial were all just another adult imposition to be endured. We were far more interested in our own forthcoming out-ings, of a more adventurous and infinitely more cheerful nature.

Before we could go on any public expedition, there was the business of having the hair cut. If we were off to the seaside for a day's outing, maternal insistence came into play and since I was long gone beyond the stage of having Mother chop and hack until she was satisfied, it was off to the local barber on Saturday morning - youngsters were not catered for on Saturday afternoons because there were older sheep to shear. The tonsorial establishment of one Mr. Patrick Curtin, commonly known as Pakey or Paak, consisted of the front room of his small house opposite Harrington's Square, where the writer Frank O'Connor lived for a time before he took to the pen and achieved enduring fame.

Curiously, in the way that a prophet is rarely respected in his own country, O'Connor was hardly ever mentioned in the locality. He had, after all, moved to Dublin and therefore to a certain oblivion insofar as his old neighbours were concerned. Indeed, it was many years later when I finally caught up with him in print, and later still before I came to know much of his early life in Cork. Be that as it may, Pakey certainly was there, in the little gloomy room with the north-facing window through which the sun never shone, and precious little light entered, because of the general dust and the accoutrements with which it was invariably cluttered. The room was unrelievedly dismal, the walls dingy with some sort of old paint that had faded to a dark non-colour and the ceiling, which had possibly once been white, then reduced to an overall dark ochre by years of cigarette smoke.

On one wall hung the only print in the salon, the well-known image of the padre horseman blessing the troops kneeling in the mud before the battle of the Somme or some other such bloody confrontation of the First World War. It was appropriate to the place because both Pakey and his brother Jack had served in the British Army, where it was reputed that they had learned the barbering trade, both being mildly incapacitated. We never learned if they were actually wounded in action, though the suggestion was there, but certainly the style of haircut had all the hallmarks of the barrack square; short back and sides was a grossly inadequate description for a head shorn by the Curtins. Then again, the operation cost only four old pence for juveniles, so we could not really complain.

In spite of the depressing surroundings, it was an interesting place to be because invariably we had to wait our turn while Paak or Jack dealt with the other customers, and we could easily overhear the conversations, which tended to range over the whole gamut of human experience, but inevitably drifted back to the old days and the Great War. One old gentleman, tall and tottering, came regularly for a shave and while Paak stropped the cut-throat razor, this customer would carry on a conversation which was utterly unintelligible to us, but which Paak appeared to have no difficulty in understanding. The poor man seemed unable to close his mouth fully, so that the words merged into an incomprehensible sameness. Only later did Paak tell us that the old man had been badly gassed in the conflict, but that he had no trouble in understanding him because he had seen many such victims in his time, thereby lending some credence to the suggestion that he had actually been to the Front.

On quieter mornings, when only a few of us lads were present, Paak would perform for us the most awful trick with the razor, stropping it carefully and placing it on his outstretched tongue, then pressing it downwards so that the blade sank into the flesh. But no blood ever came and he told us that the secret of the trick was not to move the blade even a fraction of an inch sideways, or his tongue would be off. To this was added the dire warning not to try the same stunt ourselves if we wanted to be able to speak for the rest of our lives. He need not have worried; we were horrified by the performance, and in fact I still shudder at the memory of it today.

But essentially he and Jack were the most gentle of men, who would not tolerate any foul language in the place, at any rate while we youngsters were present. They provided a basic, essential service for the locals at affordable prices and, if they did occasionally slip out for a drink, nobody minded. This happened at certain intervals during the morning when sufficient money had been earned. Then Paak would go to the till, rummage inside, slip some money into his pocket and announce: 'I'm off Jack, see you in half an hour.' He would return from Cosgrove's pub at the Cross breathing alcohol and carry on as usual, until some time later Jack would announce that his turn for a break had come, and the same process would be repeated. They were not, however, drunkards, and none of us had ever seen them in any way incapable. It was accepted among the clientele that they were entitled to wet their whistles, and the customers would patiently wait until one or other had slaked his thirst before returning to attend to his business.

So we would be shorn, and then it was off home to the big tin tub in the kitchen for the weekly bath. The best summer clothes would be laid out and readied, together with the seaside gear, and a last anxious glance would be cast at the night sky before going to bed. If it was bathed in the pink light of the setting sun, we would retire happily, in the knowledge that a red sky at night is the shepherd's delight and that the omens for the following day were good. But no matter what the forecast, sleep would be at best an uneasy slumber; the morning would bring its own meteorological story and the vagaries of our climate suggested that anything could happen.

It is not easy to erase dire memories of spending the whole day in the drenched confines of Youghal railway station while the rain sheeted down and the thunder and lightning rumbled and crackled overhead as Mother Nature put on a display of pyrotechnics which would have put any fireworks to shame. And all the time, the sandy beach beckoned, even though the waves, driven by the gale, crashed and thundered against the breakwater and cascaded on to the promenade, driven to fury by the brute force of the mighty, rolling sea. Because there were no return trains until the evening, we could only watch disconsolately as the soggy hours crawled on, dismayed that our great day out had become not just a washout, but a calamity, since it was unlikely that Mother would be able to find the cost of the fares again that summer.

But time passes and memories fade and this morning would be all right. The sun would shine. The day would be glorious. As we made our way down the hill to the station at Glanmire Road, in the company of the Murphy children and their parents, one of the Thompson's mares, which daily pulled the bread van to our very doors, was already sheltering under the huge sycamore behind the high wall, and we sang as we danced along on limbs of joy. At the station, the gates were barred against a huge multitude as the harassed railway staff got the trains ready, and black engines backed long rows of ancient carriages into the platforms on the Cobh-Youghal line. For these excursions, anything with wheels would be pressed into service, the majority of the carriages being decrepit six-wheelers from the last century, and the appellation 'First Class' meant absolutely nothing except that the fortunate occupants had more comfort at no extra cost.

Eventually the gates would open and we would be herded into some sort of orderly queues, while in the ticket office Dan Holohan and his staff would cope manfully with the unceasing demand for the vital slips of card which would give access to the trains. As the first trains pulled away, we would become fearful again. There was still a huge crowd; perhaps the overburdened system could not cope with everybody. But somehow it did. New trains were marshalled, in what must have been a nightmare for the operating people, and one by one they were sent on their way.

Finally it was our turn. Up to the barrier, where Mother would show the day return tickets, bought at privilege cost because of my late father's association with the railway. I often wondered if this was entirely legitimate, but nobody ever questioned it, in the way that the good natured railwaymen would also turn a blind eye on the rare occasions when John Murphy would take us along with his own brood. 'How many have you, John?' the ticket collector would ask. 'Eight, Bill,' John would reply, straight-faced, knowing full well that Bill was aware there were only six in the Murphy family, and grinning, he would count us onto the platform.

Then came the dash for accommodation and excitement reached fever pitch as we raced ahead of Mother to find an empty compartment, into which we all crowded, ourselves, the Murphys and any stragglers who happened to come along and could be squeezed in. Finally, when all the pint carriages had somehow become quarts, the guard would stride along the platform, carefully closing all the doors and locking them with a special key, before giving the long train a final look over, blowing his whistle and waving his traditional green flag. An answering toot from the engine and suddenly the supporting pillars of the station awning would seem to move past the windows, and it took a second or two to realise that it was we who were sliding slowly out of the station.

Gradually the locomotive got hold of its heavy load and speed increased, over the girder bridge across the Glanmire Road and heading for Dunkettle, with the great silver sweep of the upper estuary on the right and Blackrock Castle standing sentinel over the old fishing village at the other side of the Lee. On to Cobh Junction we chugged, getting the inevitable piece of grit in the eye as we looked out of the open window to glimpse the hard-working engine up ahead when rounding a curve. A brief respite at the Junction, where yet a few more passengers were somehow crammed in, with the help of the station staff who would come to each compartment and shout: 'Any room for a few small ones in there?' Then, as the Cobh line swung away to the right, we were on a single track and began to count the passing stations with mounting excitement: 'Midleton, Mogeely, Killeagh ...' and, with our voices rising, 'Youghal!' as we rolled along past the first of the sand dunes and the holiday homes at Clay Castle.

As the train disgorged its enormous complement of passengers, which flowed like a human tide out to meet the incoming sea, we would take time to wander up to the front to see the engine and chat to the driver and fireman, perhaps even to be invited on to the footplate to see the controls and blow the whistle. In the sidings behind would rest long lines of the carriages of earlier trains, soon to be joined by ours as the single platform was cleared for yet another incoming train and our engine went off to be turned, the crew heaving and straining at the bars of the turntable. Then it was off to the beach for us also, to savour the salt tang of the summer air and to splash in the waters already almost crammed with bodies of young and old. The old town itself would be largely ignored in those days, which is a pity because it had a fascinating history which we did not then appreciate, concerned as we were with the passing moment and the pleasures of the beach.

Walter Raleigh came here, bringing the potato and tobacco, gifts at once beneficent and dubious, before losing his head in more senses than one. The long, narrow streets reflected the timelessness of the place, with its picturesque clock tower and its ancient archway. It seemed the sort of place that would never change, where fishermen would still tie up their boats at the little quay, and where the minor minions of maritime commerce would ply their trade. These were the surroundings that, a few years later, were to so impress American film director John Huston, that he decided to make it the locale for portion of the epic screen version of Melville's *Moby Dick*. The waterfront was duly transformed into a new England clapboarded village and Youghal's place in the history of motion picture making was assured.

But to us, it was the seaside resort that was important and it was surprising just how many people its safe and pleasant beaches could accommodate on those summer Sundays of the great excursions. Like the Statue of Liberty, Youghal always seemed ready to take in the tired and the dispirited, the weary and the work-worn and for a brief while, to refresh them and give them the resolve to face another week. Its welcoming arms encircled us all, young and old alike; its balmy sea breezes played on us for a day and when it was all over, and the great rush to the station began all over again, it sent us home content and exhausted, with the belief that it would never end, that the excursion trains would forever pound up and down the line we knew and loved so well.

There was one other outing of note, far more spectacular even than Youghal could offer. This was the stuff of high adventure, of unknown frontiers to be crossed and strange landfalls to be made. The year was 1947, in the early summer of which Mother decided that we should again visit her two sisters in Bridlington, on the east Yorkshire coast between Hull and Scarborough, where they had lived for many years. It was one thing to announce, blithely, that we were going; getting there in those grim years immediately after the war was quite another matter. There was no question of air travel, it was rail, ship and rail again and if it took over twenty-four hours, what about it?

The memory of that long journey will never leave me; the excitement of boarding the Rosslare Express at Glanmire, the long haul to Rosslare over a single line that is now in greater part closed, through Mallow and Fermoy, on to Waterford, Wexford and finally the port of Rosslare, where we boarded the Great Western Railways vessel *St. Andrew* for an uneventful journey to Fishguard, arriving there at some ungodly hour in the morning. Because we were going across country rather than direct to any of the large centres of population, our journey necessitated much changing of trains. Cardiff, I barely remember, came and went in the darkness, as we left the very drab GWR train from Fishguard and boarded another headed for Gloucester, during which leg of the journey I fell fast asleep. The maroon coaches of the LMSR were a distinct improvement as we left Gloucester for Sheffield, to the contrapuntal, sing-song 'right away' of one of the station officials as he got the green flat from the guard and gave the driver the go-ahead.

I was fascinated; this never happened at home and I had never before heard 'right away' being sung out like that. The fascination soon palled. The journey became something of a marathon, as we passed Chesterfield with its crooked spire, one of many which loomed up on the horizon, all looking exactly the same to my unpractised and very tired eyes, as the pounding train dragged itself past town after Midland town, until I was convinced there was some sort of conspiracy, and that in reality we were merely going round in a huge circle.

Of course we did arrive eventually, some twenty-seven hours after we had left Cork, but what fascinates me now, in retrospect, is that in spite of the complexity of our journey, the many changes of train, and the fact that the railways were in a parlous condition after the war, we did not miss one connection, having changed again at Sheffield and Hull before getting, at the heel-end of a weary evening, the final local train for Bridlington. While some of the locomotives were in relatively good condition, there was no doubt that others were not, and some of the famed Stanier Black Fives that dragged us across the Midlands were being threshed unmercifully as their crews fought to keep time with inferior coal and run-down motive power. Conversely, the Shire class of the LNER which brought us on the final stage of our journey appeared to be in fine mechanical fettle and looked elegant as well - Geordie pride perhaps?

'Beautiful Bracing Bridlington,' as the tourist literature put it, was a typical British seaside resort of the day, complete with esplanade, promenade, a huge variety hall known as the Spa, seafront gardens complete with floral clock, elegant hotels and, of course, hundreds of boarding houses which catered for thousands of visitors and from which the town's landladies made hay while the sun shone. Best of all, it had a harbour with a whole fleet of pleasure boats, ranging from the converted tug *Yorkshireman* to the purpose-built and, in descending order of size, *Yorkshire Belle*; the beautiful teak *Bridlington Queen*, the *Boy's Own* and the *Princess Marina*.

Sea-crazy as I was in those days, their very presence was like maritime manna and I would spend every last shilling - which was what the round trip cost - on successive journeys to Flamborough

Head and back to the little harbour at Brid. It mattered not in the least that all five vessels went by exactly the same route to exactly the same place and that, very probably, we saw exactly the same porpoises gambolling about the bows. If I had nothing to do and a shilling in my pocket, I would be away on one or other of the boats, usually standing up in the bow and holding on to one of the stays, as she tossed and pitched in the rough waters of the Head, and I believed myself to be a veritable Captain Ahab in pursuit of the Great White Whale.

While I was one of those who did not need any persuasion, there was plenty of stentorian inducement for others. Salty types in old navy jerseys and peaked caps bestrode the harbour ramparts bellowing, with lungs of fire: "Oose for sailin'?; Sailin' on the Yorkshire Belle, 'oose for sailin'? or 'urry along now for the *Boy's Own*, just leavin'.' And so it went on, with each competing vessel somehow filling its own complement, and chugging out of the tiny harbour to the great North Sea and the jutting brow of Flamborough Head, some four miles away.

In a very short time I came to love the Yorkshire folk, with their blunt approach to life, their outspokenness, their unfailing good humour ('It's being so cheerful as keeps us going'), and even the broad accents of the Dales, which at the outset I had considerable difficulty in understanding. One of my aunts who had spent the greater part of her life in Bridlington managed a large guesthouse for a character called Arthur Duffield, whose full-time employment was in the local gasworks and who, on the evening of our arrival, took me to see the sea, which was but two minutes' walk from the guesthouse. He chattered incessantly as he showed me the way, presumably pointing out the local landmarks, but I was hard put to understand more than one word in three, a difficulty which he volubly brushed aside and continued on with the very one-sided conversation, constantly patting me on the back, and giving me half a crown when we finally arrived back at the guesthouse.

This was a large, high, four or five-storied building, one of many stretching along Vernon Road, built in good solid Victorian red brick and with gardens back and front. In the house next door lived a colourful parakeet on a perch in the front window, and I would have great fun making it talk, which it did in squawking tones as it bellowed obscenities in broad Yorkshire. Visitors apart, there were some characters resident in the guesthouse also, notably one very elderly and rather doddering soul called Mrs. 'Oughton, who in the middle of a meal would suddenly stand up and announce to all and sundry: 'I'm going to wash me,' and summarily disappear.

But the great benefit of the boarding house, as far as I was concerned, was the fact that it offered ample opportunity for remunerative employment. Arthur Duff, as he was commonly called, would give me all sorts of little errands and tasks to perform and my aunt Margaret, who for some reason had the pet name of 'Todo', would induce me to vacuum the place every Saturday - for a consideration, of course. So I was never short of 'brass' in the colloquial term, and even if much of it was spent on the pleasure boats and the boundless amusements of the esplanade, there always seemed to be more where that came from.

It could not last, of course. My other aunt, Annie, with whom we were staying, was a cook in a local school and it was she who suggested to my mother that, in order to make some friends and stay out of possible trouble, I should attend St. George's for the last month of the summer term. Despite my protestations, it was all arranged. She had spoken to the Head and he was willing to have me. My mother was now working, as was my sister, and my temporary incarceration seemed a very good idea to everybody, except me. In due course I was interviewed by Mr. Austin, the Headmaster, who welcomed me to St. George's, which was a secondary grammar school, and he put me into the care of Mr. Arundel, who was First Form classmaster.

I was then aged eleven, had finished fifth class in primary school at home and here I was, suddenly pitched into secondary school. To my utter amazement, I quickly found that I knew at least as much if not more about general subjects as did my classmates; I did not then understand that our own system of education was regarded as superior to that of Britain. Even when I took part in the summer examinations, I did exceptionally well, barring of course, subjects like English history which I had never studied. But I quite amazed both Mr. Arundel and my English teacher, Mr. Mellor, and was told, to my utter embarrassment, that I was an example to the whole class.

But in general I liked St. George's and did, in fact, make many friends there, so that for the remainder of our stay in Bridlington my horizons were widened even further as we explored countryside and seashore, both after school and in the holiday period that followed. In spite of some post-war shortages, the resort was very lively indeed, with a great deal of entertainment of every kind, including a 'fit-up' theatre on the esplanade, which managed to provide a variety show every evening to an enthusiastic audience seated in deck chairs.

The stars of this little revue made the most outrageous claims of their theatrical experience and expertise, including one who listed several films in which he had appeared, no doubt as an extra, since his dramatic performances would never have passed muster in any other arena. Young, blonde Sadie - if that was her real name - might have been all right on saxophone and clarinet, but Jimmy's brand of slapstick comedy was of the very lowest order, consisting mostly of belting the rest of the small cast across the face with wet rags. The Spa provided more sophisticated shows, to which I and my school pals would gain entry by the simple expedient of climbing the surrounding wall from the seaward side, when the tide was out, and enjoying this free performance all the more.

In some respects, the place was a curious mixture of the optimistic and the world-weary. The war may have been over, but there were still some German POWs lingering about, in their drab purple uniforms with black patches sewn on breast and back, doubtless as targets for the gunners if they had attempted to make a run for it while the hostilities continued. But nobody seemed to pay any attention to them any more, and they strolled about apparently unconcerned and certainly, as far as I could judge, unhindered by the locals. For the majority, it seemed that the war had run its course and they were now bent on enjoyment, with hundreds of soldiers, either newly demobbed or on leave, holding beach parties with their girls, with much singing and twanging of guitars and banjos.

'Beautiful Bracing Bridlington' was also booming, full of life and good humour in that summer of 1947. The hotels and boarding houses were stuffed to capacity, the seafront was a blaze of flowers, and everybody was spending as if there was no tomorrow. Even when the last bus of the East Yorkshire fleet left the front at midnight, leaving in its wake a queue of disgruntled travellers who could not be accommodated, the smaller and much more flexible private service of Williamson's would come along to pick up the stragglers and pack them in, reminding those still remaining that it would be back in fifteen minutes for them. Such were the great days of private enterprise!

On a return visit some years ago, I was saddened to discover how lovely Brid, like so many other seaside resorts, had deteriorated. Gone were the fine hotels, their sites having been turned into car parks. Most of the boarding houses were closed up or let out in flats. The whole place looked tired and dishevelled and the flowers had all gone from the seafront, including the floral clock. Only one pleasure boat of the original five now voyaged to Flamborough Head, the old *Yorkshire Belle*; two others, the *Boy's Own* and the *Princess Marina* lay rotting in the inner harbour. Only elderly couples, it seemed, patronised the place, sitting in the sun or tramping briskly up and down the esplanade, sniffing the salt air and no doubt resurrecting old memories of younger days and better times.

Old glories soon fade, but those early days in Brid left me

with a love of Yorkshire and its fine folk that has not diminished. I have been back several times, and have found new enchantments in the Dales. But I do not think I want to re-visit Brid, because it is no longer the place of my youth, where the halcyon hours of one golden summer sped by on wings of youthful excitement, novelty, entertainment and interest.

*　　*　　*

We came home that September, again through the Black Country of England, leaving behind my sister who is long since happily married in Leeds, and I had to pick up the threads of life at the North Monastery, to which I had then changed, and where I had been Confirmed just before leaving for Bridlington. The solemn ceremony had taken place in the North Cathedral, the presiding Bishop being Dr. Daniel Cohalan who is remembered, among other things, for having excommunicated members of the old IRA during the War of Independence. He is also reputed to have said, on hearing of the death of his contemporary, the Church of Ireland Bishop of Cork, Cloyne and Ross: 'Now he knows who the *real* Bishop of Cork is!' The North Monastery, officially known as Our Lady's Mount, was - and still is, though much changed in character - situated on the high ground in the northside of the city, a curious mixture of old grey and newer red-brick buildings. The large school, primary, secondary and technical, is run by the famed Christian Brothers, founded by Ignatius Rice in the last century.

They were reputed to be tough men, these same Brothers, and I was perhaps fortunate in that my first teacher was an affable layman, a Mr. Lynch from Cobh who was popularly known as 'Long Lynch', to distinguish him from another teacher of the same name but smaller stature. In the way of things in those days, our class shared a room with another, without any partition, and we dreaded the days when Long Lynch would be absent through illness, because then we would be left to the not too tender mercies of Bro. –, who was wont to wield the leather like any galley-master would wield the whip, and without any apparent reason other than to satisfy his own quite evident tendencies towards sadism. It was my opinion then, and I have not changed it over the years, that the likes of Bro. – should not only have been debarred from the classroom - any classroom - but kicked headlong out of the Order as well.

I once saw him catch a youngster, no more than ten years old, throw him across a desk and beat him savagely until he was exhausted, simply because a local butcher had complained that somebody had stolen some sausages from his window, and the lad in question was believed to be the culprit. There was no discussion, the lad was given no opportunity to speak, the butcher's word was accepted without question and the youngster was summarily thrashed. We could all have told Bro. – that even if the lad did steal the sausages, it was probably from sheer hunger; he was from a broken home and his father was unable to manage even the simple business of feeding the pair of them. The Brother's excesses did not stop there. For any minor infringement, real or imagined, he would line up the entire class and proceed to leather them savagely, until his own uncontrollable fury was fully vent and the thirty odd pupils were reduced to small, whimpering shreds of humanity.

In retrospect, what is amazing is that this sort of savagery was allowed to take place without anyone interfering. The teachers seemed as terrified as the rest of us to open their mouths; the Principal must have known what was going on, but he never intervened. In fairness to the Brothers, I must add that there were only one or two bad apples in the monastic barrel. The tragedy is that, being neither Christian nor brotherly in their outlook, they tended to blacken the characters of all the rest, the vast majority of whom were decent, dedicated and, more often than not, good humoured men who went to extraordinary lengths to educate us.

When I finally entered the Scholarship Class, with about nineteen others deemed to have a chance of qualifying for a Corporation Scholarship, and therefore free secondary education, the amount of their free time that our two Brothers gave up for us was literally limitless. Bro. Hallissey did, it is true, have a fiery temper, but we were never ill-treated in the way described, and more often than not we could defuse his anger and reduce him to howls of laughter with a daring comment such as: 'Watch it, Brother, your blood pressure is going up again,' and we would all relax and get back to work. Bro. Loughnane, who I believe later went off to South America, was again no easy taskmaster, keeping us at it in the certain belief that we were always capable of more, but when we were really in trouble, he would rush to the rescue.

Once, when I had flunked for the umpteenth time in algebra, which was my particular Achilles Heel, instead of getting the round telling off which I expected, he asked me instead to meet him in the Shop after school that afternoon. There, amid the new books and pencils which were sold on the premises, he sat me down and quietly explained that since I seemed to have a problem with the course, perhaps we two had better go over it again, from the very beginning - otherwise I would not get the Scholarship.That good man subsequently gave up many of his afternoons, and patiently coached me until the time came for the examination. It was typical of the dedication of the Brothers that when I emerged from the algebra exam, 'Locker' was waiting outside the door, examination paper in hand, to check the results with me. The delight on his face when all my answers tallied with his is something I shall never forget and my stammered thanks were brushed aside with the simple words: 'It was worth it all, for both of us.' Needless to mention, I duly got the coveted Schol.

In those days, the Mon was a very nationalistic place. We were expected, as a matter of course, to converse in Irish, and indeed all subjects except English were taught through that medium. Happily, thanks to Small Jack and St. Pah's, I had no problems at all, being fluent in the native tongue, though I must admit that trying to learn Latin through the medium was a mind-boggling exercise involving a treble-think every time we tackled a new piece of Livy. Even scientific terms came naturally after a while, though much later on, at Leaving Certificate level, when for some strange reason everything suddenly reverted to English, we all had to think twice about terminology. But we were never allowed forget that we were Irish, in mentality as well as in fact, and this was reflected in our games, our speech, our singing, and not least, our drama.

The annual Mon plays were something of an institution in the city, attracting huge audiences, not least of young ladies from nearby educational establishments who would flock to watch us perform *Robert Emmet* or the saga of the 1916 Rising, complete with burning GPO, blank bullets and all the high drama of the executions. Our beloved Brother Diarmuid Ó Briain (Bob) was the mastermind, and often he would summarily haul a few of us out of class - to the annoyance of the teacher - to polish the script, move a few props, or erect some scenery, so that we all felt very important in the scheme of things even before we trod the boards on opening night. Those plays, more perhaps than anything else, gave us participants a great sense of maturity and confidence, especially those who, like me, were not born hurlers or footballers, destined to shine on the sportsfield.

Later, when I had left the Mon and was heavily involved with youth clubs, a little group of us, lads and lasses alike, decided to put on a play. Lacking a venue, we approached Bro. Diarmuid, who was then Principal, and hesitatingly asked if we could borrow his hall for a few nights. Smiling, he took my arm in his famous iron grip and whispered: 'Ná bac le sin, beidh an Harty againn' (Never mind that, we'll win the Harty Cup), as he had always done. Bro. Diarmuid liked to get his priorities right, and only then did we get down to business, all of which was conducted in Irish, of course. When he realised that the play too was to be in Irish his eyes lit up. Of course we could have the hall, for as long as we wanted, and there would be no question of a fee. The play, a comedy about the tribulations of a garda in love, was a hugely successful, if outrageously amateurish, production and nobody was more pleased than Bob, for whom our affection had remained undiminished down all the years.

It is against this sort of background, of years of much happiness and only a few moments of trauma, that I must and will stoutly defend the Irish Christian Brothers against unwarranted criticism, and often naked hatred. There may have been a few blackguards in the Order, men who probably had no true vocation in the first instance, who had no business either in the Brothers or the teaching profession, and who were probably there because they had nowhere else to go - some of us came to subscribe to the belief that they came from large families who could not otherwise have afforded their education, and that they took their frustration out on the youngsters.

But I match these few against all the very good men I met, and I find the balance overwhelmingly in favour of the latter. Without the Brothers, this country would today be a much poorer place. They educated successive generations when nobody else would, and to that extent, they can be said to have helped in no small way to lay the foundations of modern Ireland. They gave generously and unswervingly of themselves and their talents and, in doing so, they gave us not only education, but a sense of our own dignity and a code of conduct to carry us through life.

Inevitably, because it was so far away from home, the Mon broadened my horizons in more ways than one, bringing me to distant parts of Cork and introducing me to sights, sounds and smells that did not pervade our own semi-rural area. The route to school, for instance, brought us past Collins' Barracks, where the first of the wayside clocks, just visible over the high wall of the barrack square if you stood on tiptoe, reminded us of the need to get a spurt on or face the ire of the teachers.

From the top of very steep Fever Hospital Hill, named after its most notable building - a place that struck terror into those obliged to go there in the special fever ambulance with such terrible diseases as scarlet fever and worse - came the second timely reminder from the famed pepperpot steeple of St. Mary's, Shandon. The time on the four faces of the clock, the biggest in the city, if not in the whole country, was never the same, and since two sides were visible to us, it was a question of taking one's pick and hoping for the best. The explanation offered for this variation was the force of the prevailing winds, which slowed some of the hands, but whatever the truth of the matter, Shandon was always known as the Four-faced Liar.

Reaching its head out of the valley of Blackpool almost to the same height as Shandon, which stood on higher ground, was the equally well-known red-brick shaft of Murphy's brewery, gaunt, often belching smoke from the brewing process - and how high? Well, according to one bright pupil of the Mon, whose class were given the task of estimating its height by way of trigonometry, it stood at one hundred and forty-two feet, plus Mickey Mebser. Asked by an intrigued Brother to explain this unusual calculation of vertical measurement, the bright lad replied: 'Well sir, in order to work out the angle, I took the top of Mickey's head as the baseline, rather than lie on the dirty ground, and did me sums from there.' I understand the genius in question was commended for initiative but not for accuracy. What Mickey Mebser felt about it all is unrecorded, which is perhaps just as well.

Just around the corner from the brewery, as we neared the end of our long trek, was an uphill, narrow, dingy lane known to us as Denny's Lane, or more often, the stinky lane. Occupied on both sides by the Denny bacon factory, it was the source of the most foul smells, especially on killing day, when determined men in aprons and big wooden clogs herded loudly squealing, protesting hordes to the knife. If the screaming was some sort of portent of Hell, then the smell was surely another of the likely torments to be endured there by the wicked. It is impossible to describe that all-pervasive thick fug, which seemed to lie on the surrounding area like an invisible smog. It even penetrated as far as the school itself, so that often, on hot days, even the hardy Brothers would be compelled to order us to close the windows.

At the top of the lane were a few houses, in one of which lived one of my classmates. When I asked him one day how he and his family managed to live with the smell, he looked at me blankly and asked: 'What smell?' In those days, environmental inconveniences were taken for granted as being part and parcel of the industrial process; Denny's gave good employment in the area and there was nothing on record to suggest that the foul odour was in any way harmful. Similarly, Goulding's fertiliser factory at the mouth of the Glen would at times emit a sulphurous gas that, when sniffed, seemed to reach right down to the toes, and many local people suffering from heavy colds would take a walk in the Glen just to 'get the tubes cleared out by Goulding's'. I know from personal experience that it was an effective, if temporary, cure.

There were other diversions along the route to the Mon, like the fine old drays of the brewery, hauled by beautiful Clydesdales with huge muscles and furry hocks, clomping along steadily, the very epitome of equine strength, with their jingling, highly polished brasses. A little further in towards the city, the building firm of Eustace's had a steam lorry, I think an old Foden, which was still in service in the late forties, a venerable, vertical-boilered wagon that snorted and spluttered its slow way through the flat city streets, all the while belching out smoke and steam on its ten-miles-an-hour progress with loads of bricks, cement and miscellaneous building materials. On the way home, if we were heading to the Library, which was often the case, the route took us down past the old butter market, from which the merchant princes of an earlier century purveyed the goodness of the lush hinterland all over the world, thence to North Main Street, once the principal thoroughfare of the old city.

There, once a week, would be parked an ancient Ford Model T, battered beyond belief, bereft of many of its fittings, bald of tyre and with bits hanging down everywhere, coloured a delicate shade of grimy black and old rust, but still motoring. Laden with the produce of the countryside, it was owned by a market gardener who came regularly to sell his wares to the many shops in the area. Rusting and decrepit it may have been, but its one-eighth-inch thick plating gave the impression of utter indestructibility; this thing would go on forever and, if it broke down, the local blacksmith would surely be able to fix it, so unsophisticated were its innards. With so much of interest all around us, it is a wonder that we ever got to school, or home afterwards.

While we were all influenced by Mother Church in one way or another, it would be wrong to conclude that we were goodie-goodies. But the influence was there, coming from our homes, where in many instances the Rosary was said every night, and our schools, where the Catholic ethos was very strong, so that in our everyday lives, we automatically saluted the passing priest, in case he might be carrying the Blessed Sacrament on a sick call. Reared in this sort of environment, it was scarcely surprising that even toughies like us, as we considered ourselves, could be persuaded occasionally to attend evening devotions in the chapel on the hill. Benediction did not last very long anyway, and there was a certain pleasure in listening to the lovely Latin 'Salutaris' and 'Tantum Ergo' and breathing in the rich waft of incense as the priest swung the censor in our direction. There was peace here, away from the troubles of the day and perhaps the trepidation about tomorrow; the peace that comes of the predictable and the enduring, the simple and the unchanging.

St. Joseph's, as churches go, was not very big, and we knew every pillared arch and every statue, every stained glass window and every painting of the Stations of the Cross. We knew too the tall figure of the much-loved Father O'Connor, senior curate, whose clothes were never other than slightly shabby, and who was reputed to give away in charity almost as much as he received when collecting the twice-yearly dues from people who could ill afford to give. His deep voice would drone the well-known ceremony and he was always patently delighted to see any of us youngsters present, coming to the gate afterwards to chat to us and ask after our parents. We came away, at peace with him, with ourselves and with the world, after this brief interlude. If there are times when it is good to be alone, there are also times when it is good to pay communal homage to the Creator, to feel the benefactions of cosy, traditional rite among friends and neighbours, and to be refreshed.

But we were growing up and more pressing duties were being thrust on us, like attendance at the annual parish Mission which, once optional, was now being considered compulsory. This was one of the big events of the year, with visiting Missioners, usually Redemptorists, being brought in for the occasion of spiritual renewal. They were mighty men of God, those same Redemptorists, men with 'words of learned length and thundering sound' and they not only 'amazed the gazing rustics ranged around', they terrified the living daylights out of them, so much so that backsliders who had not seen the inside of the church for years were cajoled back into spirituality. The first week was reserved for the women, and from them we would get some indication of what the Missioners were like. There was always a 'quiet Missioner' and a 'hard Missioner', the first usually coming out to soften up the audience with a few jokes and stories before the other emerged to get the real message across.

We youngsters, who went along for the entertainment as much as anything else, usually sat in the very front seats, from where we could see the Redemptorist swaying back and forth in the high pulpit as he bellowed out his message of salvation, his voice rising from a muted hiss to a shattering roar as he delivered his punchlines. Often we thought he would topple out of the pulpit in his zeal, and you could hear a mouse cough in the church as he thundered the message of repentance and the way to a new life. Hellfire and eternal damnation were the foundations on which the majority of the sermons were laid in those pre-Vatican II days: be prepared, for you know not the day nor the hour.

'There are men here tonight' (the voice would begin to build up to a great crescendo), 'who, if they do not repent of their sins and turn to God, will not be here next year.' And so it went, one spiritual horror following another, until the very last night of the Mission, when we would renew our Baptismal promises to renounce Satan and all his works and pomps, of which one tale, probably apocryphal, is told. 'Do you renounce the Devil?' asked the Missioner, repeating the time-honoured question. 'We do,' came the response, in an emotionally charged atmosphere.

'Louder, let me hear you!'

'We do!' came the great roar and from the very back of the church, the added words, 'the bastard'.

The extraordinary thing is that these were the very kindest and most understanding of men, both in the confessional and outside the church, and they would listen patiently to long catalogues of sins and omissions, and deal in the most gentle manner with penitents. As a result, they were much loved and, in some parishes, were actually chaired from the church at the end of the Mission. They were effective too; people went to Mass who had not been there for years, others gave up the drink that had been causing havoc in their homes, at least for a brief time, for human nature is full of the sort of frailties that the Missioners were trying to root out.

In our own small place, Danny, one of the mildest of men with a leaning towards 'the drop', would be at seven o'clock Mass every morning during the Mission, and at each of the evening ceremonies, and we would no longer be able to persuade him to give us a few verses of 'The Groves of Sweet Glanmire' as he made his unsteady way home down the lane in the dusk.

There was one night on which we youngsters were discouraged from attending. 'Tomorrow night we will be dealing with an

adult subject, and I do not want to see anyone under the age of six-
teen in the church.' So we stayed away, but we knew full well what
was going on. We may have been green, but we were not cabbages,
and casual conversations overheard the following day would confirm our views.

'Begor Jack, he gave 'em the country roads last night!'

'He did so, and the passion wagons as well.'

The evening ceremonies over, we would make our way home,
downhill past the Three Horseshoes pub, in which we did not have
the slightest interest, and on to the forge, which was a source of
undying fascination. Even at that late hour, there was a fair chance
that the smith might be working and we would huddle in a little
group outside the door to watch.

In scenes reminiscent of Dante's Inferno this big man (were
blacksmiths always huge in stature?) would bring the fire to a billowing orange furnace as he pumped the bellows with a wooden
handle rather like the shaft of a horsecart. With a long-handled pin-
cers, he would extract a bright red horseshoe from the fire, carry it
to the anvil and, bang, tap-tap; bang, tap-tap, he would strike literally while the iron was hot, keeping the rhythm of the anvil. Flying
sparks, the soft roar of the furnace, the peculiar, pungent odour of
smoking hoof as the final fitting was made, and the hiss of steam as
the shoe was plunged into cold water before being expertly nailed
in place, combined to give our young minds a certain vision of the
sort of hell the Missioner had been talking about. We watched, full
of awe, until the smith, busy and tired, finally asked: 'Have you
young fellows no homes to go to?'

Of course we had homes to go to, basic by today's standards,
with few of the modern comforts. Bathrooms, for instance, were
conspicuous by their absence, the Saturday night dousing being
executed in a big metal tub in front of the kitchen fire, while toilets
were invariably outside and often not even adjoining the house.
There was the front room, or parlour, the kitchen-cum-living room,
a few bedrooms and that was it, while some of the smaller homes in
the area consisted merely of one room plus scullery downstairs and
two bedrooms above. Surprisingly from these, the little homes of
Cork, many of them situated in tiny lanes and squares, came some
of the largest families and finest people, reminiscent of the sturdy
young men and comely maidens of de Valera's famous vision. How
they all managed to cram into these tiny homes is still a mystery to
me, but, ragged though some of the children may have been, they
all seemed happy, while the toil-worn parents were always ready to
welcome small strangers like myself for a cup of tea and a slice of
bread and jam with their own offspring.

Many of these same offspring, my young friends and neighbours, were to rise to positions of eminence in later life. From a small house in Glenview Terrace, at the top of the Glen Lane, for instance, came Tadhg Ó Ciardha, one of the large Carey family, who went on from brilliant studentship to become President of University College, Cork. Former Taoiseach Jack Lynch was born and reared in a relatively small house at the foot of Shandon steeple, and there are numerous examples of people coming from what would nowadays be seen as very cramped homes who subsequently attained eminence in various sectors of national life.

Indeed, it can be said that as the fledgling nation began to find its feet, it was the ordinary people – many of whose parents had been active in the struggle for independence – who, through dedicated scholarship and ambition, developed not only the methods but the dedication necessary to help set the country on its feet. That these youngsters were so motivated was due almost entirely to two major factors: the influence of their parents, who scrimped and scrounged under the most unfavourable conditions, and often at great personal sacrifice, to educate them, and a system of education which, in spite of its many detractors, consisted largely of the most dedicated teachers, who were fully aware of the conditions in these houses.

These small city homes were as picturesque as they were cramped. On the wall outside the front door would hang a birdcage during daylight hours, its tiny occupant, be it finch, linnet or canary, singing fit to burst, truly a bird in a not too gilded cage. The caged canaries I could tolerate, because they were bred in captivity and would certainly have perished quickly had they been freed, but I could never reconcile myself to trapping little wild things like linnets and goldfinches and confining them, like the prisoners by the rivers of Babylon, to sing forever behind bars. The trapping was carried out in the Glen and the surrounding area with a treacly stuff called bird lime, the ingredients of which remain a mystery, but which was spread thickly on the branches of a bush, a decoy bird being placed nearby to attract another victim. True, the captives were well looked after, but it always seemed to me that this was no compensation at all for deprivation of the basic right of every bird to take wing and soar at will in the blue heavens.

Inside the houses, often behind a half-door, the top portion of which could be opened in fine weather while the bottom remained closed to keep out unwanted animals, was the parlour with its oil-cloth covered table, its dresser stocked with common delph for everyday use and perhaps some fine China for ornament, its bright fire and the picture of the Sacred Heart, under which rested an oil lamp, constantly burning. In reality, these small city homes compared almost exactly with their counterpart country cottages. Living where we did, we were familiar with both, though our own houses were larger and more commodious, making up in space what they lacked in cosy intimacy.

It was to these homes that we would return at night, to sit by the fire of turf or wood blocks – but never of coal because of the wartime shortage – to read incessantly, since television was unheard of and few had the wireless. My own reading was both constant and catholic, because having an insatiable appetite for the printed word, I gobbled up mentally everything I could lay hands on. Everybody began, of course, with the comics, the *Dandy, Beano* and *Knockout* and later progressed to the teenagers' *Champion, Hotspur, Adventure, Rover* and *Wizard.* Then along came the most wonderful of all, the brand new *Eagle* setting very high standards of entertainment and information, with its advanced concept of travel in outer space with the intrepid Dan Dare and its famous centre-page spread of cutaway drawings of the mechanical marvels of the day: steam locomotives, aircraft, submarines, ships, turbines and so on.

Some of our elders tended to discourage this interest in comics and indeed some teachers abhorred them as being too superficial and too badly written. I did not then, and do not now, subscribe to that view. They may not have been classics, but they did inculcate in many of us the reading habit, and generations of youngsters who began with Frank Richardson's famed Billy Bunter went on to much more serious matters, myself included. They also stimulated our imaginations and in their own none too serious way helped our mental development. Even today I would far rather see a child reading a comic than watching the television set or a video.

From the comics we progressed to more technical offerings like the *Meccano Magazine*, when we could afford it, or perhaps the *Boys Own Paper*, a now mostly-forgotten journal that had a great deal to offer in terms of general interest reading, even if it did have a distinct Imperial flavour about it. Inevitably, this obsession with the printed word led to membership of the City Library, for a few paltry pence a year. Situated on Grand Parade, this beautiful limestone building was a successor to an earlier Carnegie library on the South Mall. To us youngsters, even its appearance inspired respect, its long corridor, which we had to traverse to reach the Children's Department, being tastefully panelled in dark mahogany, with fine engravings of old Cork and some paintings, mainly by local artists.

Even in those days of austerity, it spoke quietly of elegance and the rightness of things, of scholarship and information to be found in excellent surroundings and, not least, of an endless supply of material for our entertainment and edification. Even without the aura of respect it commanded of itself, woe betide any youngster who grew boisterous; he or she was quickly and very firmly tackled either by the tall, uniformed porter or else by one of the library assistants, who was known to us as a veritable female dragon, and who would tolerate no nonsense.

The first section beyond the lobby was the reading room, where the daily newspapers and some periodicals were kept, and it was here that I first became acquainted with journals such as the *Illustrated London News* which I would peruse in fascination, at the same time watching surreptitiously the antics of the old men, some of them vagrants who would come shuffling and sniffing in to while away a cosy hour on a cold day. Some of them could not see very well and had large magnifying glasses which they would skim across the pages, bending over them like lepidoptorists studying some new, rare and fascinating species. The stillness here, and indeed throughout the building, was broken only by the occasional asthmatic cough or splutter and, in the lending departments, the hushed murmur of voices as books were exchanged.

There, in the quiet splendour of the Children's Department, I first became acquainted with all of the junior classics, starting, like everyone else, with *Treasure Island*, the now almost forgotten *Children of the New Forest*, the epic frontier works of Fenimore Cooper and of course, William, Biggles and all the rest. From there too I took home, with much dithering because we were allowed only one book at a time – an irksome restriction long since removed – works on the lives of the great engineers, on the building of such wonders as the railways, on the Suez and Panama canals and, through a schoolboy fascination with the sea, on ships and sailing men. I remember reading, tucked up cosily in my little corner by the fire, Richard Dana's great work *Two Years Before the Mast* and many similar tales of the terrible hardships endured by the old salts of Cape Horn.

In my mind's eye I would journey with them through the Roaring Forties to Valparaiso and Tierra del Fuego, the land of fire, and onwards to Australia in the days of the *Cutty Sark* and the great grain and tea races, while St. Elmo's Fire spluttered and spat around my royals and to'gallants, and the iron men of the windjammers ate hard tack and drank cocoa instead of the daily rum ration – cocoa because they found it kept them warm longer than the rum. I voyaged up the Amazon and wandered with the Conquistadores in Peru of the fabled Inca gold, little knowing then the foul treachery of the Spanish and the awful slaughter they visited on an innocent people.

So the Cork City Library became an integral part of my life, as indeed did the frequent journeys to and from there. These, in many ways, were as full of interest and education as were the books themselves, for a youngster with eyes to see and a mind to wonder. My usual inward route took me first down Summerhill to the top of the Tunnel Steps, from where I had an aerial view over the railway station at Glanmire. Often my wanderings would coincide, intentionally with the departure of the Day Mail for Dublin and I would stand for ages watching the last-minute preparations: the sudden blowing-off of the safety valve of the huge green engine, as an anxious fireman built up every possible ounce of pressure for the tough climb ahead, the lowering of the red and white semaphore signal, the shrill blast of the guard's whistle, the burst of steam and water as the driver cleared the cylinders and then, the first blast of smoke and exhaust steam from the chimney as the regulator was opened and the locomotive took hold of its heavy train. A half revolution and then the huge driving wheels would spin, frantically trying to grip the track, until the regulator was eased and then gently opened again and away she would go, gouging and belching and straining, under the tunnel, the carriage wheels clacking over the points, until the tail-end of the last carriage disappeared, leaving behind that peculiar, lonely emptiness of the station when the train has gone.

With its going, so would I, down the steps and across to the busy quays, all the berthing spaces filled with ships from all over the world, from the little tramps to the great grain and coal boats, with dockside room at such a premium that several more might well be lying in the roads at the big swinging basin, awaiting their turn to get in to discharge. Those that were berthed were surrounded by activity in the way that a queen bee might be surrounded by her ardent workers. At the Innisfallen dock, men were already loading the limited cargo and the few cars, which had to be craned on board in large slings. Soon now the emigrants, going for the first time or returning to Britain – usually to London or the huge Ford plant at Dagenham, from which they earned the soubriquet 'the Dagenham yanks' – would arrive and there would be the most harrowing scenes as the vessel pulled away.

Elderly mothers would hold up Rosary beads and in loud voices, to be heard above the tumult of departure, exhort their sons and daughters to remember to say their prayers; tears would run down cheeks and the stern rail of the vessel would be a mass of sadly waving arms. On one historic occasion, a huge man from the northside of the city was heard to bellow down to his weeping wife: 'never mind about me woman, feed the finch!' But even these comical priorities could not mask the dolefulness of departure, and the necessity for going reflected the grim state of the economy in the late forties and early fifties.

A little further up towards the city centre, perspiring dockers, tough men though they were, laboured in steamy, dirty holds at the filthy work of shovelling coal into huge buckets which were hoisted away by the overhead cranes. Others scurried, ant-like, down gangways, carrying on their stout shoulders large sacks, bales and boxes. Years later, a docker told me of the day when one of the noted local stevedores called him aside.

'Tell me Tommy, why are you going more slowly then the others?'

'Well, 'tis like this, sir. The sole is falling off my boot (pointing to the flapping sole), and if I go any faster I'll fall out on my head, load and all.'

'Oh we can't have that, Tommy,' said the stevedore, reaching into his pocket and pulling out a huge wad of notes held together by a stout rubber band. Tommy, delighted, thought the price of a new pair of boots was on the way. The stevedore peeled off the rubber band, handed it to Tommy and added: 'There, that'll keep your sole in place. Now get on with it'.

Moored right next to Brian Boru Bridge, a Scherzer rolling lift (bascule) structure built in 1905, lay the Clyde vessel *Glengarriff*, part passenger ship, part cargo, but mostly cattle, which rested in a nearby lairage before the long haul to Liverpool. Driven through the streets, they would cause serious delay to the then sparse traffic, especially if a few young and frisky bullocks decided to make a bolt for it before reaching the lairage. Brian Boru Bridge itself, like its companion Clontarf Bridge on the south channel of the Lee, could also cause serious delays, when the centre 62-foot span was raised to allow the passage of a coaster to or from the upper reaches of the river.

Nowadays these bridges are fixed, but at that time, little sailing smacks like the *Carbery Queen* would come right up, almost to St. Patrick's Bridge, with cargo for the brisk coastal trade. There too came a little vessel from central Europe, bearing Hungarian and Czech refugees from heaven knows what terrors. For many years it lay moored there, known locally simply as 'the refugee ship', until its occupants achieved some sort of national status from a sympathetic government. (One married a lass from Ballingeary and their lovely, talented daughters subsequently became prominent on the local musical scene). From there, it was but a few steps to the city centre proper and the library, with a head full of travel, vicarious adventure and the wonder of it all.

But life was not all books. There were other forms of entertainment on those gloomy, cold winter nights, when the homework was done. A little group of us would gather in John Murphy's house across the way to while away a few hours playing cards, mostly simple games like Sevens, Beg O' My Neighbour and the more intricate 45 and 110, amid much bickering and hilarity. This was a sort of urban version of the rural rambling house, where neighbours would drop in uninvited, and after the nine o'clock news (John's was one of the few homes to have 'the wireless'), the story-telling would begin, the tales being interrupted by such huge guffaws of laughter that we often wondered if the very large lady in the room overhead would come crashing down on us. Owing to the very curious construction of the house, John's family did not occupy this room, though they did inhabit that directly above it, on the top storey!

If Sarah's brother Frank, who had deserted the railway for life as a ship's stoker, happened to be home, we would be regaled with strange tales of faraway places. Frank was a tall, thin, angular man who, in addition to his fund of anecdotes about such far-flung places as Bone in North Africa and Miami, before it was as fashionable as it now is, once took young John and myself to the docks to see his ship, the *City of Waterford*, guiding us right down into the very bowels of the vessel, from where we emerged feeling very claustrophobic indeed, and wondering how anybody could possibly work there. He once promised to bring me back a Bowie knife from America, but as it happened, neither he nor the knife ever appeared again and I lost track of him completely.

Inevitably, on those nights, the story-telling would revert, in the best tradition, to ghost stories, and we would sit listening very silently to tales of the Banshee, the keening woman spirit who is supposed to presage the death of somebody from the families of the O's or the Macs. More gruesomely, somebody would swear that they had seen the dread 'Headless Coach' and while the wind tore at the roofs and the old elm across the way, we would shudder as we could all but hear the wild, thundering hooves and see the fiery eyes come blazing down the lane. Later, we would rush across the short few steps between the houses, with many a backward glance into the inky blackness, to hurry up the stairs by the flickering light of a guttering candle.

Because of wartime shortages, we did not have electricity in the upstairs portion of our house at the time; the work of wiring had been interrupted by the hostilities, so we relied heavily on an old paraffin oil lamp and on candles. The lamp was reasonably elegant, standing on a brass base with a red glass oil bowl and a long, curvaceous glass funnel which shielded the wick. The candlesticks, however, were purely utilitarian, consisting of a wide, saucer-like enamelled base with a small handle for the finger or thumb, and a simple tube to hold the candle.

We had also used a gas lamp in the kitchen when I was younger. It gave off a soft, gentle, hissing light from its flimsy mantle, a little filigree thing of such delicate construction that it broke literally at the touch of a finger. It served us well for years, but when I was about six, a man from the gas company came and took it and its attendant piping away, because some neighbour had finally persuaded my mother that we did not need both electricity and gas. She watched it go as she would oversee the departure of an old friend, and when the electric light was switched on she did not, as was her custom, welcome it with the greeting: 'The light of Heaven to our souls', but instead said very quietly: 'There goes a little light that has seen us through many a dark night'. It was, in more ways than one, the end of an era, and small though I was, I was touched by a strange sadness.

*   *   *

The deepening winter brought other considerations, not least meteorological, and while our wise old schoolmaster would tell us solemnly that 'snow is all right on Christmas cards', we all longed for a white festive season. I do not recall it ever happening. Frost, yes; snow, never. For several weeks before we would look expectantly at the icy night sky, as if our gaze could of itself bring the desired result. My sister and I would place little saucers of water on the outside window-sill and, in the morning, rush out anxiously to see if it had frozen. Often it had, but there was no sign of snow. Wake as we might to roofs covered in hoar frost, which for a moment, in our post-slumber daze, had us fooled, there was nothing more substantial. Frustrated again, we would look elsewhere for our excitement, of which there was plenty.

The very first sign that Christmas was at hand was the window dressing of the shops at the Cross, where the Kelly sisters and others would replace the more mundane displays with holly, tinsel, cakes, a few toys and other goodies, and decorative red crêpe paper. With frozen noses pressed to window panes which rapidly became fogged over with steaming breath, we would survey the contents of each display and conduct our own best-dressed window competition. This was the prelude; the great symphony was yet to come, and it consisted of many movements, all building to the magnificent festive crescendo.

First, there was the business of getting school out of the way before we could even begin to enjoy ourselves. The pre-Christmas exams would be undergone and the results handed out; nothing very traumatic there as the majority of us were able to cope with Small Jack's tough but fair test of our ability. Then, having wished us a happy Christmas and released us, like wild animals from a cage, into the bustling world outside, he too would go off to to enjoy his break, free for a little while of the daily grind of stuffing knowledge into us. We would head for the wild places to collect holly, which was scarce enough and difficult to reach even where it did grow. But usually our lack of success was not disastrous, because a few pieces could be scrounged from a sympathetic milk-man or nearby railwayman, who would bring it home from his up-country travels and distribute it generously among the neighbours.

Most prized, of course, was the red-berried holly, with the variegated coming a close second. It would be carefully sectioned and hung over pictures and mirrors and then the decorations, twist-ed paper stringers and lengths of tinsel stowed away since last year, would be strung across the ceiling, to transform the room for a few brief weeks. Largely, we did not bother with Christmas trees, these being reserved for the posher houses on the main road, from where we could see the coloured lights twinkling the message that there was an un-bridgable gap between them and us. But it not bother us; we had our own ways, our own customs and our own pastimes.

The greatest excitement, inevitably, was brought about by the trip to town, Even when we were a little too big to visit Santa, there was more than ordinary joy in parading through the packed streets, mingling with the cheerful crowds and gaping, eyes out on stalks, at the toy and model shop windows. Most of the items we knew just could not be afforded, but there was no harm in looking and hoping and anyway, the looking was free. This was especially true of Robert Day's in Patrick Street, where, in addition to Santa's cave, a most wonderful working model railway was on display. Specially set up for Christmas, this was contained behind glass walls and consisted of a full layout with village, stations, engine shed, and all the ancillaries. It would hold us enthralled for a long time, as the little Hornby Dublo trains wound their way around the circuit, jour-neying through a Lilliputian land of their own.

Some lucky lad would receive a set for Christmas, but my own attention was usually directed to something more affordable, like the glass cases on the opposite wall full of Britain's farm animals. I had quite a collection of these, some of which, having been obtained by swapping for other items, were quite old even then and would be very valuable today. I recall a whiskered farm labourer in his smock, a milkmaid suitably dressed in the fashion of the English rural scene of perhaps the twenties, and some others, all beautifully crafted in lead and hand painted. The models then on show were more modern, because Britain's tended to keep up to date with agricultural and military developments, but they were still intriguing in their accuracy. They ranged in price from about one shilling and sixpence for a large model of a mounted huntsman or woman to a penny for a tiny chick, busily pecking at the ground, so that everybody could afford something, if they were sufficiently interested in that sort of collection.

Dragged reluctantly away, we would be persuaded to address the more mundane matter of ordering the bird, in our case a goose. This entailed a trip to the English Market, that fascinating place of local commerce where fowl of every description hung in profusion; serried ranks of scrawny necks dropping from plump, plucked bodies ready to grace hundreds of tables. In the bedlam of the marketplace, amid the lively chatter of the salespeople and customers, choice seemed to have been difficult, because the hanging birds were prodded and poked, argued over and debated, walked away from and walked back to, until finally the selection was made, honour being satisfied all round. Only then could we head for home, battered by the bustle, exhausted by the constant press of people and minds reeling from the wonder of it all.

Nobody slept well on Christmas Eve. Even when Santa had long left our home, there was still the anticipation of a present of some description which Mother had once again scrimped to buy, but it would remain a surprise until the following morning. Come daylight, and still with no sign of snow – it scarcely mattered now – I was first downstairs, to find that after my departure the night before, Mother and my sister had laid out a beautiful Christmas table, complete with candles and little decorations on the best white tablecloth and there, at my place, was the present. Trembling fingers tore open the wrapping to find inside, yes, a number of Britain's little huntsmen and women, the latter riding side-saddle in black garb, while the former were in bright red, together with some other farm animals for my collection, gleaming in their fresh paint, utterly desirable. Somebody had got the message and no matter what happened now, Christmas was complete, and vague dreams of a train set faded into the distance . . .

Of course, it all passed far too quickly, the trip to Mass, the bilateral showing off of presents to the pals, the huge Christmas dinner, the subsequent feeling of being replete and cosy and at home, while not forgetting to spare a prayer for those less fortunate, as had been enjoined on us at the morning ceremony. Before we knew it, the day had gone; Christmas present had suddenly become Christmas past, wafted into history almost in an instant with Mother's end-of-night benefaction: 'Well, thanks be to God for so much'. I sometimes felt like adding: 'and thanks be to Mother for making so much of so little'.

A long and deep sleep was rudely interrupted early the following morning by a loud and continuous banging on the door knocker, and the raucous voices of a group of youngsters raised in not too tuneful chant:

THE LIFE OF OTHER DAYS

> The wren, the wren, the King of all birds,
> St Stephen's Day got caught in the furze
> Up with the kettles and down with the pots
> Give us our money and let us be off.

These were the famous Wren Boys, who came unfailingly every year on their rounds, singing for a few pence at every house. They never had a wren, though some did make an effort and brought along a 'dummy' tucked away in a bit of a bush. Others blackened their faces and almost all were dressed in strange garb, having used any old material that came readily to hand, so that they presented a strange if not always elegant picture.

There was only one way to get rid of them and so end the awful cacophony, and that was to throw a few pennies down from the bedroom window, upon which they would sing their final verse:

> God bless the mistress of the house
> Put a golden chain around her neck
> And if she's sick or if she's sore
> May god have mercy on her soul.

With this rather dubious blessing, they would be off, chanting loudly, to the next house leaving us in peace – until the next group came and the whole process had to be repeated, until about mid-day, when they would go off to the local shops to dispose of their earnings. With their departure, we settled down to our own affairs, making the most of the remaining few days holidays before trudging reluctantly back to school in the bleak mist of an early January morning.

But we were only back a few days, just settling in again, when one morning we woke to find the world covered in a carpet of white. Overnight, snow had come at last, taking us all by surprise, though fairly weather-wise as we were, we should not have been caught unawares. For a few days a bitter wind had been blowing up the lane from the Glen, which meant it was coming straight from the north, unhindered in its icy passage by any large mountains. We got the full blast of its cold bite, which whippped at faces and hands like a lash, to send us hurrying, red-faced and stinging, into the warmth of the house and the fireside.

But overnight the clear skies had become shrouded over with the black pall of snow-bearing clouds. While we slept, they had swept over the countryside, driven by the wind, transforming it into a wonderland of white which cast strange blue and purple shadows. We were reminded that snow is not white, that it picks up and reflects the greater part of the colour spectrum, giving our surroundings a totally new and exciting appearance. In that bitter winter of 1947, against all the odds, the blizzards lasted several weeks, piling up showdrifts in the Glen as the winds tore in relentlessly from the Arctic. To our delight, the heating system in the school was unable to cope, probably because of the fuel shortage which was to become critical before it was all over. Also, some teachers were unable to make the cross-city journey to school, so on the second or third morning of the snow, we were all sent home and the school was closed.

Delightful though our circumstances now were, we soon tired of snow-balling and sliding down a slope in the Glen on an old piece of sheet iron. Young John Murphy and I found a new occupation in feeding the many birds which now abounded in his father's garden. Too weak from cold and hunger to fly, they became almost tame, so that we had no difficulty in catching thrushes, blackbirds and sparrows in our hands, where they would lie, terrified, but unable to flee. How many we rescued from death during that savage winter I do not know, but we scrounged every crumb and heel-end of bread we could find, together with little bits of fat and anything else that came to hand, and fed them in the garden that was utterly changed in appearance. All around us, the landscape had taken on a new look, full of gentle, rolling white hollows, as the harsh contours of the land were ironed and smoothed by the piled-up drifts. Old gnarled trees assumed a new dignity in their surgical white coats. Hedgerows glistened with leaves suddenly turned into diamonds, beckoning the wan sun that sometimes broke through a brief gap in the heavy, leaden skies.

We cared not at all that for several weeks the whole country, and indeed most of Europe, was locked fast in an icy grip. The nightmare of the transport people was our sweet dream and, unlike them, we hoped it would never end. While whole communication systems were frozen solid,with trains snowbound for days on end and almost every road impassable, we roamed free in the white countryside. There was a special sort of pleasure in taking the dog into the Glen at evening, when the whole world was still and white and our feet left tracks in the crunchy snow.

Soon, still more would come toppling from the heavy grey sky, to hide all traces of our passage, but meanwhile, the dog did not quite know what to make of it all. He raced across the newly laundered landscape, rolling in the the drifts, snorting with glee as his hind legs tossed up great clouds, as a snowplough might, and he fell into hidden holes, to come bounding out again with a bark and a huge leap. There was no complete darkness, even at night. Whatever little light was there was picked up and magnified by the all-pervading snow, so that even in what would normally be total darkness it was possible to see, and with some care, to avoid now-hidden hazards.

In due time, news drifted in that the Lough, on the southside of the city, was frozen to the point where it was person-bearing. It was too far away for us to reach easily without transport, but we did see pictures in the *Echo* of people sliding happily on its icy surface, and would willingly have joined them but for lack of buses – possibly the only time when the transport chaos hit us directly. At the very beginning, a few brave drivers had managed to get their vehicles as far as the Cross, but as the conditions worsened rapidly, we all had to pitch in with canvas bags, ashes and what little grit we could find to place under the rear wheels, so that they could turn and head off back to the city before they became snow-bound.

Mayfield, of course, being so high up, was utterly out of the question. Worried bus crews, on reaching the Cross, took one look up the hill, shook their heads and apologetically told their clients that they would have to walk the rest of the way home. It was a long and unpleasant trudge, the more so since most of them had shopping bags and some were quite elderly. In fact, as the snow became packed, it must have been a hair-raising task getting the buses back downhill to the terminus. Passengers were refused admittance; only the two-man crew travelled as the big vehicles crawled and slid, often sideways, down the hill, grinding along in low gear at less than walking pace, the drivers, very rightly, wary of even touching the brake.

Somehow, in spite of everything, the essential commerce of the area continued. Snow and ice or not, the milkmen somehow managed to get through, even if they were very late. They came muffled up to the eyebrows against the biting weather, and even their hardy hands could not handle the freezing commodity they sold without the aid of fingerless mitts. Like the famed Pony Express, the postmen also made their perished rounds, even if deliveries were restricted to one per day in the worst areas. But Paddy Buckley left his mare in her old stable across the road, coming once a day to feed her and ensure her comfort. He reasoned that there was no point in trying to go anywhere with that huge, heavy cart and risking his precious animal going down under it. That, for him, would be economic disaster, the end of his career as a carrier, and Paddy was not ready to retire yet.

Even John Murphy, for once, had to neglect his beloved garden, apart from a bit of hasty tidying up. The ground was crowbar-proof in its icy solidity and John's fork and spade were carefully put away in the greenhouse until the great freeze-up ended. Meanwhile, there were other, more pressing problems. The Collins family, who lived in one of Goulding's cottages in the Glen, normally drew their water in buckets from a pump on the main road, because they did not then have it on tap. When the pump froze, they had to depend on the neighbours, but some of us had our own problems. In our own case, the leaden feed pipe entered the kitchen from a hole in the ground outside the house, there being some two feet of pipe visible before it entered through the wall. Of course, after a few days of sub-zero temperatures, it froze, despite being hurriedly wrapped in old sacking. In due course, old Maurice Hayes arrived with a plumber and when the latter applied some heat to the pipe, it split, 'which was only what I expected it to do anyway', he commented. But, watched by a small audience, he got out his big stick of plumber's solder and his blowlamp and set to work, filling the crevice with fresh lead and then making a large solder ball around the whole repair to strengthen the affected area. Then, with a flourish, he took a rag wrapped in grease and showed us how he 'wiped the joint', smoothing and finishing it, so that it looked like a huge bulge in the middle of the old pipe. But it worked and we had water flowing again; Maurice re-wrapped the pipe very carefully, lagging it against the extreme cold again. 'All we can do now is hope that it will hold,' he said, as he and the plumber went off to tackle the next emergency.

Keeping the home fires burning was another problem. Coal for domestic use was still unavailable and we had to make do with turf and timber. The former was often anything but dry and hard, the latter often difficult to obtain. It was not uncommon, once the fire had been lit successfully and was burning fairly well, to stack sods of turf on top of the hot range to dry them out for the rest of the night or even the morrow. Dry, they would blaze heartily, giving out great heat. Wet, they were worse than useless, using up our small supply of valuable kindling in a futile attempt to create any sort of blaze. The best they would do was to smoulder frustratingly, giving off a lot of smoke but no heat. During weather like this, it became common to bank down the fire before retiring at night, so that it could easily be brought to life on the following morning, meanwhile drying what turf was piled on the range during the night. It was a self-perpetuating cycle, with the fire being used to dry the turf which in turn was being used to keep the fire burning.

If we were lucky enough to have any timber blocks to hand, much the same process was employed. It was useless, in weather like this, venturing to Paddy Frawley's sawmill off Harrington's Square for a barrow or box-car full of blocks, because he could not get any supplies of timber from which to cut them. So, no matter how badly they might be needed, his screaming circular saw, driven by an ancient petrol engine, was silent when it was most wanted. That same engine was so decrepit that when the saw, which it drove by way of a long belt, was running, it needed a constant flow of water to keep it cool. A long rubbery hose leading into the radiator gave the impression that the engine was somehow running on water alone.

And so we survived it all, without too much hardship and certainly with a great deal of outside entertainment, until the morning when we woke to find that what had been icicles were now drips. The hand that then clutched at our hearts was icier than the conditions of the past few weeks. A big thaw had set in. The magic of the blizzards and the coming of the ice-man was at an end. Worse, we would soon get a clarion call to say that school was open for business once again. In this fluxy world, we were sharply reminded, there is nothing so certain as change.

There were other outdoor spectacles of considerable signifi-
cance in our young lives, perhaps the most notable being that
which was signposted at least a week in advance by Father
O'Connor during the announcements at Mass: 'On Sunday next, the
men and boys of the parish will assemble outside the Church at
2.30 pm and walk in procession to the Grand Parade, where
Benediction of the Most Blessed Eucharist will take place.' There
was no further exhortation because there was no need for it. The
announcement alone was enough to galvanise people into frenetic
activity in the intervening week. It was the spark that set off the
powder keg of old and cherished tradition. During the following
days, as we made our way home from school, there was no shortage
of free entertainment as we stopped to watch the local men and
women giving the small homes of Dillon's Cross their annual face-
lift.

Even those normally unemployed would be hard at it, cleaning and scraping, white-washing and painting. Men trudged off to
Carroll's yard in Anglesea Street for bags of lime which were mixed
with water to make the whitewash, and some of the more enterpris-
ing added some colour to the mix, so that when they were finished,
the row of single-storey houses looked like something from the sun-
splashed Mediterranean, and the whole place took on the appearance of a holiday resort. Meanwhile, of course, there was much
humour as the workers were constantly chaffed by onlookers, with
comments like: 'Begor Mick, I see you're turning the dirt inside out
again' or 'I suppose t'oul coat of wash will hold the place together
for another year.'

But behind all the banter, there was an air of high purpose
and determination. The annual Procession was nigh and the place
would have to be clean, in accordance with the decrees of simple
faith and old custom. Ladders were borrowed, windows and doors
were re-painted and then the latter were hung with bright striped
covers to keep off the glaring sun, and so prevent blistering of the
new paint. Finally, the flags and bunting were excavated from old
boxes lying in lofts and hung up, and many of the little windows
were dressed with special shrines dedicated to the Sacred Heart.

Often these were veritable works of art, carefully constructed
from sprays of flowers cut specially for this great occasion. Those
who did not have gardens of their own simply went into the surrounding countryside and gleaned what they could, or scrounged
from neighbours. The centrepiece of the display was invariably a
statue or framed picture of the Sacred Heart, usually removed from
its normal place above the little red light in the living room. By
Saturday night, the final touches had been put to this mammoth
bout of neighbourhood decoration, and the evening sun bounced off

walls that ranged in colour from the purest white to various pastel shades of pink, ochre and blue. By any standards, it was an amazing transformation and the atmosphere was comparable to that of fiesta time in warmer climes, so that for a while we could imagine that we had been transported to a totally different place.

Depending on age, we young lads might or might not actually walk in the Procession. It was generally assumed that those who had been Confirmed had become men, in the Catholic sense at any rate, and participation was *de rigeur* for them. Even for the rest, there was the indirect involvement of touring the area to determine who had the best window display, and watching the Procession passing on the following afternoon. Compared with the hectic activity of the previous week, this was almost an anti-climax, even though it was the reason for the whole upheaval.

Crowds, mainly of women and children, stood along the pavements and joined for a brief while in the hymns and prayers as the long human crocodile, headed by a senior altar boy with a high-staffed Crucifix, passed along. Next came the clergy, the other altar boys, the Confraternity and the rag-tag and bobble of male humanity, from the active to the decrepit, all on the same mini-pilgrimage, heading, not east to Mecca, but west to Daunt's Square, on this one special day. Suddenly it was all over. The Procession disappeared out of sight and the flags and bunting were left whipping and snapping in the afternoon breeze. In its blaze of new colour, the Cross began to doze again and a sense of contentment descended on the whole area. The traditional ritual had been observed, the old practice upheld, and all things had been done with due decency and respect.

When we'd see old Johnny walking slowly towards the city, carrying by its special handle an old lead-acid accumulator, we knew that another big event was near. Preparing for the day of the big match was taken just as seriously as getting ready for the annual Procession. Everything had to be ready in good time; nothing must be left to chance, especially the vital wireless. Around our place, and especially in the country areas, not everybody had mains electricity. Rural electrification, that huge programme of resource development which revitalised the whole nation in the forties and fifties and brought a new brightness to many a home and farm, had still not come to some places.

Indeed, some people had refused to accept the new wave of power which was rapidly sweeping across the land in one of the biggest and most significant developments ever seen in this country. Some simply felt they could not afford the new scheme. Others, more hidebound, held out on the grounds of superstition, and it only needed one obdurate person in a group to delay connection for all the rest. But mostly it was a question of finance, which is why old Johnny could be seen plodding his slow way to the city with his ancient battery, which he was taking to be re-charged in anticipation of the big day.

In one sense, Johnny was fortunate. Living in a little cottage on the road to White's Cross, he did not have electricity, but at least he had a wireless set, unlike many people in the area, including ourselves. It may have been battery-powered, but it worked, and he and his friends could hear the vital broadcast on Sunday afternoon. It was something no true-blooded Corkman would want to miss, and the lengths to which people would go to hear it were quite extraordinary. The Munster Hurling Final, after all, was one of the great highlights of the year, and a Cork win at Thurles was the gateway to Croke Park and the ultimate glory of an All-Ireland medal.

Much of the preparation passed over the heads of us youngsters. Our place in John Murphy's living room across the way was assured, the only stipulation being that there was to be no talking or clowning during the match. But for the days before we, like our elders, would earnestly discuss the prospects of a Cork win, bandying about the names of people we knew only by reputation. How many goals would Christy Ring score? (There was never any doubt in our minds that he would!) Our local hero, Joe Kelly, we did know, and our anticipatory attention would naturally be directed to him, but other names too rolled easily off our tongues as if we had known the players all our lives, names like those of Din Joe Buckley, Willie John Daly, Joe Hartnett, Jack Lynch and all the rest.

They could not have known of our adulation, even though they might have guessed it. They may have been removed from us, but they certainly were not remote. Each god-like figure bestrode our little lives like a veritable Colossus, engendering the sort of awe in which only youngsters can hold their heroes. We may not have been hurling fans in a big way, but by heaven, when it came to the Munster Final, we were as good as anybody else at whipping up the enthusiasm.

With the coming of the great day, excitement became white-hot. At the Cross, little groups of men would sit in the sun on the low wall after Mass, animatedly discussing the day's prospects. For once, the pubs would empty early, as the Sunday morning drinkers made their way home to get the dinner over and find somewhere to listen to the broadcast, whether in their own homes or elsewhere. Often, the little houses which did have the wireless could not contain all those who wanted to listen, so the magic set would be placed on the sill of the open window, and the crowd would gather round outside, sitting on the few chairs available or on the dusty pavement, careless of their Sunday best.

Finally, the great moment would come, when the stentorian tones of Ireland's most famous broadcaster, a then young Mícheál Ó hEithir, would boom forth the traditional words: 'Bail ó Dhia oraibh go léir, a cháirde, agus fáilte go Dúrlas Éile ...' Nobody could set the scene better. Nobody could more quickly bring the excitement to fever pitch, even before the game began. In graphic verbal description, all the pomp and ceremony of the occasion would be laid before us, as if we were there. In our mind's eye we could see the marching band as well as hear it in the background. This was the high summer of our content, this hour or so of the Gaelic Sunday, as we wriggled on our chairs and waited for the great contest to begin.

It astonished us that Mícheál was so utterly knowledgeable, that he knew not only the players, but the subs, the dignitaries, the mentors, right down to the essential bottle boys. How could one small head carry all he knew? But it did, unfailingly. And his familiar pre-match preambles, well laced with the sort of graphic description of which only he was capable, took us literally all over the world, as 'by courtesy of Radio Brazzaville, through which this broadcast is being relayed', he sent messages of goodwill from relatives to Irish clergy and nuns scattered across the globe, to our missionaries in the deepest jungles of South America and in the scorching deserts of Africa. It was a virtuoso performance from a man who was to become a legend in his own time, an artist of the microphone, whose distinctive voice and delivery remain alive in many a memory today.

At last, after the National Anthem had been played and sung, and the great pre-match roar had gone up even before the end of the Anthem, the pitch would be cleared and the ball thrown in. It was then that Mícheál really came into his own, his voice weaving and bobbing with each turn and twist of player and ball, reaching a crescendo of dramatic power as a score seemed imminent. And so expert was he at judging the game that it usually happened. His was the very stuff of high drama, as he single-handedly built the game into a fury of excitement, so much so that one old fellow who only once travelled to a Munster Final came back with the report: 'Sure, 'twasn't that great at all - next time I'll stay at home and listen to yer man.' As the play ebbed and flowed, with first Cork and then Limerick in the lead, we agonised, bit our nails, shouted in triumph and groaned in despair.

The powerful, almost metallic, broadcasting voice pierced our inner depths as the commentary flowed on like a great and remorseless tide. Two minutes to go and Cork were two points behind. The great Mick Mackey had struck again. Despair was everywhere. Then suddenly: 'Joe Kelly has the ball. He passes it out to Christy Ring.

He grabs it out of the air, turns, hops it on his stick, turns again - and it's a goal!' In the ensuing bedlam, we hugged each other as we shouted. Even the normally staid John Murphy permitted himself a hearty cheer. The relief in the room, as in hundreds of other rooms across the city, was palpable. Ringey had done it again and in the midst of the euphoria, we knew that the post-mortems would go on for days, as the game was re-played in pubs, offices, homes and shops, on factory floors and at the local creameries. The afficionados would be at it for weeks, hurling each stroke over and over again, until they came to Ring's last, great, glorious bullet-ball that almost burst the back of the net.

If radio entertained us only infrequently, we rejoiced in it when we could, until the day came in 1951, when we finally acquired our own wireless. Radio Éireann was then broadcasting for only part of the day, its transmissions beginning with sponsored programmes at 1 pm, except of course, on Wednesdays, when we had 'Hospitals Requests'. At that time, the country, which for years had been racked with TB, was making a valiant effort to rid itself once and for all of this killer disease, and the special TB sanitoria were crammed with patients. Whole families were split up; husbands and wives were separated for years on end. Children too languished in these places and the Wednesday programme must have been a boon to countless thousands who needed a bit of cheer as they struggled along the long road towards health.

It is difficult now to revive the horror of TB, known to some as consumption. In many places the disease, while prevalent, was almost unmentionable, a veritable death sentence; like insanity or nervous disorder, a sort of unwarranted slur on a family, to be talked about in whispers, if at all. In the schools, we were all vaccinated with the sugar lump vaccine, which I remember brought my own arm out in a huge and painful lump. I found it curious that this pleased the medical people, but apparently it meant that the vaccine had taken and I was more or less guaranteed immunity.

But even this was not enough for the Brothers, who would constantly preach to us about staying out in God's good, healthy air and above all, staying out of packed dancehalls and cinemas, where we would be sure to contract the disease. A few of the more zealous added to this the fact that we would also be keeping away from occasions of sin - though it was difficult to imagine just what sort of eternal damnation Hopalong Cassidy would have led us into!

Be that as it may, the Wednesday afternoon programme had a huge listening audience, heavily larded as it was with the top tunes of the day from a place called Tin Pan Alley, wherever that was, as well as the more traditional favourites. But in early summer, as the May breezes began to tickle the standing crops and the birds fed their fledglings in the garden, one melody could be guaranteed to top the list every week. Scottish tenor Father (later Canon) Sidney McEwan brought tears to many an eye with his beautiful rendering of the lovely May Hymn, better known to many as 'Bring Flowers of the Rarest'. It was then unusual enough to find a singing priest, but one who sang so charmingly was certainly unique in our experience. Adulation is a poor enough word with which to record the response that he aroused in this country, and not least in the sanatoria.

When some years later he came in person to sing at the City Hall, the place was thronged, and he received many ovations. With him, I remember, was a very large and well-proportioned soprano, whose name I cannot now recall, but who shimmered majestically on to the stage with all the grandeur of a galleon under full sail. She too had a magnificent voice, but as far as the audience was concerned, she might as well not have been there. She was accorded a courteous reception in recognition of her fine singing, but plainly the audience had come to hear Father Sidney, and that was that.

The wireless was very new to most of us and there was a certain magic in being able to trawl across the wavebands, where the names of the stations came up in green lights, picking up incomprehensible broadcasts from the far corners of the globe. Where, for instance, was Hilversum, and Allouis? Radio Luxembourg we knew, if only for its Irish and Scottish request programmes. They too had huge audiences in this country, and one of the chief delights was in listening to the unfortunate presenter struggling manfully with place names like Drogheda, Cobh or Youghal. Meanwhile, back at home, Radio Éireann was slowly extending its entertainment range and we listened avidly to the first of the radio soaps, the famous 'Kennedys of Castle Ross'.

Of even more interest was a show called 'Take the Floor' compered by the incomparable Din Joe (Fitzgibbon), to become famous as the only radio programme in the world on which Irish dancing was taught. As Rory O'Connor and his dancers beat out the steps, Din Joe called the sequence, in square dance fashion, and the popularity of dances like The Walls of Limerick, the Siege of Ennis and the Haymakers' Jig grew enormously, especially at the crossroads dances. And all the while the little green magic eye reassured us that the station was right on the button, and the big box in the corner continued to hold us in wondrous attention, even if Radio Éireann, then limited in resources, still broadcast for only part of the day, and not at all on certain days like Good Friday.

The wireless was a fairly hefty instrument, full of coils and valves and transformers, all adding up to a big and non-transportable package. Even the supposedly portable outfits of the day still needed mains electricity and, anyway, could not be carried about for long in the hand. Portable simply implied that they could be taken from room to room, to be plugged in again. It was some time in the early fifties when I first read, in the *Meccano Magazine*, that never-ending fount of information on matters scientific and engineering, that somebody had developed a thing called a transistor, which was only an inch long, would replace the valve in the wireless and would transform the radio of the future. Nothing seemed to happen for many years and our old wireless remained in the same place, gobbling up the odd valve but continuing to serve us valiantly. The *Meccano Magazine*, it seemed to me, had got it all wrong. I should have known better!

Much as we loved the radio, there were other entertainments. Of course the cinema cost money, if only a little, but then a little is a lot when you do not have it. There were, at my count, eight cinemas in Cork in the fifties, varying from the sublime Savoy and Capitol to the more economical Assembly Rooms, Imperial and Lido. Some were less salubrious than others and of one, which had better remain nameless, it was said that you could go in crippled and come out walking - with fleas!

In time, we sampled them all, without, I must add, any noticeable ill-effects, following the fortunes of our favourite stars of the time. Undoubtedly the Savoy was the queen, with a large and varied programme and the added attraction of the huge organ that rose magically out of the floor in the front of the screen, to remain for about ten or fifteen minutes while Fred Bridgeman played a selection of melodies for a sing-along. So popular was it that Sunday night audiences, mainly courting couples, all held pre-booked tickets and nobody could get in until somebody else had dropped out.

However, because both Mother and an aunt, Molly, of beloved memory, were both working in the Palace during my teens, that naturally became my mecca. John Treacy, Neilus Farrell, Timmy O'Leary, Dan Cronin or his brother Neilus, whoever happened to be on the door, would allow me instant admission, and if manager Bill Ahern knew anything about it he said nothing, it being tacitly accepted as one of the perks of relationship to the staff. In addition, Mother was entitled to a free pass to the other houses, which she handed on to me, so that at any given time I had access to all the cinemas as well as to the Opera House. Richer in entertainment was I than all my tribe, but of course this sort of superfluity palls too, and more often than not I would gravitate back to the Palace, as much for the chat as for the film.

There, in the old back bar behind the gods, one or other of the staff would regale me with tales of the days when the Palace was Dan Lowery's music hall, attracting all the best acts in these islands

One of the few surviving pictures of my father as a fireman on the GSR.

The author, aged about 18, with 'Rex'.

The authors' mother.

John Murphy, railwayman, gardener and brother of noted Cork sculptor, Dr. Seamus Murphy, R.H.A.

'Nana Mac' (left) and Nora outside the little shop.

Mr Tom Nott, for many years Foreman Printer at the 'Cork Examiner'.

An overcrowded platform at Youghal as excursionists pour from the train of old six-wheeled carriages.

Youngsters helping with the harvest, as we did in the Doctor's fields behind our homes.

It was impossible not to be impressed by the elegance of the funeral procession, with its finely crafted hearse drawn by two jet black plumed horses.

Anticipation – a horse waits to slake its thirst while another guzzles noisily from one of the many drinking troughs in the city.

Patrick Street in the author's childhood. Note the absence of traffic, the bicycles and the shawled lady.

Cork Locoyard in 1953, when the author worked there. The absence of any large express engines, except No. 397 on right, suggests a late afternoon picture.

The legendary T.E. Lawrence on a new Brough Superior SS 100 (guaranteed to reach 100 mph), with manufacturer George Brough in October, 1930.

Johnny Creedon (left) in typical pose, holding his audience enthralled at a Mass Rock near Inchigeela.

Eighteen or twenty Linotypes made quite a clatter . . . A scene in the Examiner *printing office before the arrival of the new technology.*

A reaper and binder of three horsepower! By the late forties, the tractor had replaced the horse on heavy work such as this.

and beyond. There too I was told that Harry Lauder was once booed off the stage by a discriminating Cork audience because they felt he was not giving of his best. I loved the Palace, as much for its old-world atmosphere as anything else. With its red and gilt decor, its ornate boxes beside the stage and its dedicated staff, it epitomised for me the theatre-cum-cinema, the very essence of more gracious times and above all, the world of the music hall that I had never known, and would love to have experienced.

Before those free-entry days however, when a bunch of us were heading off to the cinema on Saturday afternoon (to go at night was unthinkable because of the cost), the venue was very much a matter of what we could afford. The Coliseum and the Lee were favourites, because they both had 'fourpenny hops' and in addition were deemed by our parents to be respectable. Of some others, and in particular the Lido, it was rumoured among schoolmates that instead of fourpence, empty jam jars to that value would be accepted at the door. I cannot vouch for the veracity of this, but certainly jam jars were at a premium in the city at that time, and especially in late summer and early autumn when the firm of Ogilvy and Moore were busy buying blackberries for jam-making. This in itself was quite a little industry among some of my school friends, who swore that there was pots of money to be made picking blacks, but when some of us subsequently saw people arriving at the jam factory with whole carts full of the berries, we decided that we had little chance of matching this sort of industry, which presumably was organised on a large family basis.

Only slightly lower than the Palace in my esteem was the old Opera House, with its triple-tiered auditorium, the high gallery rearing up over the dress circle, and often approached by the outside iron steps which clung precariously to the north wall of the building. There was another, interior entrance from the side door next to the Crawford School of Art. The ticket office was presided over by elderly, frail Miss Twomey, who was known to us all and would sell us our tickets for the annual pantomime. It was to the gods that we usually went, unless we were being taken for a special treat by Mother, who always insisted on going to the dress circle. Those early pantos, in truth, did much more than just while a few magical hours away for us. We would come away afterwards full of the shining-faced wonder of the snow effects, the revolving stage, the human horse and the fairy queen. They introduced us to the world of theatre, so that we wanted to go again and again.

It was there, for instance, that I first saw Shakespeare done 'properly', and began to understand his great works as they were meant to be ingested: not from a dry book at school, but on the living stage. Anew Mac Master, that giant of the touring companies, had brought his troupe to Cork for a Shakespearean season and, since we were then studying *Julius Caesar* at school, we were given an afternoon off to go and see the performance. This attendance was obligatory and indeed very noisy, but a few nights later I went along to see *Othello* and to my amazement, the house was full to the doors. I was lucky to get a seat in the gallery and to this day, I do not think I have ever seen an audience so enrapt. As Iago prowled about the stage, sowing his evil seeds of suspicion, that great, full house was utterly silent, so caught up in the drama that nobody dared even to cough.

It was the greatest tribute to a group of actors and actresses that I have ever witnessed and it characterised the sheer professionalism of the old touring companies. There were others, like Carl Clopet and Phoebe Bradley-Williams (how did all theatre folk have such grand names?) who brought us everything from melodrama to comic relief and, of course, there were the musicals, not least the opera. Tenor Thomas Round came to sing in *The Student Prince* and I must have seen the show at least four or five times; Chris Sheehan as 'The Red Shadow' introduced me to *The Desert Song* and there were others, all building me up inexorably towards grand opera itself.

In a darkened house, just after the lights had gone down, the curtain parted and on to the stage strode a bearded tenor who began to sing *La Donna é Mobile*. The bubbling music, the elegant, colourful dress, the delightful backscenes, the gestures, the sheer magic of it all, captivated me that night and when *Rigoletto* had ended, I vowed that, whatever else I had intended to do for the week, it would have to be ditched in favour of *Il Trovatore*. Many of the arias I knew, because I had heard them on John Murphy's record-player, he being a great opera fan, and they had but mildly impressed me. Only on stage did they sparkle as their composers had intended; only on stage did they live.

Culture, however, comes in many different guises, and Italian opera was far removed from the very Nationalist spirit that pervaded the Mon. This spirit was bound to have its influence on most of us, and in our daily lives it was expressed in different ways. Many who were expert with the camán or the football boot found their outlet on the sportsfield; some went on from the ranks of the Mon Harty Cup (hurling) and Corn na Mumhan (Munster Cup, football) teams to become All-Ireland stars, treading the hallowed sod of Croke Park and bringing glory to their native city and county.

Others less gifted in this sphere, like myself, took different directions, roads leading into music, drama, literature and, in my own case, deep involvement in Gaelic culture as epitomised by the Gaelic League, and a now little known organisation called An Réalt

(The Star). This was the Irish-speaking section of the Legion of Mary, a lay apostolate founded by the late Frank Duff and whose most noted member, apart from himself, was the lovely Edel Quinn, who died at a tragically young age when serving the Legion in Africa.

It all began accidentally, as these things so often do. I was a member of a team representing the Mon at a secondary schools' quiz, conducted in Irish and organised by one of the local branches of Conradh na Gaeilge - or Gaelic League, founded in 1893 by Eoin Mac Neill to promote the use of the Irish language. The quiz was held in an old building called An Grianán, in what was then Queen Street, near the glorious Gothic Capuchin church of Fr. Mathew, the Holy Trinity. That we won that section of the quiz is a matter of history and little interest, but the whole atmosphere of An Grianán, despite its knotted floorboards, its aura of decay and its decidedly uncomfortable surroundings, was irresistible.

I was content in the Irish spoken here, in the whole ambience, in the company of like-minded souls and, best of all, there were actually nice girls and Irish dancing - not the competitive step-dancing, though that too was available, but the old Irish folk dances of our forebears. At first, the steps were difficult and my footwork decidedly clumsy, but time, practice and expert tuition soon brought some proficiency, so that after a brief period, complicated dances like the Sixteen-hand Reel and the High Caul Cap presented no terrors. It was like entering a whole new world, of music, of dance, of old tradition, of new friends and almost before I knew it, I had become a member of the Conradh.

It is something I have never regretted. This was not the sentimental Kathleen Mavourneen stuff of stage-Irishism, but the real thing; a digging back into the roots and finding gems of literature, poetry, songs, dance and of course, spoken Irish, which seems to me one of the most romantic languages in the world. It can also be one of the most vitriolic, as I subsequently discovered when conversing with an aged poet from the Ballingeary Gaeltacht, who gave me a graphic example of bardic skill with an extempore composition in which he called down at least forty different curses on an imaginary enemy without once repeating himself.

While maintaining links with the Conradh, I subsequently, and by way of association, joined An Réalt, where our duties as part of the lay apostolate included running weekly youth clubs, where again the main emphasis was on matters Irish. Gradually the evenings became more filled with activities of this nature, and it was fortunate that I was about to complete my education and take my Leaving Cert. exam, because eventually An Réalt occupied more and more of my free time, as indeed was the case with most of the members. In those pre-television days, it was not at all unusual to have over a hundred young boys and girls present at our club nights, which were directed by different members and held several evenings a week. The recipe rarely varied: music, dancing, singing, a lecture in Irish on some topic of the day and the inevitable collection to defray the expenses of the hall. This was in Dún Mhuire on the Grand Parade, presided over by the gruff but essentially kindly caretaker, Charlie O'Leary, who was much addicted to snuff and whose suits would invariably be ruined by a fine dark brown dust.

Occasionally we held outings to places of interest. Sometimes, on summer evenings, we cycled out from the city, to Inniscarra or Ovens, into God's good air, and more than once we were known to hold a roadside ceilidhe, once to the utter astonishment of a party of American visitors near Blarney, who stopped their bus, climbed out and with expressions such as: 'Gee honey, get a load of this! isn't it cute!' had cameras clicking busily. At other times, we hired buses and took off for a whole Sunday out, to Killarney, Courtmacsherry, Ardmore or wherever the spirit moved us, always finding someone who would bring along an accordeon, fiddle or flute, so that the day would end with a rousing ceilidhe in the hotel where we were having tea. It is no exaggeration to say that enduring friendships, and not a few marriages, resulted from these outings, when we were all young, idealistic and literally as fit as fiddles from all the dancing.

These were the days of the great ceilidhe boom, when thousands of Irish people tuned in every Saturday night to Radio Luxembourg to listen to 'Irish Requests' and 'Scottish Requests', and even when the announcers got twisted into knots with Irish place names, nobody cared, as long as the music was diddling out of the wireless and the rhythmic beat of reels and jigs was filling the room. Jimmy Shand became a household name and the 'Flowers of Edinburgh' became as well known as 'Molly Malone'. At home, other bands were beginning to emerge: Pat Mc Garr and the Gallowglass, Dermot O'Brien's fine outfit and, more locally, the Blarney and the Shandon Ceilidhe Bands.

The Irish people, it seemed, just could not get enough of it, either in the ballrooms or the platform dances, which were frowned on by the Church authorities of the day, who feared all sorts of dire consequences as the lads and lasses made their way home through the darkened countryside. There were grim, puritanical sermons about the immorality of it all and about the dangers of occasions of sin, and some platforms were actually compelled to close, while dancing of any type was totally banned during Lent. Yet the boom continued.

Jimmy Shand visited the Arcadia ballroom in Cork in the

autumn of 1954, and eager crowds waited outside the door of the jam-packed hall, in the hope of being allowed in if anybody come out early. Inside, so great was the throng that it was impossible to dance; the audience stood or sat quite happily listening to the music, and as I chatted to this very modest genius of the accordeon keyboard during a break, he told me he was quite overwhelmed by it all. 'I had nae expected anything like this', he said, 'and I doot if I've ever seen a more enthusiastic crowd back at hame.'

But the dance cannot last forever; the time comes when the pipes and drums must be laid to one side, when a crust must be earned and when involvement with youth clubs and cultural matters, rewarding though it may be, does not put any bread on the table. It was time to look for some sort of living. University education, regrettably, was out of the question, because even if I had got a Scholarship, which I did not, the ancillary expenses would have been too burdensome. The household needed an urgent injection of finance by way of a regular weekly income and, while I had some irons in the fire, there was as yet no sign of them reddening. Come the autumn with its russett glory and its first soft sighs of the dying year, I was in the same position as many of my erstwhile classmates: get some work and get it quickly, not easily achieved when the Irish economy was in tatters and the *Innisfallen* was still taking its weekly quota of emigrants on the doleful sea journey to Dagenham.

There were few options and the offer of a job, any job, was grasped with the iron grip of a drowning man on a passing piece of flotsam. So when one afternoon a railwayman cousin called with the news that he could have me appointed to the locomotive department, provided I was prepared to start immediately, there was no argument, no soul-searching. Let the future take care of itself. This was here, it was now and it was real.

Athick autumn mist rose from the river to mingle with the heavy grey pall of smog over Cork city centre, and an anaemic early-morning sun struggled to penetrate the ochre gloom as, clad in borrowed plumage, I freewheeled downhill on a late September morning to the staff entrance of the Córas Iompair Éireann locomotive works at Glanmire Road. The plumage, overalls and cap (I had my own boots!), was borrowed from my cousin, fireman Connie Lynch, because as a temporary cleaner, I was ineligible for supplied protective clothing and had to provide my own. I was setting off, as had my father and many of my relatives before me, to become a railwayman. At eighteen, it was something of a great adventure to begin my first real job in life and, being a railway enthusiast anyway, I was looking forward to working with the huge machines that daily belched steam and smoke as they traversed the iron arteries of the nation.

At the little watchman's hut at Water Street I reported to a tall grumpy character who, I was to learn, was forever yelling at us youngsters to hurry up or we would be late for work. If we were, we suffered by being docked a quarter of an hour's pay anyway, but the way he carried on, you would think the money was coming out of his own pocket. At all events, he handed me a card which I duly punched and, having parked my bike in the rack, walked on towards the loco shed, arriving two minutes early, just before eight. There I was directed to the Loco Foreman's office at the back of the building with the words 'You're new, you'd better go and see Patcheen'. There, seated at a rough wooden desk and with a bright fire burning behind him, was a low-sized man in a suit and soft hat, who, I decided, must be the Foreman, Mr. Patrick O'Sullivan, otherwise Patcheen.

At my entry he glanced up, wrote a line or two and then looked up again, startled. 'Good God, boy, you must be Dinny Cramer's son.' Considering that he had never seen me before and that my father had been dead for eighteen years, I thought this recognition was a remarkable achievement, but he quickly explained it by saying: 'You're the spittin' image of him.' Rising, he put a friendly arm around my shoulder and guided me out, right down to the back of the shed with the words: 'Come on, I'll introduce you to Jerh (he pronounced it 'Jurr') Cunningham, he will be your boss; just do what he says and you'll be fine. And give my regards to your mother.'

Anything deeper than the Stygian gloom of Jerh's little store it would be difficult to imagine, that is, after we had knocked and the door had been finally opened. During the wait, a passing driver grinned at Patcheen and said: 'He won't be out for a while, Boss, he's oiling his leg with the company's oil.' 'That's enough of that now Mick,' said Patcheen, and with a warning glance at me he added: 'Poor Jerh has a wooden leg, but he's a decent man and I won't have him mocked.' When Jerh finally limped out, tall and angular, I was introduced and he handed me the tools of my trade: a metal scraper, a few rags and a small bundle of cotton waste. 'You're here to clean dirty engines, Sonny (I was soon to discover that everybody on Jerh's little team was Sonny), and you'll have to make do with that for the day because you won't get any more, so don't waste it.'

Foolishly, I had imagined that, being a newcomer, I would be started on something small. I could hardly have been more wrong. Up the shed we paraded, Jerh and I and five others, all of them new, all temporary because the beet season had started and all the full-time cleaners were out on the road as temporary firemen, past rows of dead engines and into the open air at the front of the building. There, with a gentle hiss of steam from its safety valve, stood No. 409, one of the big green express locomotives used on the Cork-Dublin run. 'That one,' said Jerh pointing to it, 'has to be off shed by half-ten, so get on with it; you and you (pointing to me and another lad) cab and boiler, you and you (to two others) motion and bottom-work, and you and you (to the final pair), tender, and don't forget the back.'

It's a long way from the ground to the top of the boiler of an express engine. Added to that is the fact that to get at the very top, you have to stand on the handrail and steady yourself with one hand while you clean with the other, all the while watching that safety valve in case it blows off with an ear-shattering screech and a powerful gout of scalding steam. Later, when we became accustomed to the job, we would have a quick glance at the pressure gauge in the cab before we started, so we would know the state of the boiler, but this morning, we were all green and nervous. But slowly the job was done, washing down with used diesel sump oil which somehow, dirty though it looked, cut through the grime, and polishing off with a carefully measured piece of Jerh's precious cotton waste. Almost before we knew it, 409 was finished and Jerh, after a few minor quibbles, announced his satisfaction. 'Right now lads, off to lunch, and remember you have only fifteen minutes.'

Considering that we had only been on duty for just over a couple of hours, and that we were not due to finish until four o'clock, I felt it was an extraordinary time to break for lunch, but rules were rules, so off we trudged to the cleaners' messroom, which consisted of a long wooden hut with old tables and benches. First, of course, there was the business of washing hands, which may seem a simple operation, but it was not. The soap supplied seemed to make no difference at all to the accumulated grime, a mixture of oil, soot, coal dust and grease, which had got into the very pores, and which remained almost immoveable. Then a passing fireman took pity on us rookies. 'Look lads, you'll never get that stuff off with soap. What you need is some sand from the bucket there. Mix it up with the soap lather and scrub your hands carefully; then wash the whole mess off.' We did and sure enough, off it came, taking some skin with it, but at least our hands were clean. Only then could we get down to making the tea.

We each had individual caddies, little divided boxes which contained tea on one side and sugar on the other. This was unceremoniously dumped into our tin gallons, which were filled up with boiling water and allowed to brew. The top of the gallon was used as the cup and milk came from a separate bottle, in most cases an old naggin whiskey bottle with a screwed-in paper cap. There was almost complete silence as we chewed our sandwiches and drank our tea, until Jerh stuck his head around the doorpost and shouted: 'Come on lads, time's up, back to work.' With the express gone away, there were a myriad of other jobs to be done: secondary engines to be cleaned, old sleepers to be chopped up for firewood, parts which needed the fitters' attention to be cleaned down and so on. Two of us were allocated to clean an old tank engine at the back of the shed, and we were hard at it when I learned my first lesson about familiarity breeding contempt.

I was leaning inwards to wash down the red buffer beam, between the buffers of the loco I was cleaning and that adjacent to it, when I was unceremoniously hauled out of the eighteen-inch gap by a burly driver who literally took me by the scruff of the neck. 'If I ever see you doing that again I'll kick your arse, young fellow,' he boomed. 'Why, what have I done wrong?' I protested. 'Look,' he said, pointing to the gap between the two sets of buffers, 'never get in between these again, you could be crushed to death if some idiot reverses that line of engines further up the shed.' 'But surely they are all dead and have their brakes screwed down,' I said. 'You don't know that they have, and never take that chance,' he replied. 'Take nothing for granted while you are working with engines. If you have to get in there, get under the buffers, but never, ever, get between them. And another thing, never go under an engine unless it has the red NOT TO BE MOVED board hanging on it.'

Then, patting me on the shoulder he grinned and said: 'You'll get used to it, but take care of yourself. You have only one life, you know.' It was typical of the fatherly manner in which we youngsters were treated by the vast majority of the senior staff, a sort of caring that made us part of the large family of the railway and that seemed to be part of the job. I once heard one engineman roundly bawling another out for using bad language 'in front of those youngsters;

they could be your own sons, you know.'

By the time Pat, my companion, and I had finished cleaning the old engine, which was a sort of dirty dark grey in colour and which did not seem materially better after our labour, though it satisfied Jerh, it was time to wash up and go home. We were both tired. It was physically exhausting work, with much stretching and bending as we strove to reach almost inaccessible places, and our muscles, unused to such work, were not yet hardened to it. But at the end of the day, it was good to swill off the muck, get a grunt of satisfaction from Jerh and go to clock off, with the admonition to be on time next morning. On the way home, I called to see my cousin Connie's mother, just to let her know how I had got on. When she opened the door, the poor woman looked at me and burst into tears. Astonished, I asked her what was wrong. Drying her eyes, she put an arm around me and said: 'Oh Tim, when I saw you in those overalls and that cap I thought for one moment it was your father I was looking at.' I had enough sense to take both off before going home to my mother!

Life on the railway may have been dirty, but it was never dull. As the days wore on, I became accustomed to the more routine jobs and began to value the friendship of the railwaymen, who were among the kindest, most cheerful and helpful people I have ever worked with, men who, even when they were busy, would take time to answer questions and explain the workings of the great iron beasts they drove and fired. At that time, the locomotive yard was a hive of activity. Manpower was relatively cheap and the railway provided good, secure employment for hundreds: drivers, firemen, cleaners, fitters, gland-packers, shunters, carriage cleaners, porters, carpenters, painters, signalmen, ticket checkers, inspectors, a host of clerks, wheel tappers, boiler washout teams, loco coalers and two characters who lived in a little hut in the middle of the yard. I never did discover just what their function was, though occasionally I saw them filling the tanks or tenders of thirsty engines.

The nature of most of these occupations was self-evident, but for the wheel tappers who, I discovered, walked the length of a train while it was standing in the station and, using a hammer, tapped each of the wheels in turn, as one would tap a bell, to hear if it was sound or damaged. It was a job which demanded a good ear and more than once I heard some jocose comments about 'bloomin' piano tuners' as they went about their work.

On many occasions I was invited on to the footplate and allowed to take a huge engine, under strict supervision, down to the coaling bank or off to the turntable. Off with the steam brake, blow the warning whistle, put her into full forward gear, crack open the regulator and feel the thrill as the giant snorted steam and began to move slowly away, all the while leaning out of the cab to watch the 'road'. Then would come the instruction: 'Ease her up now and brake gently,' and we would roll to a stop, with a pat on the back from the driver and a quiet 'Well done, lad, we'll make a top link driver out of you yet'.

Of course, we youngsters were not supposed even to touch any of the controls, let alone drive an engine, because we were under twenty-one and so were not insured. But provided there was no messing about, the shed Foreman usually turned a blind eye if he saw us moving a locomotive to a more advantageous place for cleaning, or taking an engine to be coaled or turned for a driver who wanted to grab a quick cuppa before starting work. It was, we found, possible to move a loco with only a few pounds of steam on the clock and often we exploited this in order to break the monotony of cleaning. The smell of burning coal, mingled with that of hot oil and steam, and the excitement of actually driving one of those great horses of the iron road, albeit only for a hundred yards, remains fresh in the memory to this day. I was a railwayman, and by heaven was I enjoying it!

It cannot be denied that working with steam locomotives was a very dirty job, but there were compensations, especially for an enthusiastic youngster who was managing to combine work and interest. In 1953, Glanmire locmotive yard was still full of the most colourful collection of engines from another era and from the many old companies that had been absorbed, first by the old Great Southern in 1926 and then into the nationalised CIE in 1946. They were all to be seen: the works of the great railway Chief Mechanical Engineers of the past: the express engines of John A.F. Aspinall, who revolutionised the loco works at Inchicore and later went on to become famous as the CME of the Lancashire and Yorkshire Railway; the little suburban tank engines of Harry Ivatt, who found fame on the Great Northern Railway of Britain; the famed 101 or J15 Class goods engines of Alexander McDonnell,which lasted over a hundred years and two of which are now preserved and still steaming.

Their designer came to something of a sticky end when he transferred to the North Eastern Railway and was unable to get on with the Geordies, lasting only a few months in his new post. There were too the Woolwich engines, as they were commonly called, because they were bought in a job-lot of kits of parts from the SECR in Britain, having being produced at Woolwich arsenal in order to provide jobs after the First World War. They were most used, from Cork at any rate, on the Rosslare express, and lasted until the end of steam.

Added to those were the huge express designs of Watson, the

400 Class, of which, when they were first produced, the designer is said to have stood outside Inchicore and watched one of them struggling up the bank on a test run, muttering to himself: 'She will ... she won't ...' She did, but only just, and they were later modified and rebuilt into fine locomotives, powerful and free-steaming. Then, of course, there were the three magnificent 800 Class engines, built specially for the Cork-Dublin line with its very steep gradients at both ends and named *Maedhbh*, *Macha* and *Tailte*, after legendary Irish heroines. They were commonly mis-named the 'Queens', only *Maedhbh* herself having been a queen, but that was enough to title the whole class in the minds and the hearts of the men who drove and fired them. I remember standing one morning in the yard, waiting to be allocated my next job, when *Tailte* came steaming gently in after a major service and re-fit. She was resplendent in a new coat of paint, and I thought I had never seen anything quite so magnificent as this huge locomotive in her light apple green (as distinct from the rather drab CIE dark green) with black and lemon lining and bright, polished metalwork. These three were the pride of the fleet and even in those economy-conscious days, were treated as such. I never saw any of them leave the yard dirty, and there was hell to pay if they did not get the best coal.

One afternoon, Patcheen came up to me carrying a little canvas bag and a small fire shovel. 'Go up there, on the back of the tender of 802, and fill that thing with slack and bring it back to me,' he said. I did as I was told, but my nose was at me, as the lads would say and, on arriving back at his office, I watched him tie the little bag and attach a label. 'What is all that in aid of, Mr. O'?' I asked.' He grinned. 'The down Mail was late coming in yesterday and the driver blamed the coal,' he said. 'Now they want to analyse it in Dublin. Let 'em analyse that!' It was typical of the way in which the Foreman stood up for this loco crew, but also typical of the fact that bad coal would not be tolerated on the 800s.

Generally in those days, crews were rostered to whatever loco happened to be available, but some old stagers had the same engines week in, week out, and would be very upset if they were changed for any reason, such as repairs or overhaul. Many of them treated their charges like babies, and went around them lovingly at every stop, doling out oil into their bearings when no oil was needed, and fighting with the stores man for extra supplies. Often they would cajole us cleaners away from some other job to give the spectacle plates (windows) an extra wipe, rather than waste their own precious bit of cotton, or to sweep down the footplate while the fireman was busy at something else. Jerh would play hell if he caught us, but we were always ready to oblige these fine old men, who had given a lifetime of service to the railway, and who were putting down their last years on short local runs or shunting turns. It was in our interest too, because these drivers would be the first to offer us a turn at the controls when things were quiet and to explain the workings of the various locomotives.

One of the benefits of the morning eight-to-four shift, apart from the obvious one of having a normal working day, was the fact that it offered an occasional opportunity for what was known as 'going up on Pat.' Pat was a tiny, four-wheeled, jerry-built steam engine that worked high on the gantry above the loco coaling bank, the gantry running from the bank out on to the quayside where the coal was unloaded from a ship into hopper wagons, from which it was in turn dumped onto the bank. About once a month, when the ship was in, Jerh, when allocating the morning's work, would turn to one of us lucky ones and say: 'You, Sonny, go up on Pat.'

It could be something of a mixed blessing, because it all depended on who Pat's driver for the day was. If it was Tommy, everything was fine and you would have an interesting and indeed very amiable companion. If it was another, you could be saddled with an old grouch for the day. It was my good fortune, on the few occasions when Jerh cast a kind eye on me, to be partnered by Tommy, by then pushing on a little in years and probably not quite able for main-line driving, but fully in control of his tiny charge with its vertical boiler and frames made from an old tender, a sort of Heath-Robinson affair that Inchicore had turned out, with typical economy and not a little ingenuity, to do a specific job and no more.

Going up on Pat meant promotion for the day, in our eyes at any rate, because instead of cleaning, we were actually firemen, at least in theory. I suspect that Tommy would have been quite capable of running the little engine single-handed, but there was probably some rule against this. In any event, when I arrived on the tiny footplate, he gave me a quick lesson in the delicate art of firing a locomotive. 'There's nothing difficult about this one, and you won't lose any sweat,' he told me. 'Just chuck a few briquettes in there every so often, keep the fire nice and bright and keep the bars clean. And don't forget to watch that water gauge or the boiler will run dry and the pair of us will be blown halfway to Youghal.' And so we chugged backwards and forwards on the high gantry, bringing the loaded hoppers to the bank and then returning them empty to the waterside for another load.

Of course, when the grab operator knocked off for his morning break, we did likewise, Tommy sending me to buy a couple of cakes in the shop across the road. 'Save your sandwiches for lunchtime; we'll knock off again at one o'clock.' (Two lunch breaks? No wonder everybody wanted to go up on Pat!) Tommy added further interest to the proceedings by allowing me to drive the loco for a period, coaching me patiently through what was now a well-known routine, though he did remind me that we were more than twenty feet above the ground and it might not be such a good idea to crash the thing through the buffer stops. 'At the very least,' he said with a chuckle, 'Simon (Murphy, the area boss) will be very cross.' Not surprisingly, in the company of this amiable man and with such a diversity of interesting things to do, the day literally flew by and it was with genuine regret that I left Tommy at knocking-off time, while he took on another apprentice for the remainder of the day's work. And to this day, I remember his final stricture, even in my own home: 'Always keep the bars clean and you'll have a good fire.'

But things did not always go so smoothly, and there were times when you were reminded that the railway was a dangerous place in which to work, even though the fault might not be yours. I was passing along the yard one afternoon, with a little handbrush, when a driver called to me to sweep the accumulated ashes from the footplate under the smokebox at the front of the engine. 'Whoever cleaned this thing out didn't bother to sweep them away, and I'll have a right eyeful of grit out on the road. Would you mind doing the needful?' he asked. Naturally, I climbed up to oblige; it was only a two-minute job anyway. I had almost finished when, to my surprise, the loco began to move, without any warning; no shout, no whistle. I thought he was just pulling up to the water column, but we passed this and then I noticed that the signal giving exit from the yard was off. She was beginning to sway a bit now, in the way that engines with a front bogie are inclined to do, and I was clinging on to the smokebox handrail, unable to do anything else.

Picking up speed, we ran along behind the passenger platforms and in panic I wondered if this thing was going light engine to Mallow or somewhere else. Certainly we were heading for the tunnel entrance, which we hit in a cloud of black smoke and steam, and I was really beginning to worry. As we clattered over the points inside the tunnel I was hanging on for dear life and then, sudden relief - we were slowing down. In the pitch blackness the loco stopped and slowly began to reverse back to the passenger station, where its train awaited it. Relief flooded over me as I stepped gingerly on to the platform, covered in grime, to be greeted by a very shaken driver, who looked me over from head to toe, and in worried tones, said: 'Good God, boy, I forget all about you! Are you all right?' His apologies became very more profuse when, in my anger, I reminded him that he had broken the cardinal rule; moving an engine without giving any warning whistle.

But apart from shattered nerves, I was perfectly all right and was able to give a shaky laugh when the poor man said: 'What makes it all the worse is that you were doing me a favour.' Doubtless he was also afraid that somebody would get to hear of the incident and he would be in trouble, but by then I was long enough on the railway to know that you did not rat on somebody, which I would not do anyway, the more so since the whole thing was an unfortunate accident. I never mentioned the incident to anybody, and the driver and I became the best of friends.

While the drivers were undoubtedly the kings of the road, I often felt a certain sympathy for their firemen, who had to do the real work on a steam engine, often shovelling four or five tons of coal at a stint, while also watching the boiler water level and keeping an eye out for signals more easily seen from their side of the cab. Any driver was only as good as his fireman, because it was the latter who kept the boiler steaming and the engine running, at the considerable expense of his own sweat and effort. It was a backbreaking job and, given that at times the fuel was anything but the best, it could be nightmarish as the loco crew battled to keep time, often with engines that were long past their prime.

Drivers who habitually thrashed their locos were very unpopular, because in the process they were also thrashing their mates. Except on the banks, where it was flat-out in the uphill direction, the really skillful drivers were those who could keep a train moving on the very minimum of steam, so relieving the strain on their firemen. Firing, as well as being physically demanding, was also an art in itself. Fuel had to be placed evenly on the fire, each shovelful being precisely placed in the firebox - not easy on a swaying footplate - so that the whole fire burned with a white-hot incandescence, to convert water into steam and thus into power.

* * *

Night duty was irksome only in that it interrupted what was then a very busy social life, since I was involved in a number of youth organisations, but otherwise it came as welcome respite from the daily grind. There was not, in truth, a great deal to do on the midnight to 8 am shift and, in fact, the whole area seemed almost to sleep. In the half-light of the shed lamps, locomotives would wheeze and snore like living things, sending up thin streams of half-hearted smoke, their fires slumbering or just newly-lit.

Men moved about their few tasks like ghostly shadows, humming quietly to themselves, although one lad had a magnificent tenor voice and we would all stop whatever we were doing to listen to him when he started into 'Danny Boy' or 'The Old House', which he sang quite unselfconsciously as he worked. Occasionally there would be a short peep of a whistle as a loco was moved to the turntable or the water column, almost ready to take the 2 am goods off to Thurles. Apart from this, only the background industrial hum of Cork could be heard. There would be no rowdy blowing off of safety valves, no clanking of coupling rods, no jangling of worn axleboxes or squealing of flanges, as an engine moved into the tight bend of No. 8 road. Cork Loco was asleep, or nearly so.

My first task at night was to attend to the fire and sweep out the enginemen's rest room, at the back of the shed. Then, with the place clean, tidy and warm, it was time to sit down and listen to the chat and the tall stories of the oldsters as they had a cup of tea before going on duty. 'So down the bank we came, with no brake and wondering what would happen when we hit the platform. But the signalman at Kilbarry must have noticed my mate waving because he phoned Cork box and the chap there opened the Cobh line and we roared through the station, up the rise, over the bridge and stopped half-way to Dunkettle ...'

And so it went on, sometimes sombrely, often hilariously as the reminiscences came thick and fast. 'They gave me this new fireman and you'd swear he had never been on a footplate before. When we came to the tunnel I was so fed up I told him to stick his arm out because we were turning right - and would you believe, the idiot did it!' Criticism was never too far away: 'That fellow, he couldn't keep steam for a barber' or 'He's only fit for bagging daylight up the tunnel.' But in spite of all this, the loco crews stuck together and usually supported each other through thick and thin.

During my first week on night turn, one of the drivers said to me: 'Keep your mouth shut now, but about five o'clock keep a quiet eye on old Paddy's furnace over there and you'll see something interesting.' The furnace was used for drying sand, and it was where we boiled our cans of water for tea (a minute and a half on the end of a fireman's dart and they came out gurgling), so that during the night there was a fairly steady procession of men to the furnace. At five, a driver came over, plunged his caddy in, withdrew it and laid it down while he went to get his tea from his overcoat pocket. As he did, a shadowy figure emerged from behind the furnace, bent over the caddy for a moment and the retreated. The driver, who was taking the early-morning empty carriages to Cobh, made his tea, called his fireman and off they went.

I did not hear the sequel until the following night. 'Bit of trouble on the Cobh line this morning,' remarked one driver. 'Oh yes,' came the answer, 'old so-and-so had a bad touch of the trots. I believe they had to stop at every bush on the way down,' and off they went, laughing. I subsequently discovered that the hapless driver had committed the cardinal sin of having his mate carpeted for some minor infringement, and had been punished by having a whole packet of Epsom salts dumped into his tea caddy.

Apparently he took so much sugar that he drank the mixture down without even noticing.

The rest of the night was usually taken up with minor chores, such as going up to the telegraph office to collect news of the progress of the Night Mail for the Loco Foreman, and getting a list from him of which engines would be used the following morning, so that I could check that they had all the necessary tools and implements, like fire shovels, rakes and darts, oil cans and so on. In turn, I usually made another list for Jerh, noting which loco needed what, and often there were missing items, as crews would borrow from one engine in order to supply another.

In between, I would watch fascinated as the steamraiser, big Dave, would go to the furnace with a huge shovel, take out at least a half-hundredweight of blazing coals and quite nonchalantly carry this fiery mass over his shoulder to a waiting engine, hoisting himself up into the cab with one hand while he balanced the enormous scoop with another, singing cheerfully as he went. It was a virtuoso performance that never failed to intrigue me, because one stagger would surely have meant disaster - but Dave, big and burly, never slipped and soon, gurgling and wheezing in the way that steam engines did, another loco would become a living thing, spitting out little gouts of steam from its ageing joints, simmering and snorting like an old man getting up to face another day.

This, I suppose, was the essential difference between steam locomotives and the new diesel railcars that had just arrived on the scene and were being used - quite wrongly as it transpired, because they were designed only for short distance haulage - on the main Cork-Dublin line. A steam engine had a life of its own. While the diesel throbbed, the steam loco was full of the magnificent, elemental grandeur of iron, steel, fire, water, hot oil and black dust. It emanated life, in its smell as well as its noise. It was a vibrant, living thing, and its fascination lay in its overt expression of this life in terms of smoke and steam and the promise of enormous power once it was unleashed. Built with blacksmith technology it may have been; capricious too it may have been, for no two engines, even of the same class, performed the same way, but it worked, year after year, clocking up millions of miles and leaving an indelible mark on the advancement of our civilisation.

So, during the dark hours, we prepared them and watered them, filled their bunkers or tenders with coal and turned them, to send them out again for another day's work. And if the mechanical grab at the coal bank broke down, as happened once or twice, we would all be called to the shovel, for a back-breaking hour of pitching coal into the maw of an empty tender. Nobody was exempt, and while naturally some complained, nobody demurred, because everybody understood that the trains had to be kept running. I sometimes wonder what today's trade unionists would make of it all; we simply took it as part of the job!

One of the most enjoyable tasks was that of being call boy, which included going out to call engine crews for duty, usually at night, though sometimes by day as well if an emergency arose. Not only was this an opportunity to get out of the works legitimately, without any need to hurry back, but it also gave me a further chance to get to know the railwaymen's families who, almost without exception, were delightful. Many a cup of tea I had in houses high above the city, while the bantering mother or father would offer me my pick of a fine selection of eligible daughters who, of course, would get in on the act in order to add to my blushing confusion, and laugh uproariously as I came away red-faced.

The call boy role had its perils too, as I discovered one night when, after a derailment outside the tunnel, I was hastily dispatched to round up a breakdown crew. One of my places of call was an address in Elizabeth Terrace, in a part of Cork then known as Jewtown because it was here that a group of immigrant Jews had settled. In the dim light of a nearby lamp, I read El... Terrace, the remainder being hidden in deep shadow. Finding the house number, I began to bang on the door. After some time, during which I was beginning to despair of ever waking the fitter concerned, a window crashed up and a male voice shouted, 'What the hell d'you think you're doing at this hour of the morning?' I shouted that there had been a derailment and that Mr ... was to come quickly. 'Get to blazes outa that, this is Electric Terrace - he lives around the corner.'

There were other outings, when we cleaners would be sent on various errands, sometimes for Jerh, who was not averse to asking us to pop down to the betting office and put his few shillings on a big race; sometimes for one of the bosses who wanted something in town and did not have time to go for it and, best of all, a trip to the Bandon railway at Rocksavage to get some bits and pieces that were not available at Glanmire. Several times Jerh sent me off to get some gauge glasses for the little lamps that illuminated the boiler water level gauges in the locomotives, and on these occasions I would set off with a light heart, knowing that there was little if any restriction on time and that there would be no growling from the watch-house keeper when I told him where I was going. This was official business and I was entitled to make the most of it.

The Rocksavage works of the old Cork, Bandon and South Coast Railway were across the city, beyond the two bridges spanning the twin arms of the Lee, about five minutes' ride on a bicycle. Here was the terminus of the lines to picturesque west Cork, the passenger facilities at Albert Quay and, further up, the locomotive department and general maintenance area. There was not then an engine shed at Rocksavage; locomotives were stored in an open yard, and those enginemen who did need a little shelter from the weather would park their locomotives under the old iron Hibernian Bridge which carried a road over the works, carrying out the checking and oiling under this very dubious roof.

Nearby was the paint shop,which was my destination, because it was here that the gauge glasses were cut and parcelled up for me. Of course, I would have to wait, even if a supply was ready, because the decent west Cork men would not dream of letting me go on my way without having a cup of tea. 'Arrah, sit down, boy, and take your ease for a while. Jerh can wait; when the good God made time, he made plenty of it,' would be the comment. There was an air of calm around here, a sort of unhurried activity that was completely at variance with the often frenetic work of Glanmire. I would have the tea, and then be taken into the paint shop proper to see work in progress on rejuvenating old carriages, now glistening in their new coats of dark green, almost ready for further service after generations of pounding the rails. Or somebody would take me with great pride to the loco yard. 'I'm going to light up old *Argadeen*, come and have a look at her.' And I would be given the history of the Timoleague and Courtmacsherry Railway as I inspected the little engine built by the Hunslet Company of Leeds in the last century, now being steamed for the last excursion of the summer.

The Timoleague line was very lightly laid, and only *Argadeen* and a few other engines were permitted to use this roadside tramway which ran along the seafront at the edge of the lovely Argideen (spelled differently from the engine, be it noted) Vale and estuary. Saint Molaga built a monastery there, and yet another engine was named after him. The place is also commemorated forever in Irish literature in the lovely Irish poem 'Machnamh an Duine Dhoilíosaigh' (Thoughts of a Lonely Person) by Seán Ó Coileáin, and known in Seán Dunne's translation simply as Timoleague Abbey:

Oíche dom go doiligh dúbhach	One night I sat sadly
Cois fharraige na dtonn dtréan	As the sea's waves surged,
Ag léirsmuaineadh is ag lua	My mind torn asunder
Ar choraibh crua an tsaoil.	My life's hard course.

But Rocksavage was a long way from Tigh Molaga (the house of Molaga), or Timoleague. Soon, *Argadeen* and her tiny sister engines Nos. 90 and 100 would be trundling their excursion coaches along past the old Abbey, but meanwhile, history lessons over and the gauge glasses tucked safely away in my overalls, I would have to thank my genial hosts and make my way back to Glanmire and to Jerh, who would accept them with a wry, knowing grin and tell me that I might as well go and wash up; it wasn't worth while starting anything else now!

Life in the shed may not have been all beer and skittles, but we generally managed to knock some little fun out of it. Come New Year's Eve, a particularly tetchy Loco Foreman on night shifts issued a decree stating that there would be none of that whistle-blowing business in his shed. Work would go on as usual, and there would be no celebrations. This, of course, was unthinkable, especially to people reared to tradition, and in a city where the wailing of ship's sirens and the shrieking of loco whistles were part and parcel of welcoming in the new. We all knew from experience that even small children were allowed up late to hear the racket, and they would be sadly disappointed if it did not happen. Party-goers, among whom we would not be included, might sing 'Auld Lang Syne' until they were blue in the face, and people might still throw loaves of bread against the inside of the front door, reciting the old, anxious half-prayer, half-superstition: 'Keep out the hunger for the year', but if there were no whistles, the whole thing would fall flat. So a plot was hatched.

One of the senior firemen approached us one by one and directed us towards a heap of old scrap at the top of the loco shed. 'Get some heavy bits of brass or iron and some pieces of wire, and make them into weights which you can hang on something. Then hide them until nearly midnight, and I'll be back to you,' he told us. So we scrounged, and found and fashioned our secret weapons. Near midnight, he appeared again. 'Now, there are about seven or eight locos with enough steam up to blow a whistle. When you hear a peep from No. 88, hop up on the footplate of the loco nearest you, hang the weight on the whistle cord - and run like hell before Jimmy sees you.'

At three minutes to midnight, there came the expected 'peep' from No. 88. From the darkest corners of the shed emerged a group of shadowy figures, darting about like wraiths and as they vanished again, the whole place erupted in a wild cacophony of screaming whistles, to add to the din created by the ships at the quays. Jimmy came dancing red-faced out of his office, but we were all going about our normal business, straight-faced as we could manage. Honour had been saved; tradition had been preserved. The railway workers could look the world in the face on the way home in the morning.

At the end of the beet season, in January, I still had ambitions to become an engine driver, childish perhaps, yet merely following in the family tradition, and with the advent of the diesels, everybody kept telling me that by the time I was fully qualified 'it will be a much cleaner, better job, though you'll have a few rough years yet.' It was not to be. One day I was sent for a medical, before being made permanent. I made all the usual noises, breathing in and out and saying 'Ahhhh' and '99' on request, and not worrying too much because I felt sound in wind and limb and was certainly quite fit. Then the doctor gave me an eye test and having made some notes, sent me off about my business. That was on Monday.

On Thursday, one of the lads told me I was wanted by the Stationmaster, and I duly reported to his office, wondering what it was all about. In his hand he held a little piece of paper and sitting me down, said solemnly: 'I'm very sorry, Tim, but I'm afraid we will have to let you go.' 'Why, what have I done wrong?' I asked, totally dismayed. 'It's nothing like that,' he said quickly. 'It's your eyes. According to the Doc, your left eye is weak, and because of company regulations, we can't employ you any longer. Collect your pay, and don't forget you have one week's back-money due to you.' And with more apologies, he led me out, devastated. I was not even allowed to finish off my week's work.

My career was in tatters; my little world of camaraderie and good fellowship, not to mention the job I loved, had collapsed around my ears. Worst of all, I could see perfectly well, though if I did shut my right eye, things tended to blur a little. They were blurred for another reason as I said goodbye to my friends and trod my lonely way home.

Those who are, or ever have been, unemployed will not need to be told that there is nothing quite as devastating to the human spirit; that nothing so totally and so quickly devalues the personal sense of worth, of usefulness, of contribution, of satisfaction, of all the things that the working person tends to take for granted. For a youngster summarily thrown out of work, it mattered not at all that a weak winter sunlight was shining outside the front door, that the very first snowdrops had tentatively peeped their perky little heads out of the frozen ground to herald the approach of spring, that the icy grass in the Glen was deliciously crunchy under foot, and that the bare trees stretched their hoar-white talons skywards as if in supplication. Happiness, ultimately, is within oneself, regardless of circumstances, but at times it needs a little encouragement.

In the remainder of that bleak January of 1954, there was none. True, there was the Glen, but not every waking hour could be spent there, paradise though the place was, even in winter, perhaps especially in winter, when it was all but empty of humanity and a special sort of peace descended on the place while even Nature itself slept before its slow awakening to yet another year. There was reading and there was my evening involvement with An Réalt, both of which helped to keep me sane. But at the back of it all was a certain sense of hopelessness, of the knowledge that the future stretched miserably along the time-dragging days into an uncertain horizon.

I was young, healthy, idealistic, active with the vigour of youth, ready to tackle anything, yet condemned to idleness so dire that I might almost have been given a life sentence in some grim and dreadful penitentiary, where the gates to any sort of personal achievement had been slammed with a loud and terrible finality, never to be re-opened. The relative inactivity could be coped with; the uncertainty was far more difficult. Keeping busy became a preoccupation, almost an obsession. Yet, without a goal, therapeutic occupation becomes pointless almost to absurdity. The job situation in Cork was such at that time that when one cleaning firm offered one job for an operative, the queue of applicants stretched for several streets, around several corners. Some, I found, even had University degrees.

Yet, out of this darkest night came yet another bright dawn, or early afternoon to be precise. On a Monday early in March, as a gale rattled the slates and sent the rooks swaying in their high, newly-built eeries in the nearby trees, Fred, our landlord's agent, came as usual to collect the weekly rent. Having chatted away for a while, he was about to leave when he said, casually: 'By the way, the Boss was asking if you're doing anything at the moment?' When I explained that I was not, that I had several applications in several different establishments, with no sign of anything emerging, he said: 'Right then. If you want work, come out to the yard at eight tomorrow. Bring overalls and wellingtons or solid boots. We have plenty for you to do.'

The relief was inexpressible, even when I had explained to Mother and she had queried whether I knew that I was about to turn myself into a farm labourer. I replied that I did know and I did not care. Anything was better than hanging about and it would do until such time as something else turned up. At that stage, a Micawberish attitude seemed to me to be the only solution to a very pressing problem, and there was no further maternal opposition. That night I picked out the least worn of my old railway overalls, gave the boots a good coat of polish and I was ready for the next phase of my life.

The gale had abated and a bright sun shone cheerily in tune with my spirits as I headed off the following morning, to walk the few hundred yards between home and the mini-estate of Jim Rice. His property embraced a small farm, a large garden, the remains of what was once a prosperous dairy and a large number of houses in the area of Dillon's Cross, all of which, of course, required maintenance of one form or another, as the majority were quite old. Jim, recently returned home from Canada to take over the property, was there to greet me, a tall, well-built man with a ready smile and a slight Canadian accent. Like Fred, Jim was Protestant, but of what exact persuasion I did not know, though I was aware that he was a regular lay preacher in one of the churches in town, and a man of no small dedication to his own beliefs.

As I was subsequently to discover, he was also very Christian in the best sense of that often misused appellation, being very tolerant of other beliefs and always fair and just in his dealings with his fellow man. I had been a few months in his employment when there occurred the Feast day of Ss. Peter and Paul, on 29 July. I attended early morning Mass and arrived in due time for work to find Jim standing at the gate of the yard. 'What are you doing here today?' he asked. 'You are supposed to have the day off.' When I said that I knew nothing of this he said: 'Oh yes, that's the arrangement; Fred gets the bank holidays and you get the church holidays, and isn't today one of your church holidays?' When I said yes, he asked if I had been to Mass and, reassured on that score, he added: 'Well, as you are here, would you mind bringing the cattle up from the Glen and I'll get on with the milking?'

I duly brought in the few cattle and went off about my business for the remainder of the day, but when I got my pay packet on Friday, it contained extra money. On querying this with Jim, he answered: 'That's your overtime.' 'But I didn't do any overtime,' I said. 'Oh yes, you did. You brought up the cattle for me the other morning and you are entitled to half an hour's pay at overtime rate.' When I protested that this was ridiculous, that I would have brought in his cattle if I had just been out walking my dog, he grinned and said: 'That's beside the point. I asked you to work. You did it and you are entitled to be paid for it,' and he would brook no further argument.

The third of our little team was Dan, whom I judged then to be somewhere in his late forties, tall, raw-boned, cynical and rather taciturn, yet with a dry humour that emerged when he cast a critical eye on things, as was frequent. 'You wouldn't see the likes of that in the Bon Secours Home,' he would say disparagingly as he picked up a new shovel, tested it in his hands and then discarded it for his own well-worn one. What the good Sisters of the Bon Secours had to do with shovels was, to me, unimaginable, and remains one of life's little mysteries, but Dan tended to pull his criticisms out of thin air and try as we might, we could never make any sense of them, though the intention was never in doubt. Nor did he believe in over-working himself. That same new shovel was cast aside not because there was anything wrong with it, but simply because, being new, it had a much bigger blade than Dan's old one, and could therefore carry a greater load at every shovelful. 'Whatever you do, don't take Dan's shovel,' Fred warned me, 'or there will be murder.'

The Boss, as Jim was commonly known, knew the score well and tolerated Dan's little foibles with overt resignation. Dan would give his pound of flesh, but not an ounce more. He was always on time for work, steady and reliable in the nature of the old-style farm labourer, but he resented being pushed, or hurried. Fred, on the other hand, black-haired, determined and sturdy, was very much the Boss's man. If there was a foreman among us, it was he, but he was considerate while being very conscientious and I got on well with him. He may have been the spark to Dan's tinder, but when Dan became caustic, Fred would simply grin and let him blow off steam, after which Dan would wink at me and walk away to his work, his honour satisfied.

On my first morning, Dan was sent off on some business of his own, and Fred and I settled in to digging a deep drainage trench for a new house that was being built in the Chapel Field, where the Boss had sold some sites. Fit enough when I left the railway, I was no longer so after the period of enforced idleness and soon the muscles began to creak and blisters began to appear on my hands. Fred took pity on me and would let me alternate with the pick and the shovel, to ease the muscles, but never was a coffee break so welcome as the first one on that March morning.

Lunch was thirty minutes, taken on the job because it was not worth going home for such a short period and anyway, as Fred explained, we would not always be working so near home. He also explained that I could opt for a half-day on Saturday, as he did, but of course I would have a half-day's wages deducted. This meant that I would earn four pounds, seven shillings and sixpence, which was the current agricultural wage rate, less the half-day's pay stopped - considerably better than I had been getting on the railway and rather more than I had expected. Suddenly, my life had taken a distinct turn for the better, and though I was absolutely exhausted at the end of the first day's work, it was with a feeling of enormous satisfaction that I bade Fred farewell and trudged wearily home.

Gradually, as the muscles began to re-assert themselves and the hands began to harden, the work became easier and much more varied in scope. There is a common perception that a labourer is somebody with no education to speak of, little knowledge and few skills, yet little could be further from the truth, especially in our set-up, where we were expected to do any job that came long at least competently, if not expertly. There is a certain skill even in the basics, like mixing a gauge of concrete or plaster correctly, painting a door or window, fixing slates on a gale-blown roof, or laying a drainage pipe to the correct incline. When one enters the realms of agriculture, as we also did, then the need for skill becomes even more apparent, so that the most valuable asset any farmer can have is a knowledgeable labourer who can turn his hand to a whole host of important tasks.

There was much to learn and, as Fred pointed out, I might as well pick it up as I went along, because even though I expected to move on to other things, 'knowledge is never any load and it will all come in useful to you in the future'. In due course I became confident enough to be sent off on my own on certain jobs, and in turn gained the confidence of the Boss when he realised that I could and would work without any supervision. So it was that in a very short time I could paint, hang a few slates, or repair an old door quite competently, but I never did achieve any skill at the craft of plastering, though I could throw up the first rough coat.

Then too there was the Boss's garden, to which I was sometimes hived off - mostly, I suspect, when he had no other work for me, but generously kept me employed until something more urgent turned up. There I would spend happy days in the spring sunshine with my peas, beans, potatoes, fruit and even some flowers, planting and tending, weeding and cleaning, keeping the front lawn in good trim and generally looking after quite a large area.

Attached to the side of the house was a large greenhouse, very dilapidated, and on several occasions I attempted to persuade Fred that something ought to be done with it. Given the necessary permission, I reckoned I could have renewed it in a few weeks, and the work could be done sporadically when I had time, but apparently the Boss had neither the inclination nor the money to have it taken in hand. It was a pity, because it was originally a magnificent old building, going into rapid decay for want of a little attention. A beneficial sideshoot of all this gardening was that it encouraged me to tackle my own patch with the knowledge gained at Jim's expense. I don't remember any of the crops failing, and if I did not actually develop green fingers, there were at least no disasters.

In many ways, labouring, while it can be boring if not approached in the right frame of mind, is easy, given adequate health and strength. There is little or no pressure, work is taken at a steady pace, and the results are always there to see and take satisfaction from. Always a believer in doing things to the best of my ability, I would take pleasure even in a newly-painted door or a correctly-working window sash. Again, this sort of work gave the mind time both to relax and to be busy with other things in no way related to the job in hand. Most of it was outdoors and it was very pleasurable to set off in the morning knowing I would spend the day on top of some high roof, from where I could see the rest of the world at its work far below. There is a certain power, a stretching of the imagination and the senses, in being in high places, and what to some may appear to be the very mundane task of repairing a broken chute or hanging a new slate can, in fact, turn into a fresh adventure of the mind.

Equally, there was much simple joy to be got from a day in the countryside, repairing a broken fence or laying a new one. The weather was exceptionally benevolent that spring and early summer. I do not remember any prolonged period of rain, and the physical grind of digging holes for the fencing posts and humping the heavy concrete things about was more than compensated for by the feel of the sun and wind on the face, the wonder of nature all about, the certain knowledge that everything was shooting from the good earth - including, of course, the weeds.

In every garda station and post office in the country, there used to be a notice warning of the presence of three noxious weeds - thistle, ragwort and dock - on agricultural land, and of the penalties to be incurred for permitting them to flourish. Nowadays they are probably controlled by chemicals, but when the Boss told me one morning to go and clean up the Glen, as he put it, I had to resort to the scythe. After a very short time, I began to realise how the old-time reapers must have felt. Using a scythe means using every muscle in the body, and a few more that you never realised

you possessed. As more and more green blades fell before my flashing silver one, I began to ache, and it was a distinct relief to have to
stop every now and again to sharpen the scythe with the honing
stone. But, as Fred pointed out when I made my muscle-creaking
way back to the yard that evening, it was all good practice for what
was to come. Next week we would be saving the hay.

On a bright, beautiful morning at the end of May, as little puff-
balls of cloud scudded across an azure sky and cows lowed contentedly as they drifted their stately way back to the Glen after the milking, we all piled into the Boss's old Morris Eight and set off for
Ballinhassig, where he had some fields under hay that had recently
been cut. On the way, we stopped off at a hostel in the city to collect one further but vital member of the team, the man who would
build the hayrick. Johnny Mac must have been in his early seventies, and when I finally managed to root him out of the hostel, he
seemed to be quite incapable of any kind of hard work.

That initial impression was quickly dispelled, however.
Johnny was as tough as old boots, as gnarled as an ancient oak tree,
as lithe as whipcord and as silent as the grave. Bent over with the
weight of many years he may have been, but the truth was that
when it came to haymaking, he could work any of us into the
ground. It was rumoured, darkly, that once during the Troubles he
had killed a man with his bare hands. Those same hands had a grip
of iron, springing like old branches from arms that could shoot a
pikeful of hay fifteen feet into the air and land it with precision just
where it was wanted. Johnny's place, however, was usually on top
of the rick, because he was the master builder, the man on whom
we all depended to get it square and level, to place each pikeful so
that it stayed where it was put, to build like a brilliant stonemason
would build a great cathedral, firm, enduring, steady against the
ravages of wind and time.

But first there was the more mundane business of turning,
drying and gathering in the hay. As we approached Ballinhassig, a
solitary magpie blinked black and white at us from his roadside
bush, causing Dan to look for another. 'One for sorrow, two for joy,'
he muttered dismally, while we all laughed - with the exception of
old Johnny - and the Boss observed to Dan that surely he was not
superstitious. 'It's all very fine for you to laugh,' grumbled Dan, 'but
remember, it's your hay and if it rains don't blame me.' As the sun
blazed higher in the heavens and it was getting warmer all the time,
we felt Dan's pessimism was a little unfounded. He was, in fact,
merely stirring the pot to see what new piece of nonsense he could
knock out of the day, but this morning there were no takers, and he
went back to puffing away at his Woodbine.

The first field was a big, ten-acre expanse, lined with long swathes of mown hay which we treaded slowly, turning it over so that it would dry thoroughly in the sun. By the time we had finished, it was lunchtime and the Boss's wife had made tea in the nearby haggard, with piles of jam sandwiches, in addition to whatever food we had brought ourselves. Dan, as ever, had to have his grouse, audible, of course. 'Look at that,' he said, pointing to the pile of sandwiches, 'you wouldn't get the likes of it in the Little Sisters. What we need is a good bit of hairy bacon and some cabbage and (eyeing the Boss sternly), a pint wouldn't be out of the way either.' Fred nudged me and grinned. 'He has some hope - the Boss is totally anti-drink,' while the man in question simply smiled and said: 'You'll have plenty of time for a pint after work, Dan,' to which Dan, never one to lose an argument, retorted: 'Aye, but will you pay for it?'

After lunch, we began to build the now fully dry hay into small cocks, about the height of our own heads. To the unpractised like myself, it took some time to ge the hang of it; the hay kept falling in the wrong places and sliding off the half-built cock, but soon everything began to come together and there was great satisfaction in seeing one cock after another assume its conical shape, temporarily secure against any sudden summer storm. It was blisteringly hot work, so that the sweat, which at first began to run off us, soon dried in the furnace of the afternoon sun. A great peace had fallen on the sun-hazed land, unbroken by the earlier clatter of the mechanical rake. Only the distant soft cooing of pigeons and the sibilant hiss of hay on pike broke the stillness, punctured by the occasional grunt from Dan or Johnny as they swung yet another pikeful upwards.

There was a steady rhythm to the work now: gather, consolidate, lift and position, all the while building inwards slightly from the wide circular base until the final sop was placed on top to complete the cone, and yet another cock. By five-thirty the field was finished and we laid aside the pikes with a sigh of relief. I gazed longingly at a nearby stream, but Dan glowered at me and said: 'Don't even think of it. If you dive in there now you'll never come out. You're overheated, and you'll die of heart failure when the cold water hits you.' I thought he was exaggerating, but Fred nodded. 'He's right, you'd be better to cool down gradually, and anyway, we're ready to go home.'

For the next two days the work continued in the same vein, so that the pitchfork became almost an extension of the person, turning, lifting, flicking - like another arm, ever present but almost unnoticed - until two more fields bore their regimented crops of haycocks, stretching across the acres like golden-ochre pieces on a chessboard. We did not have a mechanised cock-lifter, and the fields were so near the haggard that it was not worthwhile to reload all the cocks on to a cart and draw them to the embryo rick in that fashion. Instead, old Dolly the white mare was brought in and a long, looping rope attached to her collar. This was then simply slipped around a haycock, which was dragged along the road to the rick site.

Inevitably, as the day wore on, Dolly became tired and Dan grew impatient with her. Like himself, she could be coaxed but not driven and eventually, in exasperation, having roundly berated the poor beast, Dan handed her over to me. I quickly found that a pat on the neck and a quiet word would get her going again and, with a little petting, she carried on without any further tantrums. Meanwhile, old Johnny was laying the foundations of the rick inside in the big barn roofed with corrugated iron. Stomping around his rectangular area, he carefully spread the hay that Dan, Fred and the Boss were pitching to him, leaving a slight hollow in the centre and building from the edges inwards. Slowly, as more and more hay was piled on, the rick grew, and with it the amount of work necessary to pitch to Johnny, until that in turn became quite exhausting.

It took two full days to build that big rick, but even then our problems were not quite over. Johnny suspected that the rick was beginning to heat, possibly because some of the hay was not quite as dry as we had imagined. Left to itself, it could have ignited in a conflagration of spontaneous combustion, so that immediate action had to be taken. Johnny said there was nothing for it but to cut a ventilation shaft down through the centre of the rick and we had to set to work with hay knives, working alternately. Carving out the packed hay was not too difficult, given constant sharpening of the knives; the problem was that as the shaft became deeper, so too did the danger of suffocation. Nobody was then left stay down for more than a few minutes, with a rope attached, and was hauled up and replaced when the Boss gave the order. It was indeed suffocating down there, in that small, very hot space, breathing foul air and hay dust and it was not too difficult to imagine just how the rick could ignite.

Eventually, Johnny pronounced himself satisfied and we all breathed sighs of relief. The remedy must have had its effect, because the rick survived intact, providing valuable fodder for the following winter. The satisfaction of viewing the fields of stubble as we headed home was tempered by the knowledge that we would all have to spend some time removing the ticks which were even now beginning to pester us. It was perhaps just as well that we were moving on to other work.

After the frenetic activity of the haymaking, there were other days of relative calm, days when the work was light but tedious, like picking and stemming blackcurrants and gooseberries in the garden. In the curious way that the world wags, I was picking to fill the big bowls for the Boss' kitchen, where once as a child I had picked to eat, with the permission of old Mr. Rice, who would invite us into his domain. It was a pleasant occupation, however, undemanding on either mind or body, and tinged with a certain nostalgia. But even this palls after a while and it was good to get back eventually to more active business, like treating the cattle at Ballinhassig against warble flies. While I loved working with the gentle cows, which always seemed so contented and biddable, there were others, wild young heifers and bullocks, and even getting them penned so that they could be treated was quite an affair, involving much running about and shouting. Once corralled in the haggard however, the rest was relatively easy.

The warbles took the form of huge lumps under the animals' skin and the treatment was to rub in a concoction which, if I remember rightly, was designed to make them emerge before they could do more damage by depositing eggs and so spreading the menace. At any rate, it had to be done, though we all collected a few bruises from high-spirited beasts that kicked and bucked, and often knocked us against the sides of the pen. Young cattle too had to be de-horned, in accordance with new regulations which insisted that this be done. Calves were dealt with easily, by removing the embryo horns with a caustic stick, a little painful no doubt, but they soon recovered.

Bought-in animals that had not been treated and that had fully grown horns needed the attention of the vet, who sawed off the protruberances amid much bellowing and roaring, while we attempted to hold the firmly-roped beasts steady during his ministrations. The vet assured us that it did not hurt, but the way the creatures bucked and reared they might as well have been in some terrible torture chamber. We, of course, collected more bruises, and the operation was usually accompanied by some swearing, though not when the Boss was about, because bad language in his presence would have brought a quick and severe reprimand.

One of the great attractions of the work was its almost infinite variation. Rarely were two days the same, unless we were renewing an old building which, between stripping and re-plastering, re-flooring or making an old stairway safe, painting and decorating, could take several weeks. As the hot summer slowly yielded to an early autumn blessed with gentle, soothing breezes, and as the Great Artist began to paint the gorse on Shepherd's Hill in hues of blazing russett from a palette of reds, vivid oranges and browns, I was bronzed, fit and enjoying myself hugely. The work was no longer any great burden, the Boss was considerate, my companions were amiable, and I loved being out in the fresh air, doing something useful.

I was not, however, under any illusions. There was no use in pretending there was any real future in this, and while there are numerous instances of labourers turning to literature and making a great success of it - as for instance, Irish scholar Dónal Mac Amhlaoibh, who discarded his hod to write of the lot of the emigrants in England - I was looking for something more secure. In any event, winter was coming on as, inexorably, season follows season, and it was quite likely that the Boss, for all his good-natured accommodation, simply would not have any work for me. Once again, prayers were prayed, and answered.

*   *   *

I have often felt that events which are to have the most profound consequences in life happen in the oddest way. Arriving home, unusually, for a quick bite of lunch on an afternoon in mid-September, I found a letter from the Secretary of *The Cork Examiner* awaiting me in the midday post, to inform me that I had been due for interview that morning at 10 am! Undaunted, but a little worried, I cleaned up, told Jim Rice where I was off to, was wished the best of luck and set off.

The main offices of *The Cork Examiner* were situated, appropriately, in Patrick Street, at No. 95, which curiously enough for such an august institution, consisted merely of a doorway set between two shops. One was the butcher's of Messrs. O'Flynn, the other a grocery store which some years before had been a branch of the London and Newcastle. It was one of the first outlets in Cork to offer trading stamps, which my aunt Shaddy used to collect, and with which she used to redeem little bits and pieces of utilitarian value for her lodging house. But it was into No. 95 that I made my way, up the long stairs and into the beautiful main office, panelled in rich mahogany and with a high, polished brass railing finishing off the large semi-circular counter, behind which worked clerks on high stools at sloping desks.

Having already prepared for possible interview, I knew that *The Cork Examiner* had been founded in 1841 by John Francis Maguire, Nationalist MP for Cork in the British Parliament. He had supported the Liberator, Daniel O'Connell, in the movement for Catholic Emancipation and when that was achieved, turned his attention to the matter of Repeal of the Union, again giving his unstinted support to O'Connell. His reason for establishing *The Examiner* in the first instance was simple: he felt that the ordinary people of the Munster area had no public voice, the existing newspaper, *The Cork Constitution*, being Unionist and aristocracy-orientated.

In his very first Editorial, on 31 August, 1841, he set out the objectives of the new paper: to report without fear or favour the proceedings of the region, to do everything possible for its advancement and to maintain a politically independent stance. It was a very powerful Editorial, in which Maguire took many swipes at the Establishment and one which was to set the tone of *The Examiner* for generations to come. When Maguire subsequently devoted more and more of his time to politics, he appointed a young Editor, Thomas Crosbie, a gifted journalist who saw the newspaper grow and develop from a thrice-weekly afternoon paper to a morning daily. Crosbie was an astute Editor, well aware that *The Examiner's* following rested largely in its rural roots, and those early papers were full of the minutiae of daily living as well as of the momentous events of the times. So esteemed was he in the world of journalism that he was once offered the post of Leader Writer of the *London Times* at the then princely salary of £700 a year, but the offer was withdrawn when it was found that Crosbie was a Catholic.

Meanwhile, he had a few other strings to his bow. *The Examiner* was one of the founder-members of the Press Association, the British-based news agency, and Crosbie was one of its top correspondents. In the days before Marconi and his trans-Atlantic cables, he scooped the rest of Europe with news of the ending of the American Civil War by the simple expedient of going to meet the incoming liners at Cobh (then Queenstown), getting hold of the American papers, and wiring the details off to the PA in London, long before the liners arrived in Britain.

Crosbie succeeded Maguire as proprietor of *The Examiner* in 1867 and on Maguire's death, made full provision for his widow and family. Thereby began a dynasty which saw the Crosbie family emerge as one of the most prominent in Cork, and a newspaper which was to become so well respected within its own area that it became known simply as 'the Paper' - the implication being that any others simply did not matter! It was to this hallowed establishment that I duly presented myself on that sunny September afternoon, fully convinced that I was wasting my time, that the job was already gone.

John Leland, the Secretary, was small, dapper, businesslike, extremely courteous and very puzzled. 'That letter was posted early yesterday. You should have got it by first post this morning,' he explained. 'Anyway, now that you have taken the trouble to come in, do I assume you are still interested in the job?' he asked. 'We have had your name on file for some time, but this is the first vacancy that has occurred.' When I answered that of course I was interested in joining *The Examiner*, and that I hoped eventually to become a writer of some sort, he explained to me that I would have a long way to go, that I would be starting at the bottom and that some night work would be involved. 'If you are successful, you will be starting in the Reading Room, where we check the proofs,' he told me, 'and while I cannot give you any guarantees about the future, promotions from there do arise from time to time.' He seemed happy that night work was no obstacle, and that I had already done it on the railway. Then the formal interview began. It was short, friendly, and included some simple tests in reading, spelling and arithmetic, the results of which appeared to satisfy him.

I had expected to be told that he would let me know the outcome in due course, but to my surprise he said: 'Very well then, Tim, you seem to be quite satisfactory. You can begin work in the Reading Room next Monday morning, if you have no other commitments. If you have, we will honour them; otherwise report to Mr. Browne at 10 am.' He wished me luck, and on the way out, introduced me to Commander George Crosbie, one of the proprietors, who happened to be passing by and who shook hands with me, welcomed me to *The Examiner* and wished me well - and that was that. I could scarcely believe my good fortune: a permanent job, at home in my own city, with a solid future and the hope of achieving some of my ambitions, all at a time when jobs were as rare as hen's teeth.

It was the sort of interview that simply would not happen anywhere today. I did have references and my Leaving Certificate with me; I was asked only for the former, my word was taken for the latter and it was put aside without being scrutinised. There was no question of producing a C.V. - I was simply asked where I had worked before and what I had been doing. Then there was the courtesy with which I was treated, unusual enough in those days when so many young applicants were being dealt with and, most of all, there was the friendliness and the instant summing up of my suitability or otherwise. I left the office with the feeling of somehow belonging already and it was apparently the official view that if this young man had anything to contribute, it would emerge in due time; if not, he would hardly do any damage in the Reading Room anyhow. It was all very reassuring.

There was, of course, one minor snag. There always is. My starting salary in *The Examiner* would be the princely sum of two pounds and five shillings a week, with an extra five shillings for night work, which occurred on alternate months, whereas I was already earning almost double that on the land. Many years later,

John Leland, who was to spend fifty-five years with the firm, told me that when he began in 1923, his wage was one pound a week, increased by five shillings after the first year. In my own case, the drop in wages would make a considerable difference to the household budget, but there was no future in my existing employment, as Jim Rice was quick to confirm when I went to tell him the news. So I finished my week's work with him, got my pay and a warm handshake, and bade farewell to the pitchfork and the shovel.

Mossie Brown was a small man, semi-crippled from the waist down, but with a powerful pair of shoulders in the way common to those who have to walk with two sticks, bespectacled, impish and full of the wisdom of his years. When I met him on that Monday morning, he motioned me to a chair beside him and handed me the morning paper. 'Read that for a while, and don't be too bloody anxious to get to work,' he growled, 'there'll be plenty of it to do before the day is out.' Then he winked and grinned. 'Tell me, what school do you come from and what have you been doing?' When I told him he examined my hands, nodded and apparently satisfied, added: 'You'll be all right, you're a worker. Stay with me for today and I'll put you with someone else for the rest of the week ... and for God's sake don't make too much noise, my head is killing me.'

The paper duly read, Mossie picked up a bundle of printer's proofs, distributed them, retained one for himself and handed me the accompanying copy, the original text, in this instance from one of the international news agencies. 'You read that to me, and I correct this,' he explained. I began to read, slowly and carefully. Mossie listened for a moment, then amid much laughter from the others, he brought one of his sticks down with a resounding crash on the table and roared: 'For God's sake, boy, you're not in a pulpit, or giving a speech. Just read it quietly and quickly. And by the way, your Polish pronounciation is lousy.' More laughter and another quick wink from Mossie.

I quickly learned that this was the style of the Reading Room, a sort of easy informality in which we all ribbed each other. Mossie was very much the boss, and none of us young copyholders dared to call him anything except Mr. Brown, but I was also to learn that his bark was very much worse than his bite, and he would defend us to the hilt if anything went wrong or if we made any mistakes. He also looked after our welfare in another way, putting us forward for promotion if there were any vacancies in another part of the house, and generally taking a fatherly interest in us.

The work, while intensive, was quite boring, most of the relief coming from the fact that at that time the Reading Room was occupied by a bunch of very lively and some eccentric characters whose sole aim appeared to be to get as much fun out of life as possible. Joe Giltinan, who was known as Pinky, or Cast Iron, was a great devotee of Bernard Shaw and was rarely without one of the great man's works, from which he was wont to quote to us *ad nauseum*. Denis (Dinny) Murray was a lovable rascal, full of typical Cork humour and always ready to have a barney with either Mossie or Joe, but in spite of much bickering, the three were the best of friends. John Reardon was deeply involved in rowing and often found the confines of the Reading Room so restrictive that he would leap up on the table, bang his chest and bellow like Tarzan, to bring a little light relief not only to himself but to all of us.

One of the great benefits of the Reading Room was that it gave us a very useful insight into the operations of the entire newspaper. Because of our position as 'correctors of the press', as Mossie liked to call his team, we were at the nerve centre of things, dealing with everything from editorial matter to advertisements, from the printing office to finding our way occasionally into the machine room and dispatch departments, to where Mossie would send us on some errand or other. There were pranks here as well, of course, especially practical jokes played on newcomers, and I was not immune. 'Go out to the printing floor, find Billy and tell him I want the key to the fudge box,' Mossie ordered me on my second day in the office. Billy knew the ropes and was only too willing to send the fool further. 'I don't have that at the moment,' he said, straight-faced, 'try Mick in the machine room.' And so it went on, until eventually the penny dropped and I returned, red-faced, to gales of laughter. Mossie grinned. 'Don't get any big ideas in here,' he said. 'Remember you're an idiot like all the rest of us.'

Later, on the printing floor, where I was delivering proofs back to the typesetters to be corrected, Billy called me and told me there actually was a thing known as the fudge box. He showed me a semi-circular instrument into which lines of type were locked, and the box was then bolted on to a special place on the press so that late news could be run into a gap left in Page One, without the need for making a new page plate. 'And there is actually a key,' said Billy, showing me an ordinary double-ended spanner used to squeeze the type in the box. Laughing, he added: 'Don't worry, we were all caught out on that one, but don't let Brownie make a hare of you again.'

Because the printers' union was very powerful and tended to be a closed shop, we were not allowed to lay a finger on a line of type, but apart from that, all the men were ready to explain what they were doing and to answer questions. The linotype machines in particular fascinated me. They were like something devised by Mr. Heath Robinson, full of speeding cogs, twisting eccentrics, reaching arms, rumbling noises and the acrid smell of molten metal. The operator sat at his keyboard, tapped out, as on a typewriter, one line of brass matrices, each with the required letter inscribed on it, and inserted thin steel spacing strips until the line was of the required width. Then he pressed a lever and sent it away to be cast, and the fun started.

A pump squirted the hot metal into the tiny casting box, a huge arm came down, took the line of matrices, and lifted them up to the back of the machine, from where they were dropped on to a revolving worm, to be re-distributed back into their rightful place. Meanwhile, the newly-cast line of type shot out of the box and into a tray at the operator's left-hand side. And so the process went on until he had a whole column of type, known as a galley, each column having a catchline or identifying word, at its head, so that the compositors who put the pages together would know what went where.

Headlines over a certain size were set by hand, from large cases of type known as fonts and I often felt that the casehands, as they were known, were rather like little boys playing with bricks, as they placed the individual letters into their setting sticks, which were adjusted to a given column width, again padding out the lines and spaces with blanks, so that everything fitted snugly. It was not unknown, though it was officially frowned upon, for a casehand to shave a tiny sliver of metal from a letter when he was trying to squeeze a heading into a given space.

As might be imagined, newspaper production in those days was a dirty, noisy business. Eighteen or twenty linotypes clattering away made quite a din, to which was added the noise of finished pages being beaten flat and square prior to being stereotyped, the scream of the saw trimming the huge, semi-circular cast metal plates, the roar as the great press gathered speed and began to spew out the day's news. Ink and metal mingled everywhere in a confusion of grime, and upstairs in the Engraving Department, where the plates for the illustrations were made, a group of skilled men worked with giant cameras, arc lights, fire, water, acid and Monkey's Blood or Dragon's Blood - depending on who your informant was - in a strange sort of chemistry which produced from a photograph a metal plate ready for reproduction. They always seemed to me like souls possessed, determined to find the ancient alchemists' dream of making gold from lead, as they plied their mysterious craft.

All of this internal uproar was added to outside by the shouts of the Echo boys (many of whom were grown men) in the streets as they bellowed their traditional cry of 'Eeee-ch-oaaa, Evening Eeee-ch-oaaa' from lungs of truly magnificent strength. They were firmly managed by Johnny Mahony, from the northside of the city, a man who became something of a legend in his own lifetime as a very practical entrepreneur as well as a sportsman of renown, especially where beagling was concerned. Johnny was no accountant and he probably would not have been able to decipher a balance sheet if one were handed to him on a silver tray, but he knew his business and his unruly staff intimately. I never saw him write anything down; all his affairs were stored in his head: his orders, his allocations of papers to the various boys, his need for extra copies as the day progressed, and his final tally. His bank was his back pocket, from which he would extract a huge wad of notes with which to pay for the balance of his papers at the end of the day, having earlier made a lodgment, in cash of course, at the office.

At the end of the first month, when I had begun to settle into the routine, I was transferred to the night shift, work beginning at 7 pm and ending about 2 am, except for one reader and one copyholder who stayed late to correct the second edition. The reader in question was the night Foreman, Connie O'Sullivan, popularly known as Connie Dorum, a small, hunch-backed man with huge bushy eyebrows, who was quite elderly at that time. He was a staunch Republican in the best sense of that now much-maligned description, and the only time he lost his temper was when one of the lads would plant a small Union Jack on his desk for a bit of crack. Then Connie would erupt into a diatribe of vituperation against Her Majesty's government as we all roared with laughter. But essentially he was a gentle soul and he bore our high spirits with good humour, and managed to keep a sort of despairing discipline which never impinged too much on any of us.

One of the most hated jobs was reading the nightly Stock Exchange prices, which Connie would always undertake himself, I think because in some dim and distant past there had been a glorious mess-up, and one of the senior Crosbies had become a little upset when he was unable to find out how his investments were doing. At any rate, the copyholder working with Connie would regard this chore as something of a nightmare, galloping through the long list as quickly as possible. Often, Connie would nod off, to re-awaken with a start some time later. 'Where were we now?' he would ask. 'Commercial and industrial,' the copyholder would reply, having skipped several pages. 'We were not, we were only at Government Securities,' Connie would growl. It took a long time to figure out how he remembered, but in fact he did not. Shrewd as ever, when nodding off, he would allow his pen to drop, nib down, on the proof, so that when he woke up, there would be a large blob of ink at the place where we had broken off.

It was always a relief to get out at finishing time and walk home through the silent, sleeping city, meeting only the odd garda on duty, or a night watchman dozing by his brazier. Sometimes I would accompany the garda on patrol duty up Summerhill to St. Luke's Cross, where he would meet the beat sergeant and we would shorten our respective journeys with stories and jokes, while he would, of course, want to know all the news of the night. This easy companionship made the long trudge home that much more tolerable.

In spite of the tedium, I enjoyed life in the Reading Room, but it was generally regarded only as a jumping-off point and a sort of apprenticeship, so when Mossie finally told me there was a vacancy in the Commercial Department, I duly applied and, with Mossie's recommendation, was accepted. Frankly, I hated the place from the outset, except for a brief stint in the advertising office in Academy Street, where I was in daily contact with the public, and enjoyed meeting them and chatting as they placed their advertisements. But it was with a great deal of relief that, having let it be known that I really wanted to be a journalist, and having done some part-time reporting of minor matches at weekends, I was finally sent to see Pat Crosbie, then Editorial Director.

Pat was tall, broad-shouldered, extremely capable and very direct. 'Ah, young Cramer, they tell me you want to be a journalist.' He rapped out the words, machine-gun fashion as was his habit, when I entered his office. 'Right, *Examiner* editorial, Sunday night, eight o'clock. See Jimmy Cullen,' and the interview was at an end. Really, I wanted to be a reporter, but there was no point in arguing. The vacancy apparently was for a stand-in sub-editor for the summer holidays. We would have to see what happened after that. What did happen was that I spent the next few years in a sort of yo-yo capacity, reporting during the winter and editing during the summer holidays.

There is a popular image, still extant in some circles, of a reporter as a fellow in a trenchcoat and trilby hat, with a granite face and a heart of stone, hard-bitten beyond belief, unaffected by any tragedy, driven only by the all-consuming ambition of feeding the ever-gaping maw of the printing press. It is an image that has been bolstered over many years by the cinema industry and latterly, by television and video, all of which set out to portray the life of the reporter as one of unending glamour and high drama. Nothing could be further from the truth, especially outside of the great newspaper cities of the world like London, Paris, Washington and New York.

Transposed into provincial journalism, the reporter is like everybody else, earning a living in what is often a monotonous, even boring, routine job. Sitting day after weary day at the press table of the local District Court, for instance, recording the minor woes and shortcomings of human nature as reflected in cases of common assault, careless driving, after-hours drinking and all the other peccadilloes of the human condition is not exactly the stuff of the heroic. Yet it is as much part of the job of journalism as the great events of the day, which are, in any case, the preserve of the senior reporter. Like everybody else on the reporting staff, I served my time in courts and council meetings, in committees and agricultural shows, with only the occasional foray into the memorable news story because there happened to be nobody else around when it broke. But the mundane also had its fun, even if it did lack the glamour, and a sense of humour went a long way towards relieving the tedium.

Contrary to popular belief, our law enforcers are human, and reporting the proceedings of the courts in the various country towns often had moments of hilarity. In those days, when none of us juniors had cars, we were very kindly accommodated by the District Justices, who would pick us up at a given time and place on the morning of the court and drive us to the venue. One such was District Justice Seamus P. Kealy, slight of build and with a nervous tic on one of his cheekbones which could be extremely distressing for the poor man. Often on the way to the court in his Hillman Minx, which he drove with all the abandon of a veritable Jehu, he would say to me: 'Don't let me get too cranky with them today - this thing is at me again.' Even if he did get cranky, his justice was always tempered with mercy, because as he once said: 'I remember when we were being sworn in, the Minister of the day reminded us that we were the first Justices of the new State; we would be trying our own people and we should at all times remember that. I have never forgotten that.' He would also enliven the trip to the court with a useful run-down of what was on the list for the day.

One morning, grinning hugely, he told me: 'We'll have some fun today, Tim; we have a fellow caught with a bottle of poteen in his possession.' The court was in Macroom and we duly reached it as the rain spilled from leaden skies. When the case was called, Justice Kealy heard the prosecution evidence, which was to the effect that the defendant had been found at the roadside between Macroom and Inchigeela, dead drunk, with his bicycle on top of him and a bottle of poteen sticking out of his pocket. Winking broadly at me, the Superintendent concluded his case and sat down, as Mr. Kealy called the defendant.

Up the centre of the courtroom came a middle-aged man, wearing boots and a long coat which was obviously rain-soaked, and nervously twisting his battered old cap in his hands. 'Well, my man, what have you to say for yourself? What did you want with that bloody staff anyway?' asked Justice Kealy sharply. The poor fellow looked even more woebegone than ever. 'To tell you the truth, sir, I only wanted it for embrocation for me greyhounds' - at which the court erupted into laughter. The Justice thought for a moment then said: 'So you don't deny the charge, that you had it in your possession?' 'Sure, how could I deny it sir, wasn't I caught with it?' Mr. Kealy paused, looking out of the rain-lashed window. 'Tell me, how far did you come this morning?' 'Seven miles, sir.'

'And how did you get here?' 'On my bicycle, sir.'

Another pause, as the Justice made his mind up. Then: 'Fair enough, you came a long way in the pouring rain to be here and you met the case honestly, as far as I can see.' Bending down, in a stage whisper which could be heard all over the court, he hissed to the Clerk, Seán Murphy: 'Well Seán, what's he like; is he an honest man?' 'Ah sure, Justice, he's a decent poor fellow, a farm labourer with nothing previously known against him.' 'All right so,' said Mr. Kealy, 'since you took the trouble to turn up on such a bad morning, I'll apply the Probation Act, and don't be caught with that bloody lunatic soup again. It's no good for you at all. Save your money and buy a decent bottle of whiskey - and don't come up before me again.'

Mildly surprised at the leniency of the judgement, I mentioned this to the Justice on the way home. 'Ah well, Tim,' he said chuckling, 'he was a decent poor man who was caught out in his sins. It's coming up to Christmas, so how could I fine him? And anyway, I'm never without a drop in the house myself.'

Of such stirring stuff were our days composed and our system of justice meted out. There was the day when, sitting in the sunshine outside the old, tiny Halfway court at Ballinhassig while waiting for a garda car to arrive to cart him off to jail for six months, a young itinerant defendant convicted of horse theft was told by the Justice: 'I'm sorry I have to send you away, but you caused everybody a lot of trouble. Anyway, you'll be out for the summer.' Then a kindly garda Sergeant gave the young lad his packet of cigarettes. 'Put those in your pocket, because you wont get much were you're going. Tell the warder I gave them to you.'

There were further journeys, into the heart of the Kingdom of Kerry, to report on the Kingdom County Fair, the big annual agricultural show in Tralee, where I was summarily dispatched because the reporter allocated to the job had gone sick. I travelled off in the *Echo* van, piloted by an elderly driver who, I was convinced, had second sight. Blazing along the road, somewhere outside Farnanes, he suddenly stamped on the brakes when approaching a bend. 'What's wrong Dan?' I asked. 'I dunno, but there's something around there.' When we got around, at a snail's pace, a horse and cart was spread across the road while the driver opened a gate. Had Dan kept going at normal speed, the consequences would have been appalling. He was unable, to explain how or why he knew of the obstruction. 'It's a kind of instinct ... you just get this feeling when you're as long on the road as I am.'

In Tralee, there was no room at the inn, or indeed at any of the inns. The place was crammed with visitors to the Fair and I had arrived very late. At Benner's Hotel, a pleasant young lady sympa-

thised with my plight, but could do nothing about it. Then suddenly: 'Look, it's just a chance, but try the Hibernian. It's a small hotel
in the main street and he might just have a room for you.' After
some searching, because it was a small establishment consisting
merely of a hallway with a stairs leading to the hotel rooms overhead, I found the Hibernian, and a tall, dark-haired Kerryman who
listened to my tale and said: 'Sure, we can't leave you in the street,
boyeen. Come in and I'll find a room for you somewhere.'

It was at the very top of the house, and the simple furniture
consisted of a bed, an old wardrobe, a battered chest of drawers and
a washing table complete with jug and basin. My host opened the
door with a flourish and courteously waved me in. 'Leave your bag
there now, and come on down and have the tea,' and he led me to
the dining room where in due course was produced a mixed grill,
complete with home-made brown bread and butter, which would
have fed a hungry horse. As I finished, my tall host appeared again,
wanting to be reassured that I had had enough to eat. Satisfied on
this point he said: 'Tomorrow is a Holy day, so you'll want to go to
Mass. I'll give you a call at seven, you can have breakfast, and the
church is only around the corner.'

I slept the sleep of the just that night, and true to his word, my
host knocked on the door the following morning precisely at seven,
came in and put a jug of hot water on the wash table, with the message that breakfast was ready when I was. When I called him to settle the account, he scratched his head, hesitated and then asked:
'Would seven and six be too much?' When I assured him that it
would not and that I had been treated royally, he laughed and said:
'Sure, 'twas only a small room, the only one I had left, and the
biteen you ate didn't cost much anyway.' He was most reluctant to
take the ten shilling note I gave him and accompanied me to the
door to show me where the church was.

A small enough incident perhaps, but one which left me with
the happiest memory of my first overnight stay in the Kingdom, and
the thought that kindly people are far more important than the
plushest of surroundings. I had been treated with great hospitality,
had slept and eaten well, been called on time and even reminded of
my spiritual duties, as if such treatment was quite natural, which
indeed it was. Courtesy, friendliness and the caring for people are
innate in the Kerry folk, as indeed is the case in most parts of rural
Ireland. There is no pretence, no fawning, just a natural pleasure in
looking to the needs of the traveller. If there was no room at the inn,
then room would have to be found. It was as simple as that, and in
my later journeying throughout this land, I have invariably found it
to be so. Not only that, but I actually made money on that transac-
tion, because as far as I now recall, our overnight allowance in

those days was at least double the very small charge my kindly host had levied!

The easy informality of the Reporters' Room contrasted sharply with the rather rigid regimentation of other parts of the house. Our Chief Reporter at the time was the late William Spillane, middle-aged, bespectacled and quietly humorous. He also adopted the role of father-figure, forever reminding us youngsters of the virtues of thrift. He would arrive into the office about 11 am, remove the jacket of his suit and replace it with a well-worn tweed affair with leather patches on the elbows and proceed to hold forth. 'My bank manager raised his hat to me in the street again this morning,' he would announce solemnly, his eyes twinkling. 'I bet very few of you boys can say anything like that.' Then he would open his wallet, extract a twenty-pound note and wave it above his head, much to the chagrin of the rest of us, who could barely raise a pound between us.

That he had our interests very much at heart was undoubted, but waving ponies about was hardly calculated to raise the spirits of those who were forever on the verge of being penniless. One morning, as Willie was going through his act, Harry, a great extrovert and a fine reporter, but who was at times the bane of Willie's life, snatched the twenty-pound note, pasted one corner, sprang on to a high desk and stuck the note to the ceiling. 'Now Chief,' he said wickedly, 'what's the use of saving if you can't spend?' while we all roared with laughter, in which Willie cheerfully joined. But Harry's exuberant nature was to bring about his eventual downfall. More than once I was dispatched by Willie to rouse him out of bed and get him into work, and all his foibles were tolerated, if despairingly, until one afternoon the bubble finally burst.

Harry had gone to bid farewell to a friend leaving for Britain on the *Innisfallen* and, being Harry, had accompanied his pal on board, where the two ended up at the bar. On the following morning, Willie received a telegram that read: *Dear Chief, stranded in Wales, home tomorrow, send money - Harry.* Even Willie, with all his good nature, could not save that situation, and the hapless Harry was asked for his resignation. He was the first to admit that it was all his own fault, but he was a fine newsman and a genial companion and we were all very sorry to see him go. He subsequently settled in Britain and made a good life for himself there, returning occasionally to see us and to recall amid much laughter the occasion of his departure.

If he lectured us about thrift, Willie was also considerate enough to put a few shillings our way when he could. As part of his position, he was correspondent for a number of other newspapers and for the Press Association. Often at weekends, when we juniors were covering a number of sports fixtures, Willie would ask us to send a few paragraphs and results to his various interests and invariably, a few days later, we would receive an envelope containing a cheque from him. Once, when he left me a cheque for ten shillings, I queried it with him, knowing full well that the few lines that had appeared would not amount to that much. He simply smiled and answered: 'You were kind enough to oblige me, I am just discharging my own obligation and I am very grateful to you.'

He was the very epitome of gracious, old-world courtesy and it was generally agreed that Willie was an old toff. He was the very antithesis of the popular image of the hard-bitten News Editor, being totally incapable of an unkind word, even his often necessary reproaches being delivered more in sorrow than in anger. Such necessary discipline as he imposed rested in the fact that he was much loved by all of us. He had our total respect and if we erred, it was not out of any disregard for Willie, but simply through our own shortcomings or the folly of youth. His untimely death was greatly regretted and he is still remembered with affection.

When I say that much of my youth was spent on two wheels, I mean that from my mid-teens, when Mother somehow managed to scrape enough money together, I was the proud possessor of a bicycle. A Hercules, it came shining new from the South of Ireland Cycle Company in Maylor Street, and cost the then princely sum of five pounds. I had learned to ride on something far less ostentatious, an old banger belonging to my friends the Mackeys of Mackey's Cross, near Clogheen on the old Blarney Road. Kerry Lane the locals called the place, because in the old days it was the main artery leading west into the Kingdom of Kerry, past the distant mountains beyond Macroom which could be seen from Mackey's Cross. Along there, in the colourful days of the so-called merchant princes, trundled the common carts of the farmers from the hinterland, bearing butter to the market near Shandon, the largest butter market in Europe, to be weighed, boxed and sent all over the world.

Mother and I would spend several summer Sunday afternoons each year with the large Mackey family, whose father Paddy was the local blacksmith. It was there, cajoled by Margaret and Bernard, that I took my first wild, wobbling bicycle flight downhill towards Kerry Pike, with my two friends shouting encouragement. After I had discovered that Margaret had let go of the back of the saddle and I was on my own, there was literally no stopping me, and in due course, with much shouting, myself, bicycle and all ended up in a heap on the roadside. But soon I had got the balance right and I cycled like a veritable Seán Kelly, and a year later the arrival of the brand new machine opened up horizons that had hitherto been undreamed of.

For a relatively penniless group of us, a bicycle meant trips to places that had hitherto been far beyond our reach, places like Inniscarra, on the road to which Pat Holohan, son of Dan, the Glanmire station booking clerk, showed us our first optical illusion. The road apparently sloped slightly downwards, yet we had to pedal. Turn about and go the other way and the same thing happened. We were fascinated by this unexplained mystery and even more amazed at the scholarship of Pat, who was constantly putting these strange phenomena before us. Seaside resorts like Garryvoe suddenly became within reach, albeit with some effort, and even distant Youghal could be reached and returned from in a single day's outing - sixty miles in all, with the afternoon spent playing football on the beach and swimming.

Being of a technical bent, I quickly found that I had been appointed chief but unpaid mechanic to the group, forever fixing punctures and doing sundry repairs, so that in time even the mysteries of the three-speed Sturmey Archer gear became revealed. I have always had great respect for machinery, and my own bike was kept in good repair and well maintained. It was a practice that was to stand me in good stead later when I graduated to motorcycles and was forced by financial considerations to undertake my own repairs. The first of the powered machines was one of the then very popular Lambretta scooters, built by the firm of Innocenti of Milan and all the rage in the fifties. It was supposed to be the poor man's motor car and came complete with spare wheel, large windshield and rear carrier, as well as a separate pillion seat for the lady friend, which no doubt was a big selling point.

The Lambretta was very good for town work, nippy and manoeuverable in traffic, but on the open road it had its drawbacks. Even when I had removed the large, sail-like windshield from mine, its little 150 cc two-stroke engine could not be pushed much beyond 30 miles an hour. Wind it up to a sustained 35 and after a few miles it would overheat and simply putter to a standstill, to sit there until it had cooled off. Its front brake - the most important stopper on a motorcycle - was virtually useless, and the general balance of the machine was always suspect, due no doubt to the very small wheels.

On one historic occasion, when I was acting as runner for the late and very well-known sporting journalist, Tom Higgins, at the famed Clounanna coursing meeting, I scootered into the lovely thatched village of Adare in Co. Limerick to phone some results back to the office. The job done, I sat on the Lambretta and from the seat, gave the kickstarter a hefty swing. The little engine roared into life, but I had forgotten one vital thing: the kickstarter operated in a forward direction and on this occasion it had not swung back. Tearing back to Clounanna, I banked over to take the bend on a curving bridge. With a terrible scraping noise, the kickstarter tore into the road and the parapet of the bridge began to approach at an alarming rate of knots. Unable to straighten the machine out, I braked and dived off, to let the bike crash into the wall of the bridge.

I survived with a few scratches, but the machine was looking a bit sorry for itself. The kickstarter was wrecked but I was able to bump start and get going again, steering with handlebars that were anything but straight. At the crossroads a garda on point duty was full of concern for me and helped me to pull the steering straight. Then, having checked that the brakes were working, he let me go on my way, doubtless realising that even in dire emergency, the press must be served. But I was more than a little disillusioned with it all, especially when I got the subsequent repair bill.

Soon afterwards my pal Tony gave me a turn on his new Francis Barnett, a proper motorcycle with large wheels, and I was astonished at the superior riding qualities and general handling of the machine. The Lambrette, it was decided, would have to go. It was duly traded in for a 250 Jawa of Czech origin, and there began a love affair with motorbikes that was to last for eight or nine years, until I married.

The Jawa was a superior handler, very comfortable, good for just over 60 mph and in general, a nice machine to ride, but it too had its inherent faults. The quality of the material appeared to be very poor and the electrics, in particular, left a lot to be desired. It was at that time that I heard of a venerable Brough-Superior in our area and made tentative approaches to the owner. Yes, he would sell it if I was interested, and he showed me the enormous machine of 1936 vintage, with a huge V-twin, side-valve JAP engine of 1,150 cc capacity, the whole monster being accompanied by an ageing sidecar. A deal was duly done and the combination was taken home to be refurbished, though I quickly ditched the sidecar as both too decrepit and too dangerous. I could never manage to make any sort of fist of combinations, even though they were considered very safe by the insurance companies, and I was subsequent delighted to hear an old Scots engineer and vintage owner in London tell me: 'Give me two wheels or four, three-wheelers are un-mechanical contrivances.'

About that time I was writing articles for the two major British motorcycling magazines, *The Motor Cycle* and *Motor Cycling*, the editors of whom were kind enough to use some of my ramblings. One piece I wrote about the Brough brought a letter from Kent, from a chap who wanted to find out who could own a Brough-Superior that he had not heard of: apparently he knew the owner of every surviving Brough in these islands, the machines having been hand-built by George Brough of Nottingham and a marque to be treasured. Intriguingly he signed his letter 'Saff' and only after some correspondence had passed between us did I discover that his real name was Les Wombwell, that he lived in Margate, and was known as Saff because he had been born in Saffron Waldron. He also had three magnificent Brough-Superiors, which I was invited to go and see.

On arrival in Margate for a brief holiday, I found that Saff did indeed have a magnificent little collection of old motorcycles, chief of which were, of course, the Broughs, a huge 1,150 like my own but in far better condition, and two SS80s, which he had named Dick Turpin and Black Bess. He had spent countless hours restoring them to pristine condition and while they were his pride and joy, they were generously given to me to ride whenever I wanted them, while he ran his seaside café business.

Saff had been an ambulance driver in London during the blitz, but like so many who had gone through the trauma of war, it was extremely difficult to get him to talk about it. He would simply say that at times things got a bit hairy and leave it at that, but otherwise he had a keen sense of humour and we became firm friends. During my stay we journeyed to London to visit other kindred spirits, including Fred Warr, who held the Harley Davidson franchise. Even though he knew full well that I had neither the money nor the intention to become a potential customer, Fred very kindly explained the intricacies of the various models to me and took me for a gallop on one of the latest of these legendary machines.

Motorcycling in those days had much more to do with enthusiasm than anything else, and anyone showing a bit of interest was quickly made to feel at home and tended to be treated with great generosity. It is easy to understand why people who have never been afficionados, or in today's dreadful imported expression, 'bikers', could never understand why we bothered to ride these cold, wet and potentially very dangerous machines. It was impossible to keep dry on a motorbike in wet weather, despite the many ingenious devices invented for this purpose. Even the best of specialised clothing could not keep the rainwater from dribbling down the neck; a small towel shoved under the collar quickly became soaked, and the cold too tended to penetrate the bones. In spite of this, during the years of my life on two wheels, I never suffered from a severe cold.

The other side of the business, and probably that which attracted us all, was the sheer exhilaration of sitting astride a large machine, kicking it into life and then having the freedom of the roads, to go as we pleased, enjoying all the beauties of the summer countryside and easily able to slip through the heavy holiday traffic. More than anything else, motorcycling tended to teach one roadcraft very quickly, in those days when there was no formal instruction and even no driving test. The rider had to be able to sum up a given road surface quickly, to look very far ahead and to anticipate potential hazards at high speed. In a collision, there was no protection except that provided by a safety helmet; a body could be hurled hundreds of yards and end up battered beyond recognition. We became very conscious of our vulnerability and tended to take appropriate, sensible precautions. The only thing on our side was that traffic was far more sparse then than it is today, but if you wanted to fool about on a high-powered motorcycle, the chances were that you would do it only once.

Nor was it all a mere quest for speed. On the open road, the majority of us tended to cruise at or about the prevailing limit of 60 mph, though one of my office colleagues, Cyril, a Triumph fan, habitually blazed along at 80, his unprotected head turned sideways against the violent slipstream. It was only in his later years that we persuaded him to fit a windscreen, to protect his eyes if nothing else, as his Tiger 110 tore along the roads of Ireland. We never did manage to get him to wear a helmet, and his own superb roadcraft resulted in his never having an accident, even though he was quite elderly before he finally gave up his beloved bike.

Of its nature, motorcycling tends to be a fairly solitary pursuit. While we clubbed together heartily in the way that those of common interest do, everyone remained an individual. We all rode different machines at different times, and rallies of any sort, but especially vintage and veteran events, nurtured a great camaraderie. I became deeply involved in reporting motorcycling events for our own newspapers, as well as for *Motor Cycle News*, then edited by Brian McLaughlin, and almost every weekend would see me at a grasstrack, scramble or trial. For my efforts in promoting the sport locally, the Munster Motor Cycle and Car Club made me an honorary life member and drew me further into the fascinating world of the internal combustion engine in all its forms.

In the early sixties, several attempts on the Irish speed record were made on the Carrigrohane Road outside Cork, notably by Charlie Rous and George Brown. Both rode huge Vincents, specially prepared and stripped to the very bone, the epitome of naked power, containing nothing more than a frame, engine and rudimentary seat. Overseen by the indefatigable Archie Canty, club gaffer, we would repair to the closed road at dawn, to watch in awe as the lone rider faced the measured mile while the official timers made their last-minute adjustments. The huge engine would be pushed into life, drawn up to the line and then, in a burst of savage, wheel-spinning acceleration, Charlie or George would give it everything they had, the gear changes being so slick they were almost imperceptible. Records, I seem to recall, were broken, but disaster was never far off.

One morning Charlie was nearing the end of his storming run, his huge Vincent howling along at something in the region of 180 mph, when the engine seized. There followed, for what seemed an eternity, the rubber-scream of his rear, racing slick tyre on the concrete surface. As we watched in horror, somebody shouted: 'Why doesn't he whip out the clutch?' After what seemed an age, during which Charlie somehow managed to hold the bucking machine on course, the screaming stopped and so did the big Vincent. Charlie, as might be imagined, was trembling visibly when we raced up to him.

Afterwards, when I asked him what had happened, he explained that when the engine seized, he did indeed try to whip out the clutch but it was a servo clutch, gripping tighter as the engine went faster. 'At my terminal speed it simply wouldn't budge and the rear wheel remained locked,' he said. Grinning, he added: 'Like all the rest of you, I was waiting for the bang when the tyre burst, and if that happened I knew I could not hold her.' Typically, Charlie was out again the following morning, the engine having been stripped and rebuilt. Archie pulled me aside and whispered conspiratorially: 'Don't tell anybody and this is not for publication, but that engine is now running on neat Redex lubricant (which was bending the rules) - and we are all running on neat Paddy!' The record was duly trimmed.

They were extraordinarily courageous men, these record breakers, as well as being most amiable characters. Occupied as they were with the business in hand, in which we all knew life could be at risk, they always found a few moments for me, and my endless requests for publishable knowledge were invariably treated with courtesy and openness. The same was true of my friends in the Munster MMC and indeed the other clubs in the area. Week after week I reported their events and if, for reasons of other work, I could not get to a given venue, somebody would phone me at the office that night with details and results.

Nobody ever complained about what I wrote; nobody took umbrage if I introduced an element of slagging and, in fact, I think they all enjoyed reports punctuated with harmless good humour, even if it was at their expense. I must have driven the sub-editors on *Motor Cycle News* quite insane, because on one week, after a whole series of reports detailing some extraordinary happenings on the Munster circuit, each of which received a zany headline, the anguished sub finally headed my piece simply: 'The things that happen in Ireland!'

Meanwhile, my own motorcycling had undergone several metamorphoses. The old Brough languished, awaiting spare pistons that were almost unobtainable, and I had acquired a second-hand Sunbeam. Introduced first in 1947, just after the war, these were machines far ahead of their time in many respects. I first saw one in the possession of our then Parish Priest, Canon Stritch and not being an enthusiast and at that time having little knowledge of motorcycles, what impressed me most about it was its quiet, gentlemanly progress and its huge balloon tyres. Mechanically, there was a lot more to it than that. It had a car-type, in-line, two-cylinder 500 cc twin engine, a single-plate car-type clutch and best of all, shaft drive to the rear wheel, which of course eliminated the messy chain.

My first machine, dating from 1953, was the sports model, with normal motorcycle wheels, but otherwise identical to the tourer with the large tyres. In terms of top speed the Sunbeam was not a particularly rapid machine, attaining about 70 mph when pushed, nor indeed did it have the handling of such others as the legendary Norton, but it was unfailingly reliable, a gentle push on the low-geared kick-starter bringing it to instant, quiet, burbling life. The overhead cams were driven by a chain which also activated the distributor, and of the two Sunbeams that I owned in succession, none ever leaked a drop of oil, unlike some other models of the day. It was especially easy to work on when the need arose, only a few simple spanners being needed to dismantle the bulk of the machine. A very stressless motorcycle to ride, it would tour comfortably all day at 60 mph - enough to take me into the picturesque beauty of scenic Kerry and back in a day's run.

After some time the folly of youth dictated that the Sunbeams (I now had two) went, in a package consisting of one fine machine plus the other for spares, and I acquired a 650 cc Triumph Tiger 110 - just like Cyril's. It was a good, fast, workmanlike machine, but piddled oil at every opportunity, and nothing I could do would cure the irritating drips from the rocker boxes, and the rather odd oil pressure gauge mounted just above the right toe in the riding position. Several pairs of new shoes later, I decided it had to go, and in its place came a brand new Matchless 650 twin, gleaming black and chrome, and a delight to ride. Meanwhile, strange things were beginning to happen to the British motorcycle industry.

The new phenomenon first made its appearance in the Cork shops by way of a strange little machine called the Honda Benly, a little 250 twin of extremely compact appearance and reputed to go like the wind. 'Mark my words, this thing is going to sweep the market,' said the mechanic in the motorcycle shop when I called to see this stranger from far Japan. Like everybody else, I laughed. It was too small, too insignificant-looking, to capture the public imagination. But it did. It had all sorts of accessories like electric starter, flashing indicators, a gutsy, oil-tight little engine. It heralded the beginning of the end for the Nortons, the Matchlesses, the Triumphs, the BSAs, the Ariels. The latter company made a valiant attempt to stem the growing Japanese tide by introducing the innovative 250 twin two-strokes, the Leader, complete with full protective streamlining, and its sports brother, the Arrow.

But it was too late. The iron age, blacksmith technology that had pervaded the British industry since pre-war days had finally met its come-uppance. If this seems harsh, one has only to compare, for instance, the Triumph of 1938 with that of 1962. Only the suspension had been improved; the basic design remained static, although doubtless advances in metallurgy had taken place in the engine room. For some strange reason, the traditional British manufacturers had believed themselves and their designs to be invulnera-

ble. After all, they were good value for money. They went on forever, in the way that an old steamroller does. But many of them, as for
instance the BSA 350 single-cylinder engine in the 500 frame, were
grossly underpowered, brutish workhorses lacking any kind of
sophistication, huge beasts that dragged unnecessary weight about
with them. But handsome is as handsome does was no longer good
enough.

The pace of change was unremitting. Gradually, on the race-
tracks and on the roads, the Japanese models swept all before them.
The era of the superbike was about to dawn. One by one, the British
companies collapsed before the onslaught, unable to modernise,
unable to compete, unable to market. Perhaps they were simply too
many in number, too diverse, too late for any sort of realistic amal-
gamation that might have rescued something from the wreckage. At
all events, they went to the wall, which was a pity, because with
them ended a great tradition of motorcycling and indeed of the sort
of individualism that the riders of another age revelled in, when it
was possible to select from literally hundreds of different machines
emanating from one country.

Now, with one or two notable exceptions where franchises
have been bought and a few models are being largely hand-built,
the old British bike is gone. It has winged its way into two-wheeled
history, and instead the all-embracing wings of the Oriental manufacturers have darkened the skies over Britain as elsewhere.
Nowadays, if you want to see anything from an Ariel to a Velocette,
you will have to attend one of the hundreds of veteran and vintage
rallies that take place every year, where the glory of yesteryear is
paraded in all of its *concours d'élégance*, where mighty engines still
rumble into life and where proud owners, men and women who
will not allow us to forget, spend long hours refurbishing and
renewing, shining and polishing. They are the sort of people who
would not look twice at a Golden Dream or a sleek semi-racer, not
because they cannot recognise marvellous technology when they
see it, but simply because it is not for them.

For over a score of years now, one of the most popular of these
rallies has been that organised under the aegis of the Munster
Motorcycle and Car Club by the tireless duo, Paddy Morrissey and
his wife Jude, who year after year succeed in bringing to Cork
enthusiasts and machines from all over the world to take part in a
rather gruelling but highly enjoyable trip around Cork and Kerry.
Once, in a weak moment, Paddy persuaded me to take part in one
of these rallies, riding his little two-stroke Carfield, which I was
convinced was powered by a not too efficient lawnmower engine. It
was not exactly the best sort of day for that kind of thing. The rain
spilled down as we set off from Silversprings on the eastern side of

the city, heading out through Fermoy, Tallow and Youghal, where that portion of the rally was to end.

The weather would not have mattered greatly except that the Carfield had a belt drive and as it chuffed laboriously up Watergrasshill, the rain began to have its effect, the belt began to slip and the little engine was quite incapable of coping with both the slippage and the gradient. There was nothing for it but to dismount and walk beside the machine until level road was reached again. This performance had to be repeated so often that I was very late arriving at the Tallow checkpoint, where an enthusiastic timekeeper, well-covered from the elements, made signs indicative of my tardiness and goading me on to greater effort. Sitting soaking wet and already going flat out at just over 25 mph, wondering when the belt would next begin its antics, my feelings towards this cheerful individual are perhaps best left unrecorded.

Matters were not materially improved by other competitors who, on huge, powerful machines with real chain drive, would roar past, giving me a thumbs up as they vanished over the hilltop at ferocious speed. It was no consolation at all to know that, coming along somewhere behind me, was the breakdown truck and that if all came to all, both the Carfield and I could be piled into it. We did eventually reach Youghal and, while I did not figure among the placings, I was given a finisher's award, probably for sheer endurance, though Paddy, quietly smoking his pipe as usual, was kind enough not to say so.

This interest in vintage machinery inevitably led to an introduction to one John Ellis of County Kildare who, I was informed, had a very sizeable collection of old cars and motorcyles and would make excellent feature material. An inquiry brought a most courteous response. Of course I could come and view his collection, and he would pick me up at the station in Dublin. He did, in an absolutely immaculate 1929 Rolls Royce, in which he proceeded to chauffeur me to his elegant home. John was then retired from business in Britain, dapper, silver-haired and the very epitome of the old-world English gentleman. On arrival at his large house, we drove into a big square courtyard which contained what had once been serried rows of stables or loose boxes. My eyes popped as, one by one, he opened the doors to unveil the goodies inside. I had heard of collections, but had never anticipated anything like this.

Everything was covered in white dustsheets and as these were drawn away, there emerged a whole pageant of motoring and motorcycling history. All the venerable models were there, together with others I had never heard of. A Hupmobile car springs to memory, and a beautiful blue Ace four-cylinder motorcycle combination from the United States. The treasures seemed to spill out of the stables as door after door was opened. I regret that I did not then keep count of the total, but it must have run into hundreds of items, each in pristine condition - John employed a former aircraft mechanic full-time to keep everything in working order. Moreover, almost everything could be bought, provided one was an enthusiast and it was going to a good home. John kept a notorious little black book in which was recorded the cost of each vehicle and the cost of the work done to it since its acquisition - the total was the sale price. There was no bargaining.

Out of pure mischief, I asked whether he would sell the 1929 Rolls. 'Of course. Just a moment,' and the little black book appeared. 'You can drive it away for £100, that's what I paid for it and it has not needed any work.' Seeing the look on my face, he smiled and added: 'Of course, before you decide, I must in all fairness remind you that it does 12 miles to the gallon, and I imagine that the tax and insurance would be very considerable. But you would, of course, have a motor car for life.'

It was very, very tempting, but I was saving to get married and I rather doubted if I could have managed the running costs, whatever about the initial outlay. Needless to mention, it is a decision I have sometimes regretted, the more so since, much later, John was forced to sell off a large portion of his collection, and that Rolls went to America. I duly got my feature article however, and returned on several occasions to Kildare, while John continued to support the Munster Club's annual rally until very recently. Each year he would bring a different car or motorcycle, and we would all be intrigued to learn just what model he was about to delight us with.

That there is a special sort of magic about these old machines cannot be denied. We all tend to admire beauty in one form or another, and the mass-produced machines of the built-in obsolescence era simply do not have the same appeal as those built to last in a more gracious and leisurely age. Part of their appeal is their very individuality. Hundreds of the motorcycles built in Britain in the early years of the century, for instance, came from what would nowadays be termed cottage industries, little backyard workshops where would-be entrepreneurs assembled machines from parts often produced elsewhere. Many tended to use the famed Jap engine, for instance, installed in frames and ancillary bits of their own design, and some went on to become highly successful industrialists.

George Brough was a case in point. He too used the Jap motor, Castle forks, Amal carburettors and electrical components from recognised suppliers. But Brough also dreamed of producing the Rolls Royce of motorcycles, at one stage even creating his own flat-four engine with perfectly balanced, opposed cylinders. He called this wonderful machine the Golden Dream, and only one or two were built, but they were certainly well in advance of anything else available at the time. Brough was successful to the point that his bikes did indeed become the Rolls Royce of motorcycling - Lawrence of Arabia owned several, and was killed when his SS 100 skidded as he tried to avoid an errand boy who crossed his path on a gravel surface.

Brough was a perfectionist. His machines were all guaranteed not only to go, but to attain certain designated speeds. The SS 100 was supposed to be good for 100 mph; the SS 80 for 80 mph. They were. George was also intensely proud of his products. In the sixties, long after Broughs had gone out of production, I wrote an article in the *Cork Holly Bough* about the man and his machines and was astonished to receive, some weeks later, a most courteous letter of gratitude and a small supply of transfers of the famous Brough-Superior logo - the very last of his stock - which he thought I would like to have.

If Brough was successful, there were many eccentrics who were not. The early thirties brought a strange machine called the Ne'er-a-car, which could be termed the forerunner of the modern scooter. In it, or on it, the driver sat well back, almost in a reclining position and I seem to recall that it had some strange form of steering which was quite unusual in a motorcycle - if indeed it was such. Other manufacturers produced, in addition to what might be termed standard or ordinary machines, some oddities. Royal Enfield, for instance, brought out the oil-bottle Enfield in which the oil tank was made of glass, presumably so that its contents were instantly visible. Velocette, famed for its huge, powerful semi-racing and racing machines, also produced, at the opposite end of the scale, its lovely little super-silent LE, again a forerunner of the scooter, but infinitely better balanced and very much favoured by the few ladies who took to motorcycling in those days.

But the most astonishing aspect of the peak years of the motorcycling industry was the sheer variety of machines on offer. From the little ubiquitous BSA Bantam to the Ariel Square Four, there was an amazing selection, in every engine capacity, for touring, scrambling, racing, trials, sidecar work, and even more strangely, there were ready buyers for them all. With the exception of the BMW and the NSU from Germany, the Austrian Puch, the Czech Jawa and a few famous Italian marques, the British industry had little or no competition. Yet it could not survive. Now, only the preserved specimens linger on, and the memory of the famous men who rode the great marques of yesteryear: Irishmen like Stanley Woods, the noted TT rider; the Scot Bob McIntyre, first to lap the

Isle of Man at over 100 mph, only to be killed later while testing a motorcycle; Geoff Duke and Mike Hailwood, our youthful heroes, together with a host of others who have ridden into history.

On the roads, there was a sort of unwritten code of honour and I sometimes wonder if it still exists today. You never, for instance, passed another rider who was obviously in trouble. In country lanes, if a horseman approached, you stopped and shut off the engine until he and his mount had gone past, lest the horse be scared - a gesture usually acknowledged with a courteous lifting of the cap and a smile. Association member or not, you saluted the AA man on his combination, and got a wave in return, because he too was a member of the fraternity. And always in Ireland, you allowed the farm hand to drive his cows in for milking, sitting patiently until the herd had gone past. Above all, you kept an eye out for errant sheep, since many a rider had one land on his lap, in its leap from a roadside bank.

Inevitably, the day came when the Matchless had to be sold and a second-hand car bought, an old Volkswagen which the late Chris O'Mahony generously refurbished and sold to me for £200, a grand old banger that never failed to start and to go, though its top speed from a much-worn engine was nothing to write home about. There was more than a hint of sadness as Bobby Rice, son of Jim, my erstwhile employer, handed over his hard-earned cash and roared away on my beloved bike. Ever since, I can never hear the rumble of an old exhaust without turning my head to see what it is.

...

I danced with a ballerina once. It was like dancing with an exuberant feather. Her name was Julie and she was one of the late Dr. Joan Denise Moriarty's famed Cork ballet team, and as we whirled round the parish hall in the picturesque village of Inchigeela, she literally took the weight off my feet. Her twinkling toes managed to match my stumbling steps perfectly, so that the whole business of waltzing assumed a totally new dimension. I felt I had been lifted off the ground, liberated, ready to go on forever with this heady, cloud-hopping performance, further inspired no doubt by the fact that Julie was petite, dark-haired and very pretty, with eyes like black pools that you could fall into, and a bell-tinkling laugh that soared musically and easily above the rhythm of the waltz and the thumping and stomping of the neighbouring dancers.

Inchigeela is not the sort of place you would expect to find a ballerina, deep in the heart of Cork's rural hinterland, but then again, why not? Anyway, on this particular evening, Joan Denise, of beloved memory, had brought her troupe on tour to the village, as she had done in so many other places throughout the country in her trojan and single-handed effort to spread the news of this sector of the performing arts. They performed, I seem to recall, her own ballet *Casadh an tSúgáin*, the Twisting of the Rope, based, as was so much of her choreography, on an old Irish folk tale, as well as several other little pieces of sweetness and movement. Before the show she led the dancers in procession through the village to the strains of bagpipes, played by herself, kilted and Tam O'Shantered, because, she told me: 'There is no use hiding your light under a bushel if you are in the theatre. Anyway, I want to show those people that there is nothing stuffy about ballet - it's for everyone.'

Afterwards, we all, audience and ballet company, together with anyone else who wanted to come along, gathered in the parish hall for a hop, which is how I ended up dancing with the lovely Julie, in a strange place, at the heel end of a strange night, when all our emotions were a-twirl and a cascade of diamond stars beckoned from the summer sky over Lough Allua. After the bus had borne the ballet troupe away, I wandered with the restlessness of youth to the bridge beyond Johnny's mill and leaned on the old stone parapet, watching the same stars dancing on the black waters of the lake and wondering what it was about this place that kept bringing me back. Possibly it was the utter tranquillity, that ethereal stillness that comes on lake and mountain when the sun goes down, soothing the ruffled spirit and balming the troubled brow. More likely it was a combination of this and the insistent generosity of Johnny Creedon, who always had a room for me in his hotel and who constantly brushed aside any attempt at recompense with the words: 'God

Almighty, aren't you one of my own; what would I be charging you for?'

Inchigeela, for those who do not know it, is a picturesque little village in mid-Cork, between Macroom and the Gaeltacht area of Ballingeary, and the well-known Gougane Barra, the latter being also the location for the famed work of Eric Cross, *The Tailor and Ansty*. The book was not only banned, but shamefully burned in the presence of the Tailor by over-zealous clergymen in those dark (or bright, depending on how you look at it) pre-television days when, according to one sage, there was no sex in Ireland. The village is part of the old barony of Uíbh Laoghaire, or Iveleary, its place made secure in Irish literature in the famous epic poem of the mid-eighteenth century, *Caoineadh Airt Uí Laoghaire* or *The Lament of Art O'Leary*, in which his widow, Máire Dhubh Ní Chonaill, keens for her dead princely, rebel husband. It is as much a love poem as a lament, poignant in its harrowing beauty, desolate in its sense of loss and betrayal:

Mo ghrá go daingean thú!	My love and my delight
Lá dá bhfaca thú	The day I saw you first
ag ceann tí an mhargaidh,	Beside the market house
thug mo shúil aire dhuit,	I had eyes for nothing else
thug mo chroí taithneamh duit,	And love for none but you
d'éalaíos óm athair leat	I left my father's house
i bhfad ó baile leat . . .	And ran away with you . . .

Art O'Leary is buried in the lovely quiet graveyard in Kilcrea Friary, but his memory lives forever in this defiant work which reminds us that the pen is indeed mightier than the sword, that foul death may diminish but cannot obliterate, as long as poets live and write.

Immediately to the west of Inchigeela lies Lough Allua, where the embryo River Lee swells into a mighty lake surrounded by high hills and the small farms that form the backbone of this area. At the western end of the lake is the village of Béal Átha an Ghaorthaigh, or Ballingeary, Irish-speaking and known to many thousands of schoolchildren who holidayed there while improving their knowledge of the spoken language and the Irish traditions. Further west still is Gougane Barra, the peaceful oasis hidden among the brooding mountains from whence Finbar sallied forth to Cork. Still travelling westwards, we come to Céim an Fhiaidh, or the Pass of Kemaneigh, where a hunted deer reputedly took an enormous leap across a chasm in order to evade his pursuers, and where yet another famous battle is remembered in the poem *Cath Chéim an Fhiadh*.

Steeped in history the place may be, yet Inchigeela somehow

became by-passed, a little place effacing itself amid the might and popularity of its better-known neighbours, like a timid little boy among his older peers on his first day at school. It was for many years the sort of place that travellers might pass through almost without a second glance, which was a pity because it always deserved better, a fact recognised by Benedict when he composed the opera *The Lily of Killarney* and included in it an aria entitled 'From Inchigeela All The Way'. For many years that was the village's only real claim to fame, and even if its name resounded around the opera houses and concert halls of the world, few knew much more about it. But all that was to change.

It all began in the spring of 1959 when a local committee, spearheaded by Johnny, began to develop Inchigeela as a tourism centre. I was sent to cover the inaugural meeting and, on my first acquaintance with this amazing man, I was instantly bowled over by his cheerful bonhomie and zest for life. Father of a very large family, Johnny was then in his forties, a powerful, stocky man with twinkling eyes and a great sense of humour. A raconteur of considerable talent, he would grab the attention of a willing audience by pointing up to the distant mountains and beginning his tale with the words: 'Now, up there lives a character called Shanghai Jack ...' and out would flow the most extraordinary tale, to be followed by others, until his listeners were almost in hysterics.

But behind all the banter lay a man of great understanding and enormous generosity of spirit, a true Christian to whom every man was friend and even rogues were countenanced for the good that was in them. 'He's a bit of a blackguard, but sure the poor divil has his own troubles,' Johnny would say of somebody who had come under the eye of the law, and more than once he went out of his way to help someone who had temporarily strayed from the straight and narrow.

In many ways, Johnny *was* Inchigeela and while the development was very much a team effort, it was Johnny who was the driving force. He was proprietor of one of the village's two hotels, the other, the Lake Hotel, being owned by the kindly O'Sullivan family. He owned the mill and the Post Office, together with the petrol pumps, and he also kept a rowing boat for use on the lakes, the outboard engine of which I once had the dubious pleasure of dumping into fifteen feet of water. By that time, Inchigeela had begun to boom in summer, with visitors coming from afar, mostly from Britain and the Continent, and on a bright but lazy afternoon, when I too had joined the holidaymakers, Johnny asked me to take a small party on the lakes. 'Sure, you know the ould boat and you know the lake and you'll have no problem,' he cajoled me.

So I packed them in and set off through the shallows, poling steadily with one oar until we reached enough depth to get the out-board down and started. I tugged the cord, the engine roared - and promptly disappeared over the stern of the boat. It was only then I noticed that, instead of being retained by a good, solid bolt, it had been hinged on an open-ended six-inch nail. In the consternation that followed, I managed to get the party back on shore and ran off looking for Johnny, to tell him, with considerable trepidation, that his precious outboard engine was lying at the bottom of the lake. Having ascertained that everybody was safe and well, Johnny began to roar with laughter. Then he brought me across the road to the blacksmith, from whom he borrowed two lengths of half-inch iron rod. 'We'll need a grapple,' he said, bending the rods across his knee as if they were bits of twigs.

But when we went out again to where the engine lay, shining and clearly visible in the depths, all attempts at trawling it up were in vain. Enter Johnny's son Con Dan, who dived repeatedly until at last he managed to get a grip on the outboard and bring it to the sur-face, to my huge relief. But that relief was short-lived. We stripped and dried the thing, cleaned out its innards, checked it and oiled it. But it never ran again, as far as I am aware, and I was desolate. Johnny took it all very philosophically. 'Nobody was hurt, and that's the main thing,' he insisted. 'Never mind the engine, we can get another one and anyway, it was my own fault for not securing the thing properly.' And for many years after, Johnny would recount with great glee the tale of the day when I dumped his out-board into Lough Allua, 'and sure the biggest laugh I got was the look on his face when he came galloping back to tell me about it'.

I suppose if you drown a fellow's outboard it creates a sort of bond, and indeed that bond did exist between us. Later, when I was married and Johnny came to visit our house, he said jokingly to my wife: 'Didn't I half rear that fellow?' and in a sense he did. From the outset, a special relationship had developed between us; an easy friendship that demanded nothing but gave everything. Indeed, Johnny was the sort of person with whom it would be difficult not to have a special relationship if one were in frequent contact with him. Lovable, outgoing, possessed of an apparently inexhaustible fount of good humour, he had an unique kind of caring for people which made him much loved in the community.

Near midday on a certain Monday morning at the end of May, exhausted from a long winter on night duty and taking an early week's holiday, I parked my Triumph motorbike outside the Post Office and, helmet in hand, wandered in to find Johnny draped over the counter reading *The Cork Examiner*. At my entry he looked up, started and exclaimed: 'God Almighty, Tadhg (he habitually used the Irish form of my name), but you're looking terrible. Are you all right?' Reassured that I was merely tired and quite unlikely to drop dead, he said: 'Fair enough, but this won't do at all. Wait there a minute.' Reaching up, he took a small bottle from a high shelf, shoved it into his trousers pocket and bade me follow him. We walked up the street to the hotel, chatting quietly in the sunlight. On arrival, he opened up the bar, poured out a glass of sherry and handed it to me. Then he took the bottle from his pocket, poured some liquid into a tumbler and handed me that also. 'Toss that back now, don't sip it, and belt the sherry down on top of it,' he said.

Wondering what was going on, I took the tumbler, put it to my lips and gulped the contents down. It was pure cod liver oil. Grinning hugely as I choked, Johnny said: 'Come on, what's keeping you? Lower that sherry and it will take the taste away,' which it duly did. Then he brought me out to his car and as we drove up into the hills north of the village, Johnny extolled the virtues of cod liver oil. 'It'll cure everything from an ingrown toenail to exhaustion,' he chortled, 'and you'd better be back at the shop every day at midday for your dose or I'll come looking for you. Mark my words, I'll have you like a young bullock before the week is out.' At the top of the hill, we got out and walked up a steep track to where the heather lay thick. There Johnny left me. 'Lie down there now in the sun and let the breeze blow on you. Put everything out of your mind and let Mother Nature get to work and when you're ready, come back down and we'll have a bite of grub ready for you.' And off he went, whistling and humming to himself.

It was very pleasant up there, high over the sun-hazed village and the beautiful country beyond. Bees hummed as they flitted from flower to flower gathering pollen. Presently a skylark began to soar her mellifluous way into the high heavens. In the west, a London-bound transatlantic jet climbed the stairway of its own vapour trail in a rumble of distant thunder, three miles above the earth. Fifty yards away, a vixen broke cover, eyed me suspiciously and went about her business, a silently moving tawny blur against the bracken. The jet rumbled past and a great peace descended on the sun-soaked hillside. It was half-past two when I woke, feeling more refreshed than I had done for weeks. I sat for a while, savouring the beauty of it all and then, really hungry for the first time in days, wandered back downhill to the village.

In the hotel kitchen, Kate, the waitress, had a huge lunch ready. Plump, pleasant, red-haired and full of fun, she announced: 'Himself told me you'd be here sooner or later, so I put this in the oven for you. Get that down now and if you haven't enough, there's apple tart and coffee to follow - and I'll kill you if you don't eat it.' Indeed, as I was to learn, one had to be a little careful about food in

Inchigeela. Not that there was anything wrong with it, in fact the reverse was true, but they simply kept feeding you as if the Famine would return tomorrow and the land of Ireland would once again be stripped bare of all substance.

One particular day I still remember as the morning of the three breakfasts. It was towards the end of my week's holiday and, waking early, as I was inclined to do in the fine fresh air of the place, I had gone off for a pre-breakfast ramble. On my way back to the hotel, I happened to pass Connie O'Riordan's shop, where the man himself was standing in the doorway. Since he had spent almost the whole of the previous evening teaching me how to use his beautiful over and under double-barrelled shotgun in a nearby field, I had to stop for a chat. 'Come in and have a bite while we're talking,' he ordered. Connie was tall and thin, a County Council foreman and a great sportsman, and the breakfast of a couple of boiled eggs, with brown soda bread and all the trimmings, was a lively affair, as the genial and voluble host held forth on the game he had downed and the huge pike he had hauled out of the lake. It was over an hour later when I finally said my goodbyes and continued on my way.

A call from across the road announced that Mary the Chair was seated outside the emporium of Diarmuid Kelleher, and of course I simply had to go across to chat to Mary, a lovely blonde lady who bore her confinement in a wheelchair with great cheerfullness. As we talked, Diarmuid's wife emerged and suggested that perhaps I would like a cup of tea. It would have been churlish to refuse, so there was nothing for it but to go inside, sit down and tackle a second breakfast, doled out with the same generosity and volume as Connie's. Somehow I managed to escape at last and stagger back to the hotel where Kate was waiting, a certain fire in her eyes. 'Where the blue blazes were you?' she demanded. 'I have your breakfast under the grill this past hour.' 'But,' I protested weakly, 'I've already had two breakfasts and ...' She fixed me with a steely eye. 'I don't care what you had. I have it cooked and you'll have to eat it, or else ...' It never does to argue with a red-haired girl, especially when she is holding a wicked-looking carving knife in her hand!

Johnny of course, roared with laughter when he heard the tale, and then added soberly: 'Well, at least my treatment seems to be working; you weren't eating a sparrow's mouthful when you arrived.' This, of course, was quite true. I was indeed beginning to feel like a young bullock, as Johnny had put it. The stress was gone, wafted away on the gentle south-westerly breeze from Lough Allua. I was beginning to slide once again into the easy ambience of Inchigeela, the place where there was always time enough, and about which one local wag had suggested that 'we have nothing as urgent as mañana here.' Johnny was adamant that it was all due to the cod liver oil, which may or may not have been the case; I was more inclined to take the view, which I kept to myself, that it was all due to relaxation, good company and sheer hospitality

Inchigeela was a very friendly, tolerant, open place where common sense tended to overrule all else, including the strict interpretation of the law. One morning I was chatting to the Garda Superintendent from Macroom, who had jurisdiction over the area and whom I knew quite well from my work at the local court, when Johnny came along and suggested that we adjourn for a drink. It was before opening time, and as we drifted towards the hotel I teased the Superintendent: 'Really Super, I'm surprised to find a stalwart of the law bending the rules by indulging in drink before opening hours,' or words to that effect. He smiled quietly. 'Well Tadhg, you know this place now as well as I do. You know there is only one garda here. What you may not know is that I have given him specific instructions regarding early or late opening, to the effect that unless there is trouble, he is to ignore minor breaches of the licensing laws and get on with more important business.'

He paused and added: 'Look at it this way. I know full well, and so does Garda –, that the pubs here are open early on Sunday morning. The people come in from the hills for ten o'clock Mass, and the women do a bit of shopping while the men go for a pint. It's the only time they come to town for a whole week, and who am I to deprive them of their little break? They do no harm to anyone, they contribute to the economy of the village and they never cause the slightest bit of bother. I suggest to you, unofficially of course, that some bit of ordinary common sense must prevail. We will hound the rascals and the blackguards, but my policy is to let the ordinary, decent people of the area get on with living as best they can - and you know and I know that they are decent people. I don't want Garda – creating ill-feeling among the people by operating strictly to the letter of the law, wasting his time with trivial matters when he has more important things to do. And neither does he.' He grinned mischievously and added: 'You know, there is a thing called the spirit of the law and since you very kindly asked, I'm now going to have a drop of it!'

*   *   *

As the concept of the holiday village gathered momentum and the visitors began to arrive, we were indeed a merry bunch. Included in the Cork contingent were schoolteacher Declan, together with my late lamented printer colleague from *The Examiner*, Ted, as well as Fionn, who was later to present one of RTE Radio's most popular classical music programmes every Sunday evening. There too was the irrepressible Joey, who had once canoed down Patrick Street when the whole centre of Cork was flooded and who was also alleged to have ridden a motorbike to the top of Carrantuohill. With the exception of Joey, who would under pressure admit to being a bit older than the rest of us, we were all young, all extrovert, all full of the zest and the folly of youth. There too, of course, were the many members of Johnny's large family, the beautiful elder girls who caused many a heart to ache, while his sturdy sons were ever ready to join us in our pranks and outings.

Time simply did not exist in those golden days - I was once despatched to Inchigeela to cover the funeral of a local noted poet and returned four days later, after Johnny had 'phoned my boss to say that 'Tadhg looks a bit tired and could do with a rest; can he stay for a few days?' John O'Sullivan, who knew Johnny well, was characteristically decent about such an approach and duly allowed me time off, muttering about 'that scoundrel Creedon' when I finally arrived back at the office, having of course, telephoned in my report.

The carefree days were matched only by equally hectic nights. There was no such thing as going to bed early, and three or four hours' sleep was not uncommon. We banded together and put on shows in the parish hall. We danced and we sang until we were exhausted. We walked the surrounding countryside and at Johnny's suggestion, we travelled to Gougane to climb Cam Rua, journeying in Joey's old Studebaker, filling the boot as well as the interior and drawing a long, wondering look from the solitary garda in Ballingeary as he saw legs protruding from the back of the venerable wagon. Presumably he knew either the car or its owner, because the decent man took no further action.

We also travelled to Saturday and Sunday night hops in Ballingeary and there was never any problem in getting a lift. Somebody would take us and somebody would bring us home; all that was needed was to indicate that one was going and arrangements would be made without any fuss or bother. 'My car is full up, but I'll tell the brother Seán to pick you up,' and in due time Seán would arrive in a battered vehicle of uncertain age and ask: 'Who wants to go west?' It mattered not at all that we did not know Seán nor he us. In we would pile and by the end of the night we would be the best of friends, in the way that these things tend to happen in the country. There were, of course, dire warnings from Kate. 'Don't you be dancing with them Ballingeary wans now, you'll get no good out of 'em.' What good we were supposed to get out of them is perhaps best left to the imagination, but the more immediate problem was how to identify whether in fact the partner was from

Ballingeary or not.

One of the difficulties was that traditionally, the lads all stood at one side of the hall and the girls at the other. When the next dance was called, there would be a great deal of dithering and hesitation, as the lads summed up the talent from afar, rather like eyeing heifers at a fair. Eventually shyness would be overcome and somebody would brave the walk across the hall. A full-scale stampede would follow, in which the willing girls would be unceremoniously grabbed and whirled on to the floor.

At one dance I was waltzing quite happily with a lively, cheerful young lady when I saw Kate looking daggers at me over the head of her partner. When the dance ended, she accosted me. 'Didn't I tell you not to be dancing with them Ballingeary wans?' she accused. 'How the blazes was I to know where she came from?' I answered, 'and anyway, she was very nice. I don't know what you have against the Ballingeary girls.' 'Oh you'll learn boy, you'll learn,' she retorted. 'Try propping her up against a ditch on the way home and see how far you'll get.' Kate was nothing if not blunt - anyway, the possibility was rather remote; we were going home in Seán's brother's car and, in any event, I had my own girl friend and simply was not interested.

The intriguing sequel was that when we were sitting in the hotel kitchen much later, enjoying a cup of tea, Kate was last to come in, looking red-faced and a little bedraggled. 'Well, will ye look at her,' commented Seán. 'She looks like something that was dragged through a bush backwards. I'd say now,' he added, addressing Kate, 'that you had an interesting class of a night.' Kate was not to be outdone, however. 'It's none of your business,' she replied, 'but by the looks of it I'd say I had a more interesting night than you anyway,' adding scornfully: 'Sure, who'd want the likes of you!'

Some of us were a little flabbergasted by this sort of personal assault and it took a little while to realise that it was all entered into with high but well-hidden good humour and, more particularly, that Kate, with all her warnings and accusations, was merely stirring the pot and knocking a little harmless fun out of us visitors. Next morning, when somebody - rather bravely in the circumstances - asked her why she had been so late coming home, she merely grinned and said: 'Yerrah, sure a dance wouldn't be a dance without a bit of a coort on the way home.'

Breakfast on the morning after a dance could be a sombre affair, with everybody a little sleepy and even the normally irrepressible Kate a little short on repartee. But it would be enlivened by Johnny, who made a habit of coming into the dining room and stopping at every table for a chat and a laugh. Often, with a twinkle in his eye, he would burst into song, to the utter amazement of overseas visitors, to whom this form of early-morning musical entertainment was unprecedented. One such group were six strapping lads from Northumberland, all miners, who had come to Inchigeela for the fresh air and the exercise, away from the grime and the dust of the pits where they daily hacked away at the black diamonds. They were quiet almost to the point of shyness, preferring to keep to themselves, and since they spent most of their time walking in the surrounding countryside, they were rarely seen in the hotel except for meals. Again, because they rose very early, they tended to retire long before our own night's entertainment had really got under way, so that we scarcely knew them, apart from the normal courtesies of a passing salute.

Johnny decided that something should be done about it and one morning, having given vent himself to a few bars of a song, he approached the six lads. 'Come on now lads, how about a bit of a song from Northumberland?' For a moment they looked at him in stricken silence, then to our utter surprise, began to sing, in most beautiful harmony the lovely, rollicking old ballad, 'The Blaydon Races', swaying back and forth as they bellowed out the chorus. When they had finished, there was silence for a few seconds as we collected our scattered wits. Then we stood and gave them a prolonged ovation, which seemed to leave them embarrassed but happy. The ice was well and truly broken and from then on these fine lads joined in many of our outings and entertainments and became very good companions indeed. They were, of course, quickly nicknamed, and if they were late coming in for lunch, Kate would appear at the dining room door and shout: 'Anybody seen the Blaydon Races?'

There was then no lounge as such in the hotel, but next to the bar and containing a handy hatch through which drinks could b served was the parlour, where we would all gather for an impromptu sing-song in the evenings when nothing else was happening. Prominent among the entertainers on these occasions was elderly, grey-haired, gentle Doc Collins, the local medical practitioner who lived in a flower-bedecked home just up the road. Full of years and of wisdom, Doc would burst forth into a fine baritone rendering of 'The Queen of Connemara' or 'Rory Óg MacRory', and he was much loved by all of us.

Some nights, Johnny would take his old fiddle down from its perch over the kitchen fire and bring it along to produce from its melodious strings beautiful old Irish tunes such as 'An Cúilfhionn' and other local, traditional airs that were new to us. Often, the first streaks of dawn would lighten the eastern sky as we crept off to bed, with bellies full of Johnny's lemonade and porter and hearts full of song. But we were all young and airy and after a few hours we would be up and about again, off for an early-morning swim in the nearby lake before tackling a hearty breakfast and a new day.

The little cottages in the area, as distinct from the farmhouses which were larger and more commodious, were generally of one type. Whether by the twisting, narrow roads along both the north and south shores of the lake, or high in the hills overlooking the village, they were the very epitome of simple homeliness. Usually whitewashed, their tiny gardens were bursting with all the varied flowers of summer, many of them wild, but permitted to grow along with the more developed varieties, so that the whole front was often a riot of life and colour. Sometimes a tiny porch helped to keep off the worst of the weather, dog roses and creepers clamouring for space on its steeply-pitched wooden roof.

Inside the front door was a single room, with perhaps a little kitchen off the back. There was always a large open hearth, at the side of which were built-in seats of stone and a wheel that, when turned, operated a bellows to fan the turf fire, which needed such pressurised encouragement to make it blaze. Furniture was of the simplest kind, but comfortable in the way that expertly-fashioned utilitarian pieces nearly always are: a wooden table covered with oilcloth and its attendant chairs, a settle along the wall which was convertible into a bed by night, a large wooden dresser containing all the delph on the top shelves and with cupboards below, and perhaps a súgán or straw-rope chair where one might laze comfortably.

In some of these little homes, cooking was done on a range, but more usually over the open fire, where very skilled ladies could produce the most wonderful pieces of culinary art, simple but infinitely tasty. Bastible bread, for instance, baked over the open fire with another small fire on the lid of the bastible pot, was always mouth-watering in its delicacy, and even piping hot plain soda bread was a feast to be relished. Floors tended to be solid, usually covered in heavy red tiles that were well able to withstand the battering on nights when people gathered in for a scoraíocht, or song, dance and story-telling session, these being common enough in this place. Then too would it be revealed that the cupboards under the dresser held bottles of various hues and degrees of potency, the clearest being the most alcoholically lethal since it was illicit!

Sometimes the cottage would lie in its own half-acre, which would be tilled industriously to feed a family that was, characteristically, large, but roadside holdings were often less well endowed in this respect, having to make do with a small patch on which were grown some potatoes and a handful of vegetables. Irrespective of size, the welcome in these cottages would always be the same, open, warm-hearted, come one, come all, and on scoraíocht evenings, the little place would be bursting with cheerfulness, banter and good fellowship. Little wonder that we stayed up so late in these little homes where the only requirement for acceptance was a sense of humour and a readiness to take life as it came. Any scrap of meagre talent, such as the ability to give a stave of a song or play an instrument, was an added bonus, but mostly we were entertained rather than entertaining, by people who were themselves experts in the art and who drew us into their own rich culture with deceptive ease and naturalness.

In the nature of things, the Inchigeela years sped by all too fast. As the zaniness of youth gave way to some sort of maturity, we grew older - Johnny would probably aver that we grew up! - and went our separate ways. Most of us married and settled down, but few of us lost touch with the magic village in the barony of Iveleary, to which we returned on occasion to renew acquaintance with the man himself and his charming wife Gretta. My own last meeting with Johnny was some years ago when I had taken my eldest son on a fishing trip to the area. Typically, he was busy in the Post Office when we arrived, but not too busy to chat and to phone a friend up the road to find out where the best fishing was to be had. It was neither's fault that we caught nothing that day, except in my own case a distinct whiff of nostalgia.

Soon afterwards came the sad news that Johnny had died suddenly, the great heart had pounded its last, that mighty frame of bull-strength lay still. It is enough to say that at the funeral, the village could not contain everybody who came; the many thousands who had been touched by the man and his great spirit. Let his epitaph be this: that he cared for all who came his way with boundless generosity, that he introduced us to a way of life and a host of people who enriched us all, that he made this old world a better place for all who knew him, and that he gave us all a lesson in true Christian living that we shall never forget.

So passed those happy days, out and about, sharing the joys and sorrows of ordinary people, learning the business of the reporter, concentrating on honest and accurate portrayal and struggling to get it all down in concise terms fit for ultimate publication. Good, grammatical writing was considered essential; puns and slang were frowned on and usually taken out by a disgruntled sub-editor, and in the main, flowery descriptive writing was permitted only in feature pieces. It was here that the Reading Room training really paid off. We had seen it all and read it all and we had listened to the Readers' comments on given pieces: 'That's a load of rubbish; look, he can't even construct a proper sentence,' or 'Now there's a fine piece of writing. Study that, boy, and you won't go far wrong.'

I loved reporting, but the powers-that-be had other plans for me. Apparently I had been so satisfactory on the *Examiner* subs' desk that Editor Paddy Dorgan wanted me full-time. I was given no option, and was quite upset about the whole affair because I had been given a promise by Pat Crosbie that the summer of 1958 would be my last as a sub-editor. 'Do it for me for just this summer, and I'll see that you are not asked again,' he vowed. All of us would have done anything for Pat, so I readily concurred, safe in the promise of an honourable man. But poor Pat died suddenly of cancer, a huge loss to all of us and to the paper itself, and with him went the promise. Chief Reporter John O'Sullivan called me one day in early autumn and broke the news: 'I'm sorry, Tim, but they have decided that you are going to the night Editorial full-time, beginning next Sunday night.' I was devastated, but there was not way out.

Old Tom Crosbie, the genial father-figure of the establishment, listened courteously to my plea that I wanted to write, not to edit. Then, as was his habit, he walked to the window of the Board Room, tucked his thumbs in his braces and stared out into Patrick Street. 'Now listen to me, young man,' he said over his shoulder, 'I could leave you in Reporters (at which my heart briefly rose), but I won't. Tell you why. You stay there and you'll be just another reporter. Go off to the *Examiner* subs and who knows what will happen in the years ahead. That's where the avenues of promotion are. Anyway, if you really want to write, why don't you give John O'Sullivan a hand with the Editorials - and I'll be prepared to consider that as work above and beyond the call of duty, and pay you for what you write.'

In the circumstances, it was a not ungenerous offer and I knew that old Tom was letting me down lightly, softening the blow of the prospect of permanent night work. He did not once allude to the fact that, under my original terms of employment, this prospect was always there anyway. The wily old boy knew quite well that he had me over a barrel, but he was decent enough to let me figure it out for myself, and to offer an inducement as well. There was nothing for it but to bite the bullet, smother my disappointment as best I could, and take the next step in what would doubtless be considered nowadays as the career path - except that we did not think in such terms in those days.

Except, of course, for the restrictions it placed on social activities, life as a sub-editor on *The Cork Examiner* was infinitely interesting and varied. True, a great part of the job was routine, far more routine than many people who have no association with newspapers tend to imagine, but if it was approached in the right spirit, it could be both challenging and fun. What was not quite so amusing was standing at the office door at five to seven on a bright summer Sunday evening, watching the young couples strolling through Patrick Street, heading off for an evening out in the Lee Fields, the Marina, or any of the more pleasant Cork suburbs. Meanwhile, I would have to trudge up the stairs to the editorial offices to begin a stint that would not end until two in the morning, or four if one were unlucky enough to be late man.

Once inside, however, the envy and the apathy were shrugged off; there was a job to be done, a paper to get out and that was that. The fact that I had only one night off in the fortnight - except for Saturdays, because there was no Sunday paper - was an added penance, the more especially since the opportunity for a long weekend came around only very rarely with our rota system. Explaining this to outsiders quickly took the aura of glamour away from journalism - in fact, explanation became almost a way of life - but there were compensations. People are probably more curious about journalism than any other profession, encircling it in a sort of mystique which those of us involved never felt.

To outsiders, a sub-editor seemed a sort of demi-god, an assistant to the Editor, somebody about whom revolved the whole onerous business of bringing out a newspaper every day. We had to remind them that nothing could be further from the truth, that in fact there were over a dozen sub-editors on the staff and that, mostly at any rate, we just did what we were told! Some of the brighter young blades, of course, took every advantage of this common public misconception, especially when they were trying to impress the ladies. Often they were found out in their sins, and retribution came by way of a quick rupture of what had been building towards a beautiful friendship.

The work itself was demanding to the extent that concentration was essential. This was not always easy when dealing with an endless flow of stories from all over the world, spewed out by the international agencies, to end up in a huge pile on the desk. This had to be sifted and collated, retained or discarded, as the dictates of available space demanded, and the individual sub-editor had to make his own judgment on what was important and what was not. Advice was always available, but in those days, *The Cork Examiner* was planned only up to a point and the whole affair was something of a seat of the pants operation, with the obvious exception of special pages like Page One, the back page and the Editorial and sports pages.

So we churned out news stories with all the speed of sausage factory workers on a production line, reading, assessing, cutting, pasting the bits together and finally putting a headline on them. The home news desk was even more demanding, because there there were all sorts of opportunities for error, including libel, misreading the outcome of a complicated court hearing - easy to do when the pressure was on - or wrestling manically with the flimsies on which the country correspondents' copy arrived by telegram. It was, in retrospect, a Dickensian kind of operation, with us subs, as we were known, sitting at a long table under lamps with Chinese tin hats, all scribbling away furiously through the long hours of night. Only when the work was finished after midnight did we have a break, when somebody made a huge pot of tea and we took out our sandwiches.

Later, when the printers were ready, the subs allocated to page make-up would go to the stone, a huge, heavy metal slab on which the steel page frames were laid out, empty and ready for the day's news. With us we had our page layout roughs - we had no formal layout pages in those days - on which the main headlines and stories had been marked in, and which the printers would follow as best they could. Leaden mounts were found for the picture blocks and then began the process of filling the page with headlines and columns of solid metal type, the whole process being enlivened by banter and not a little swearing when something did not fit and had to be summarily chopped. Finally, the remaining holes would be filled with the fillers which a junior sub had been sending out all night and of which only a few from his night's endeavour would be used, the page was locked up tight with special squeezing bars, the type was beaten into submission with a wooden mallet and block, and the completed frame was sent away on a barrow to the stereotypers.

Paddy Dorgan, the Editor, was a low-sized, stoutish man with Khruschevian features and heavy-rimmed glasses who, utterly predictable in his habits, arrived at exactly ten past ten every night, discarded his soft hat and overcoat and, having had a quick glance at the mail on his desk, began his rounds of the subs' table with the words: 'What's for breakfast?' By then, the Chief Sub was expected to have the menu ready, the list of major stories allocated either to Page One or the back page. Paddy would usually have a word or two with us subs, but if he called you mister you knew you were in trouble about something in the previous day's paper. Then you would be called over to his desk and receive a sound ticking off, with the reminder that 'there are plenty of people out there in the street looking for a job.'

As Editor, Paddy was a stern taskmaster, but I don't think any of us youngsters regretted the training we got under his editorship. Years later, on his retirement, he said to me: 'I suppose there must have been times when you all thought I was very tough, but look at the result - I have made Editors out of three of you.' We did, in fact, think that Paddy was a hard man, but he was a very shrewd operator indeed and could smell trouble from several miles away. He was also very much a man of his time, who knew just what made his paper and his readers tick, and if we youngsters found him a little lacking in invention and innovation, he was always willing to listen to anything we wanted to do with the paper - but woe betide anyone who tried out a new idea without his prior sanction!

We tried, of course, because at that time we were a bunch of youngsters who read the other papers avidly, noting how they did things and taking account of what we perceived to be the shortcomings of our own. We were astounded to read that one large British paper had a chap called a visualiser, whose job was to draw up an artist's impression of what Page One of his paper might look like on the following morning, while we were still struggling along in the wake of Mr. Caxton. With Paddy's grudging permission - 'I don't know what they'll think upstairs' - we fought for livelier presentation, and sometimes achieved it.

We were enthusiastic, lively, full of ideas - some of them harebrained - and ready to try anything, but it was an uphill battle in a newspaper where the Foreman Printer more or less ruled the roost, at least insofar as space and the placing of advertisements was concerned. On the hectic night when John F. Kennedy was assassinated, our Editorial Director, the late and much lamented Donal Crosbie, took the historic decision to dump a paid advertisement from Page One, and succeeded only after a running battle with the Foreman. 'You can't do that, he's a paying customer.' 'I don't care, out it comes.' And so it went on, until eventually Donal got his way.

There was often a sense of high drama, as we buried popes and presidents, recorded the rise and fall of politicians, marvelled at the new phenomenon that was the Beatles, goggled wide-eyed at the mini-skirts and once, waded thigh-deep through a flooded city to get into work, later having to go out again to report on the depredations caused by the overflowing River Lee, because all the reporters were flood-bound somewhere else. On that historic night, John O'Sullivan's son, Robin, who now owns his own PR company, and I wrote, edited and laid down the whole of Page One.

On another historic night in 1969, when I was acting Chief Sub, we sweated through the saga of the American moon landing, striving to get the last ounce out of what was without doubt one of the most dramatic stories of this century. The problem was that Neil Armstrong was scheduled to step on to the moon just as we were to go to press. To hold the first edition would have meant missing all our connections and a huge loss of circulation. To take a chance and record the landing would have been lunacy, in such a dangerous theatre where literally anything could go wrong. With the active connivance of Paddy and the Foreman, who doubtless wondered what this young whipper-snapper was up to, I persuaded him to set in type two sets of headlines and introductions, the first with Armstrong about to set foot on the moon, the second noting that he had done so. We made up Page One with the first set, while Tim O'Brien, another sub, kept an eye on the live telecast. The page had just gone away when he roared: 'He's down!' We brought back Page One, dumped the existing headline and introduction, banged in the replacement and sent it away again, to catch the whole edition, the entire operation taking no more than five minutes, since the original and the replacement were identical in size and length.

A little exhausted, I was checking the paper when it came off the press, ready to go home if everything was all right, when Paddy appeared at my side. 'There's a new picture of the landing coming on the wire. Get it processed and we'll re-make Page One.' I could cheerfully have choked him, but that is what the newspaper business is all about; the fact that it was after 6 am when I finally left the office had nothing to do with it!

It was about this time that I was formally appointed assistant Leader Writer to John O'Sullivan, one of the great characters of the office. A brilliant reporter, he had in his day covered the whole trauma of the Civil War and its aftermath, together with all the great events of the thirties and forties. His oral eloquence was matched only by his style of writing, which would nowadays probably be called old-fashioned, but he was a master craftsman in the use of the English language and could deliver a logical, calculated, devastating broadside to any politician who incurred his displeasure, which was not infrequent.

His Editorial, entitled 'The Extravagances of Mr. Childers' at the time of the controversial closure of the West Cork Railway, is still referred to with some awe in the office. Later, when he met Mr. Childers' secretary (Childers was then Minister for Transport and

Power) at a function, she buttonholed him with the words: 'Mr. O'Sullivan, what are you trying to do to my poor boss!' John's reply is not recorded, but I would love to have been a fly on the wall at that particular encounter.

This, then, was the man to whom I was subordinate, writing the second Editorial and standing in for him during his holidays and any other absences. A whole new trade was to be learned, but again I had the best of teachers. 'Never be mealy-mouthed,' he told me early on. 'If you have something to say, say it, and to blazes with the consequences. Don't be bitter, but never let them get away with anything either.' It is probably true to say that between us, John, and to a much lesser extent in those days, I, shaped and honed the *Examiner* policy, which had never been defined on issues of the day. He never had to ask what to write; I rarely did, because we had both grown up in the place and both knew just what the paper was all about. On his untimely death in 1969, I carried on as full-time Leader Writer as well as senior sub-editor and can honestly say that never once did I have any proprietorial interference, whether political or otherwise, even though at that time there were divergent political views in the Crosbie family.

Though I was then totally unaware of it and extremely happy in what I was doing, things were leading inexorably towards a certain conclusion. I was thirty-four, on top of my work, happily married, full of job satisfaction and asking no more from life than to be allowed to get on with what I was doing, when one night in November 1969 the bubble burst. Paddy called me over to his desk and said very quietly: 'Can you be in here at eleven tomorrow morning for a meeting?' When I said I could, he added: 'And keep your mouth shut, this is dynamite.' I was told no more, though I suspected and, perhaps, hoped that I might be appointed full-time Leader Writer, as I had been carrying a double burden for some months. I duly presented myself at eleven the following morning, and with Paddy, made my way to Donal Crosbie's office. He told us to sit down and then announced, without any preamble: 'Tim, as from Monday next, you are to be Editor of *The Cork Examiner*.'

There was no further discussion. The details of my appointment were to be settled later, and when the room had stopped spinning around, I understood that Paddy was to become Managing Editor, a new title in the office. In theory at any rate, I was to report to him, but Donal, in typical fashion, in a private conversation with me afterwards grinned and said: 'If you want to do something with the paper, do it - and tell me afterwards.' It was probably the most generous and positive brief that any Editor had ever been given in our establishment, and I greatly appreciated Donal's support. His cousin Ted, now our Chief Executive, but then working largely in a technical capacity, took me aside later and reminded me that as Editor, I had the power to stop the press if I ever felt it necessary to do so, and I was not to hesitate to use that power if the need arose.

The immediate problem with the *Examiner* at that time was that it was largely unplanned. Page One news had come in 1961, ousting forever the advertisements that had filled the page since 1841, but the inside of the paper was rather higgledy-piggledy, with national, local, regional and foreign news all competing with each other for space - a sort of glorious hotch-potch of information spread right through the paper. Clearly, some re-definition and some proper planning was going to be a priority, but it was not going to be easy, given the manner in which the paper was then produced.

Old and long tradition decreed that in one sense, the real boss was the Foreman Printer, Tommy Nott, a man who had such an immense pride in his work that he habitually arrived for work at 5.30 in the evening and was still beavering away twelve hours later. It was Tommy who decided what size the paper would be, where the advertising went, and in effect, how much space was left for news. An extraordinarily hard worker himself, he expected the same from others and did not tolerate fools gladly. But behind a gruff exterior lurked a generous spirit, and on the night of my appointment he walked up to me on the printing floor, shook my hand and said simply: 'You'll be all right. I'll look after you.'

It was Tommy too who would conduct the editorial conference, as it was laughingly called. About ten o'clock every night, he would poke his head around the door of the Editorial room and shout across to me: 'I have twenty-eight pages and I don't want any copy (news).' He would then spend the rest of the night trying to find a little space among the advertisements for the news that we considered absolutely essential. There is, I have long known, a public perception that the biggest problem in a newspaper is finding enough material to fill it every day. Except on very rare occasions, the reverse is true; in the interests of balance, good reportage and general presentation, material has to be pruned, chopped and even dumped altogether on any given night. There is always too much. Stories are often too long and have to be edited if the public interest is to be held. Some others have to be pruned for more serious legal reasons, but the end result is the same - the constant struggle to get the quart into the pint pot.

Against this sort of background, Tommy was very rightly suspicious of any overt attempts to interfere with what he regarded as his domain. As Foreman and Production Manager, his was the ultimate responsibility for getting the paper on the street, and if a page was running late, he would growl at the sub-editor and printer putting it together; 'Come on, come on, you can beautify it after-wards. Lock it up and let it go 'way.' A master craftsman himself, he could make up a page faster than anybody and he had an apparent-ly endless store of little items (fillers) hidden away, which he would produce with a wink and drop into a small hole remaining in a page that was almost full.

Tommy too was working under considerable constraints in those days of the hot metal industry. Only a few of his Linotype machines were capable of setting type in more than single-column width, and for much of the night these had to be used for advertise-ments. Consequently, if I handed out copy to be set double-column, especially on ultra-busy Friday nights, Tommy would look at it, growl: 'I can't do that,' and summarily cast it on the pile on his desk. Much later, as the last page was being made up, the copy would arrive, set double-column as requested, and if I pointed this out to Tommy, he would simply wink knowingly and walk away chuckling.

In spite of our very good relationship, he was deeply suspi-cious when I handed him the first layout-sheet for an inside page. 'What's all this and who's going to look after it?' he demanded. When I explained that I would personally oversee its make-up, he grunted. 'All right so, but be sure you do.' The ice was finally bro-ken; a beginning had been made on page planning and once Tommy had been assured that it would work, and could actually save time and effort, he went along with it willingly. Gradually, over a period of years, the format of the paper began to improve, but it could not have happened without the co-operation of Tommy and his team.

Meanwhile, the new Editor had other problems, just like any Editor. A Dublin colleague reminded me, kindly, that 'There's noth-ing to being an Editor,' but in fact there was quite a lot, much of it routine, some of it exciting, some potentially terrifying. Every Editor, and I was no exception, agonises about his product, wonder-ing, especially after it had gone to press, whether something could have been improved, something handled better, something tackled another way. Even with the best of staff - and I was very fortunate in this respect - there is always the worry about human error and the consequent possibility of libel, in a country where the libel laws are among the most stringent in the world. On a given night, it is physically impossible to see everything that goes into a newspaper. The Editor worries not about what he sees, but about what he knows full well he has not seen, and he depends very heavily on his staff to keep the paper out of trouble. Lawsuits can be expen-sive!

Again, on a given night, there are literally hundreds of decisions to be made, and it was often a cause of some amusement to me when I would hear other businessmen commenting on the fact that they had had a rough day, with several decisions to take. Each newspaper is a unique product. No two editions are the same, nor can they ever be. Even before today is finished, we are thinking about tomorrow and the Editor, for his sins, is never off duty. He is legally responsible for his product even when he is not there, and absence, for whatever reason, is no excuse. A 'hands-on' Editor, as the *Examiner* men have always tended to be, probably works harder than most, steering and directing the course and influence of his paper, while still getting down to the practical business of actually producing it. He must also make himself as accessible as possible to the public without allowing them to impinge too heavily on his work, and indeed on his life, trying to deal courteously with eccentrics while simultaneously wishing that they would just go away.

Politicians, I must say, have never been much of a problem, the majority being reasonable enough in their demands, given that they too are responsible to the public and therefore very conscious of their image. That is not to imply that we did not have rows, especially at election time, when the drive for party publicity was at its most extreme. We tried to apportion coverage fairly, and if all the parties felt hard done by afterwards, we felt we had got it right!

In the *Examiner* of the early seventies there was much to be done. For some time, rumours of a new system of newspaper production had been filtering in. The hot metal industry, it was being said, was on its last legs and we would all have to modernise. Certainly our own existing technology left much to be desired. Ageing machinery led inexorably to poor reproduction and complaints from the reading public. Essential spares, especially for Linotype machines, were becoming hard to find and when our own Linos, especially those that had been converted to semi-automatic typesetting using punched tapes, began spitting out bits and pieces, the enormity of the problem began to filter through to us all. It had been known upstairs for some time, of course, and certain steps had been taken which were to have profound repercussions on the production of our newspapers.

In fact, since the beginning of the seventies, our Technical Director, Ted Crosbie, had been examining actively what was going on in the print industry, and he had come to the conclusion that the way ahead lay in change and adaptation. In effect, this meant a move from the traditional hot metal process, initiated originally by Caxton, to the new and very high-tech Webb Offset process, with electronic origination of material and offset printing. One of the main advantages of the system was beautifully clear reproduction, but this was not the only one. The new system would permit much greater flexibility of layout, would be cleaner in operation, more silent, less labour-intensive. It would, in fact, mean the end of the traditional craft of printing, and while we all regretted this, it was inevitable if the *Examiner* was to survive in the years ahead.

One of the first visible indications of the changeover was the construction of a brand new Vickers-Crabtree printing press, the specification for which had been laid down by Ted himself, and which was slowly taking shape in our press room. We watched as the massive foundations were laid, foundations capable of taking the enormous strain and vibration when the huge press was finally commissioned. Slowly, from these rose the bright blue frame of the machine, its rollers and webbs, its folders and electrical ancillaries.

Meanwhile, our technical people were being sent overseas, notably to Britain, for training in the new system. They came home with wonderful tales of what could be done and was being done: pages being put together with paper and scalpel instead of huge iron frames, material being set in print by computer keyboard, and in Oxford, we were told, they were actually printing full colour several days a week. They also came with grim tales of whole editions lost during the transfer process as people steeped in old traditions tried to come to grips with new and strange technology. On the editorial side, we waited and wondered. The dismal Jimmies said it would never work. I retorted that it had to work; it was coming and that was that. Finally, our chance came to see for ourselves. Donal Crosbie, Cathal Henry, then Editor of our evening paper, the *Echo*, and myself were sent off for a week to explore a number of newspapers in Britain.

Everywhere we went, we were received with the utmost courtesy and kindness. Everything we wanted to know was carefully explained to us and people went out of their way to be encouraging. In Oxford, for instance, we were told: 'Of course you can do it. But be careful. Don't get caught in the trap of trying to run two technologies together - it can't be done. You will be terror-stricken when you have to take the big jump; dump all your old machinery and go for it bald-headed, but this is the way you must do it, and you must do it overnight.' When we marvelled at their colour printing, expressing the hope that we could just do it in black and white, there was more encouragement: 'In a year or so you will print colour and you will do it beautifully, just like this. Don't be despondent, it's just a matter of getting used to it.' With this sort of good cheer ringing in our ears, we came home, a little more knowledgeable and a lot more determined.

On Saturday afternoon, 8 May, 1976, the last hot metal *Echo* page was sent away to the casting room, with a bottle of stout ceremonially poured over it and cheered by the assembled staff. Immediately, a group of big, strong men appeared in the printing office and began to rip out all the old machinery, some of it older than any of them could remember. One ancient proofing press was said to have been there since the foundation of the paper in 1841. It was a back-breaking, and to some, heart-breaking task, but by Sunday the whole area was cleared and the new composing department in place.

Computer keyboards replaced the old Linotypes; wooden cutting boards and paper page make-up sheets replaced the old steel stone where the pages had been put together for generations. On Sunday morning I held a special editorial conference in which the message was plain: get everything to the printers as quickly as we can, give them every conceivable bit of assistance, delay nothing, above all, get the pages away. Remember that this is new to everybody. We will all be floundering and everything will be slow in consequence, but the paper must come out.

On Sunday night there was an atmosphere of determination coupled with no little anxiety. This was a new and, in our house, untried system. All the test runs in the world could not compensate for a production publication and we were all full of worries. Could we get the thing ready in time and, even if we did, would the new press work properly, first time? Slowly the night wore on and the pages began to go together. We fretted around the production area, trying to keep out of the printers' way and simultaneously be helpful if they wanted anything. We wandered into the platemaking and press rooms, anxiously checking, only to be told quietly that everything was going according to plan. Finally, in the early hours of Monday morning, the last page was sent away, to be plated and bolted to the press.

We all assembled in the press room and Ted formally pressed the button on the gleaming new Vickers-Crabtree. It started with a sigh, as of a giant awakening from a deep sleep and, as Ted held the button down, it began to rumble and then roar. We all held our breath as the blank sheet rolled swiftly through the huge machine. With a bang the inking system came into play and we could see that it was actually printing. As the first copies came off, clean as the proverbial whistle, a great cheer went up to herald the beginning of a whole new era. The elegant new *Examiner* was about to hit the street, complete with fine reproduction and, above all, on time. The following day, I received a note from a reader which summed it all up: *The bridegroom you sent us this morning was beautifully attired.*

After the initial euphoria, we had to get down to the usual business of producing the paper on a daily basis. All keyed-up as